PERIODS IN GERMAN LITERATURE

VOLUME II

Texts and Contexts

PERIODS IN GERMAN LITERATURE

VOLUME II

Texts and Contexts

edited by

J. M. RITCHIE

DUFOUR
1970

© 1969 OSWALD WOLFF (PUBLISHERS) LTD.
AMERICAN EDITION, 1970: DUFOUR EDITIONS, INC.
CHESTER SPRINGS, PENNSYLVANIA 19425

Library of Congress Catalog Card Number 67–15261

FOR
SHEENA

PRINTED IN GREAT BRITAIN

CONTENTS

CONTENTS

Preface

WITH *Periods in German Literature* Vol. I there was never any intention to give a complete survey of all movements or to impose hard and fast definitions. The aim was to make both general reader and specialist student aware of the continuing critical discussion over terms like Classicism, Romanticism, Realism, etc., as they are applied to German literature. It is important to know not only how these and other terms came to be used, but also what the most informed critical opinions are regarding their continued use. The present volume passes from the discussion of period terms to individual works and a study of the extent to which, with whatever limitations and qualifications, they might be said to represent any one period or movement. Once again it must be stressed that there is no intention to "label" any work. On the contrary, each contributor to this volume is only too well aware of the delicacy with which generalizing period terms must be handled and each would prefer to emulate the tactful and discreet "art of interpretation" advocated and ably demonstrated by Staiger. At the same time there has been of recent years a growing awareness that interpretation by itself can be self-defeating and that German scholarship has perhaps been too prone in the past to stress the "timeless" and "existential" aspects of the great work of art, to the neglect of historical roots. Hence the essays in this volume do move more than a little in the direction of what Jost Hermand has recently called "synthetisches Interpretieren", i.e. placing the text in its context. No one wants a return to fact-grubbing *Literaturgeschichte* or deadening *Geistesgeschichte*. But the neglect of all history can be equally dangerous.

Different ages are not always strong in the same literary forms, hence it might be expected that an attempt to examine various works as representative of particular historical periods between the seventeenth and the twentieth centuries would encompass the full range of possible genres as they rise to favour or fall from grace over the ages. A glance at the table of contents in the present book will disappoint such expectations. Instead the reader will find a selection restricted to six novels, three dramas, one verse epic and one piece of critical writing. Lyrical poetry is not merely

in short supply—it is completely missing. Bearing in mind the
exceptional hazards involved in applying historical terms to poetry,
it is hoped to devote a separate volume in this series to a wide
range of lyrical poems. Some further explanation is perhaps needed
as to how the works analysed here were selected. In many cases,
of course, they selected themselves. Grimmelshausen's vast novel
of the Thirty Years' War is without any doubt the most famous
and vital work in the whole of seventeenth-century German
literature. But is it baroque? Clearly there are many aspects in
the book which, taken by themselves, are "unbaroque," e.g. the
various Schwank episodes, the picaresque framework, the folk-lore,
etc. This being said, a study of both its formal qualities and its
dominant themes reveal it as a typically baroque work, and indeed
as such even more representative of its age than any seventeenth-
century lyric or drama. The value of the historical "synthetic"
approach becomes perhaps particularly apparent in the treatment
of Wieland's *Musarion*. Published in 1768, at the height of literary
Rococo in Germany, it is the supreme achievement in this mode.
Many aspects of the poem are reminiscent of qualities found in
other writers—the ironic and familiar tone of Hagedorn, the
Anacreontic mood of Uz, Götz and Gleim, the humorous
sensuality of Rost, the more emotional and idyllic note of Gessner,
and so on. But Wieland achieves with his *Musarion* a heightening
and synthesis of all these achievements and Rococo epicureanism
takes on a new depth and humanity in the ideal of the golden
mean which he expresses. All the aesthetic ideals of literary Rococo
are realized in the poem's fluid verse and decorative elegance, its
tender suggestion of the joy of love, its warm humour and brilliant
irony.

It is no doubt significant that a critical rather than a creative
work should have been chosen to represent the German Enlightenment, but probably more than any other work of the age Lessing's
Hamburgische Dramaturgie reflects both the awareness of the
need for progress and the impossibility of attaining it within the
world-view of the Enlightenment itself. Lessing's relentless pursuit
of truth through reason seems indeed to render the very validity
of reason doubtful : on the one hand there is the clearly felt need
for authority and moral purpose ; on the other the equal need for
inspired genius to break through the rules of logic. This conflict, seen
here by Lessing in terms of French classicism and Shakespearean
drama, is clearly expressed in the *Hamburgische Dramaturgie*.
In the last analysis Lessing is still the enlightened man on the side
of established reason and order, but he also foreshadows the
individualism and subjectivism of Storm and Stress. This either
Goethe or Schiller could have been chosen to represent, but their

works were felt to be well enough known even in England, and
instead an attempt was made to move out of the shadow of the
giants for once and focus attention on the less well known but no
less representative figure of Lenz. Not that Storm and Stress in
general and Lenz in particular are as much in the shadow of
Goethe and Schiller as they used to be. Of recent years there has been
a remarkable revival of interest in this period. Brecht, of course,
had early taken an interest in Lenz, but the appearance of two
new editions of his works in a country like Germany, which is
notoriously barren of critical editions of any but the major authors,
is evidence enough that Lenz' literary stock is rising at last and a
true historical estimation of his Storm and Stress drama is becoming
possible.

It was the novel, not the drama, that was to become the dominant
form in the nineteenth century, despite Kleist and Büchner, Hebbel
and Grillparzer, and it is to Goethe's *Wilhelm Meister* that
nineteenth-century novelists all look back. Hence it is perhaps only
at first sight surprising to find this work examined in the context
of German classicism. The connection between Novalis' *Heinrich
von Ofterdingen* and Goethe's *Wilhelm Meister* has always been
well documented and the choice for German Romanticism was
thereby made easy, but at the same time it is important to
remember that as far as the German Romantics were concerned
the novel was *the* representative form for the age. Stifter's
Bildungsroman is widely accepted as the Biedermeier work *par
excellence* and Fontane too is widely acclaimed as the greatest
German exponent of the novel of Realism, however elusive this
"Realism" may continue to be in the German context. In this
connection it is certainly significant that Thomas Mann should
have been singled out as the representative of the *Jahrhundertwende,* a term very much at the centre of critical discussion at the
moment. Not only did his *Buddenbrooks* literally appear at the
turn of the century : everything he ever wrote is characterized by
ambivalence, looking backwards to the realist-naturalist forms of
the nineteenth, while at the same time almost unconsciously
registering the underground forces driving Germany into the
twentieth century. Consistent Naturalism in Germany is associated
with the drama despite the experiments in the novel of intriguing
figures like John Henry Mackay. And in the history of the German
theatre of this time Gerhart Hauptmann stands head and shoulders
above any of his contemporaries. But with a man of Hauptmann's
stature it is only too easy to prove that he is not a "consistent"
Naturalist, hence in this case again the major figure was avoided
and *Die Familie Selicke* was chosen to show what does happen
when the rigid doctrine of a particular school is fully applied.

This volume closes with an examination of a land-mark in the history of the German theatre : Kaiser's "classic" of Expressionism, *The Burghers of Calais*. German literature did not, of course, end with Expressionism, but this was perhaps the last major movement that Germany has seen. It might have been illuminating to attempt to discover a work representative of the Nazi Period or the Post-war Period ; indeed *Periods in German Literature* did bring the story up to date with a chapter on German Literature from 1945. However, the temptation to single out such a representative work has been resisted : it is for the future to reveal who are to be the giants of our own time—if indeed there are to be any.

University of Hull,   J. M. Ritchie.
    Summer 1969.

Grimmelshausen's *Simplicissimus*—
a popular Baroque novel

I

Grimmelshausen's *Simplicissimus*— a popular Baroque novel

K. G. KNIGHT

SIMPLICISSIMUS is the one German novel of the seventeenth century which has unquestionably survived into our own time as a readable and enjoyable piece of fiction. There are other narrative works of the period which repay attention : courtly romances of which only a few dusty copies are extant and can be consulted in libraries ; pastoral novels in which shepherds and shepherdesses act out their parts in unreal arcadian settings ; and popular adventure stories which are of interest to the historian of literary taste. But none of these can be said to have withstood the test of Time which, as the poets of the Baroque age were well aware, threatens all things, not least literary reputations. Only *Simplicissimus* displays the artistry, the humour and the contact with real life which has enabled it to be appreciated by successive generations of readers into the twentieth century.[1]

The popularity of *Simplicissimus* just after its publication in 1669 was considerable. Its success as a best-seller is attested by the large number of pirated editions which followed it and against which the author had little protection in an age when copyright was virtually unknown. Like *Robinson Crusoe* half a century later it also called forth numerous inferior imitations bearing such catchpenny titles as *Der Ungarische Simplicissimus* (1683), *Der Französische Kriegssimplicissimus* (1682) and—one of the more original—*Der Simplizianische Weltkucker* (1677-9) by the Austrian Johann Beer.[2] In 1713 the publisher Felsecker issued the last of the "old" editions of *Simplicissimus* under the title *Des aus dem Grab der Vergessenheit wieder erstandenen Simplicissimi Abentheuerlicher . . . Lebenswandel.* Then, except for occasional references to it, including a brief appreciation by Lessing, Simplicissimus suffered an eclipse which lasted for nearly a century. Like the "Volksbücher" it was neglected until it was rediscovered by the German Romantics, notably Achim von Arnim who adapted part of it in keeping with the taste of the early nineteenth century.

The true identity of the author was not revealed until 1838 when it was shown that the pseudonym German Schleifheim von Sulsfort and Melchior Sternfels von Fuchshaim, the ostensible name of the chief character, as well as Samuel Greifnson vom Hirschfeld, the supposed name of the author, were all simply anagrammatic pen-names of Hans Jacob Christoffel von Grimmelshausen who was already known as the author of two courtly novels.[3]

When the available facts about Grimmelshausen's life were discovered it emerged that he was a largely self-educated man. Born in 1621 or 1622, he attended the local grammar school of his native Gelnhausen until the age of 14. His schooling was abruptly cut short when he was separated from his parents in the turmoil of the Thirty Years' War and he spent the last ten years of the war in the army, first as a musketeer and then as a regimental clerk. Neither as a young man nor after his marriage in 1649 had he the opportunity of an "education" in the sense that other writers, who were more highly regarded, received it. For nearly thirty years he made his living in a variety of ways—as innkeeper, horse-dealer, steward and magistrate. Yet somehow, despite his domestic concerns and his sometimes uneasy relations with employers, he found time to study, to read for recreation and to write a dozen or so novels which supplemented his income and one of which is now recognized as belonging to European literature. The essential qualities of his greatest work could not in any case have been born of study or erudition ; they are rooted in his personal experience of life and, complementary to this, in an inward reflectiveness which produced his maturity of judgement and coherence of outlook.[4]

Simplicissimus is a fictional autobiography, based partly on the author's own life and rich in adventure and experiences. The book falls naturally into three parts. The first tells how an ignorant peasant boy in the Spessart, whose home is destroyed in the Thirty Years' War, is befriended by an old hermit who cares for him and gives him the rudiments of an education. After the hermit's death the boy is plunged into the "normal" world—a world of violence and greed—and at first finds himself treated as no better than a fool or a menial. He falls in with Imperial troops and meets a young man, Herzbruder, who becomes his friend, and a cunning ruthless character named Olivier. The second stage in his life begins when Simplicius gradually wins a reputation as a soldier in Westphalia by his bravery and resourcefulness and becomes well-known as the "Huntsman of Soest." He is now a handsome well-to-do young man. Popular with the opposite sex, he indulges in several amorous exploits, one of which leads to an enforced marriage. He journeys to Cologne and Paris where he wins a spectacular social success and is temporarily involved in the licentiousness of high society. Now, however, his fortune changes and the final stage of his career begins. He falls ill, loses all his wealth and is obliged to struggle back to Germany as a beggar and a cheapjack. He becomes a soldier once more and commits a number of misdeeds, especially after falling into the company of the wicked Olivier. Fortunately, however, he again comes under the influence of his friend Herzbruder who persuades him to make a pilgrimage to Einsiedeln. Here he is converted to Catholicism. After Herzbruder's death Simplicius makes an adventurous journey to Russia and Asia before finding his way home to the Black Forest. Here, after surveying his past life with dissatisfaction, he bids farewell to the world and returns to the life of a hermit. He finds a suitable retreat overlooking the Rhine where he vows to lead a life of solitude and meditation.

No brief summary of the story of *Simplicissimus* can do justice to the abundance of episodes, the comments on man and society or the visionary depth which the novel contains. But it may well be asked which qualities of this eminently *popular* work, written by a self-educated man, may be described as "Baroque." In style and form it is unlike those long courtly novels which are commonly regarded as representative of the Baroque age. It lacks the complicated plot of an *Aramena* or *Arminius*. The style in which it is written, though certainly bearing the stamp of Grimmelshausen's personality, is unpretentious, free of conventional adornments and often borders on the colloquial. As he explained in one of his prefaces Grimmelshausen was writing for the ordinary man— "Herrn Omnis." It is therefore hardly surprising that *Simplicissimus* has almost nothing to do with court life or the upper strata of society. There is a brief episode in the middle of the book where, as "Beau Alman," the hero is obliged to prostitute himself with the ladies of high society (IV, 5) and towards the end of his career he temporarily enters the service of the Russian Czar (V, 20). But the hero moves through the rest of his life on a less exalted social plane and the characters with whom he rubs shoulders are peasants, journeymen or soldiers. Even the middle class is only represented by the occasional encounter with a merchant, lawyer or parson. The conventional gentility of the upper classes, their affected manners and speech are only mentioned as a subject for ridicule. Grimmelshausen was essentially an uncourtly writer, if not downright "anti-courtly" as has been maintained.[5]

Clearly it is insufficient here to equate "Baroque" with "courtly". Indeed, if we are to deal with the literary merits of *Simplicissimus,* we must disassociate it altogether from those courtly novels which enjoyed such prestige in the seventeenth century. We must regard it as a Baroque *popular* novel—the outstanding specimen among a large number of works of this kind, now deservedly forgotten. Almost all such popular novels stem from that picaresque tradition which had originated in Spain in the previous century and was transplanted to France and England as well as Germany. But the German picaresque novel, unlike that of France and England which flourished into the eighteenth century, belongs essentially to the seventeenth. The first examples of the genre were published after about 1610 and the last towards the end of the century when the reading public was turning to other kinds of fiction such as the adventure novel or the "galant" novel.[6] And if the picaresque form of *Simplicissimus* is typical of the Baroque age in Germany, so too are its dominant themes. Grimmelshausen reiterates in prose many of the austere philosophical or religious themes on which the Baroque poets composed variations—notably the *vanitas* of earthly things, the fickleness of fortune, the deceptiveness and inconstancy of the world and the need for self-knowledge and self-control in order to gain salvation. The curious frontispiece of the first edition—with the mythical figure compounded of man, animal, bird and fish—is accompanied by verses which point to the serious purpose of the novel.[7]

> Was mich offt betrübet und selten ergetzt
> Was war das! Ich hab in diß Buch gesetzt
> damit sich der Leser gleich wie ich itzt thue
> entferne der Thorheit und lebe in Rhue.

The sources which Grimmelshausen used in writing *Simplicissimus* are many and varied, including chap-books, folk-tales, legends of the saints and compendia of knowledge. But the most important influence was certainly the Spanish picaresque novel *Guzman de Alfarache,* which was published in a German translation by Aegidius Albertinus under the title *Der Landstörtzer* in 1615. The hero of this work is a reformed rogue who sets down the story of his disreputable life with much detail but little art. He describes his humble birth, his childhood, his initiation into a guild of professional thieves and the many exploits in which he engages before his repentance in old age. At intervals throughout the story we are reminded that this account of Guzman's rogueries is intended as a warning to the reader to avoid bad company and to resist the temptations of the wicked world. Albertinus, being Jesuit-trained and having moral rather than literary interests, expands the moral digressions which the Spanish novel contains and adds new digressions of his own, but without impairing the racy and often very amusing narrative sections. In the final German version, completed in three volumes by another hand, the hero is converted to the religious life, makes a pilgrimage to the Holy Land and subsequently withdraws from the world to become a hermit.[8]

Grimmelshausen deserves most of the credit for creating in *Simplicissimus* a native equivalent to the picaresque novel with a German hero in a German setting. He had one precursor, the Alsatian H. M. Moscherosch whose works were known to him. Moscherosch's only novel, contained in the satire *The Soldier's Life,* deals realistically with the plight of an unwilling recruit in the Thirty Years' War who is forced to take part in the evil exploits of a band of marauding soldiers until he finally repents of his misdeeds and, mindful of salvation, turns over a new leaf.

Like *Guzman* and a number of other picaresque novels, *The Soldier's Life* is basically an autobiography with a moral. The chronicle of the hero's misspent life is followed by an account of his conversion and reform, rather like the testimony of repentant sinners at a revivalist meeting of certain modern sects. And in the picaresque novel the two elements—the wicked life and the exemplary conversion—are linked in the person of the hero who has passed through both experiences. But both Albertinus and Moscherosch found difficulty in making this link credible on a literary level. The great deficiency of *Guzman de Alfarache* (and even more of *Der Landstörtzer*) is the wide discrepancy of style and tone between the entertaining narrative passages and the reflections which are intended to drive home the moral. The reader is carried along effortlessly as long as one picaresque prank succeeds the other. At intervals, however, he is brought to an abrupt halt by solemn and often trite thoughts on the duties of a Christian man which have all too clearly been 'tacked on' to an otherwise diverting story. Even the most sympathetic appreciation of *Guzman de Alfarache* is forced to recognize its dualistic structure as an artistic defect.[9] It can be claimed for Grimmelshausen that he succeeded, where Albertinus and Moscherosch failed, in overcoming this dualism by bridging the gap between the entertaining narrative and the moral digressions. He has no need to step out of the role of narrator as Albertinus does, in order to put on a preacher's robe and deliver a sermon to the reader on the iniquities of the hero. Instead he makes his narrator, Simplicissimus, tell the story consistently from the point of view of an old man reviewing critically but sympathetically the joys and follies of his youth. The life he is describing is both his own and yet not his own; he is both involved in this life and detached from it. While identifying himself with the younger Simplicius he still preserves his freedom as story-teller and commentator. Occasionally he appears to be carried away by the memory of the child or youth which he once was. He dwells with mingled amusement and sympathy on the naivety and social blunders of the callow youth. Or he looks back almost with envy on the audacious young man filled with vigour and zest for life.

More rarely there is a note of regret at his former pride and vanity. But the reader is never in doubt that the same person is telling the story throughout, for every chapter bears the stamp of his personality and his humour.

We cannot appreciate fully Grimmelshausen's ability to enter into the story while maintaining his detachment from it unless we take account of the part played in his work by irony, a quality which is most conspicuous in his style. Attention was first drawn to this by Richard Alewyn in a short stylistic comparison of Grimmelshausen and Johann Beer which was intended to show that Grimmelshausen, who had for long been regarded as a "realistic" writer, in fact frequently referred to people, events and scenes obliquely, substituting one word for another or adding ironical "asides".[10] There is a conspicuous example of sustained irony of this kind in the very first chapter of *Simplicissimus* where he gives an ostensibly "serious" account of his father's dwelling :

> My father . . . had his own palace . . . the like of which no king could build with his own hands. . . . It was decorated with lime and instead of arid slate, cold lead or red copper covering its roof there was straw on which fine corn had grown. And just so that he could make a show of his nobility and wealth, my father had the walls round his castle made, not with stones which are found by the wayside or dug out of barren earth, and still less with wretched bricks which can be baked so quickly—no, he took for this purpose the wood of the oak, a fine useful tree, on which sausages and fat hams grow and which needs over a hundred years to reach maturity. Where is the monarch who would do the like?[11]

The whole of this lengthy passage is a mock-eulogy of the hovel in which the hero spent his early years. The walls of the peasant's hut are painted in "the most durable colour in the world"— black with soot; the floor is covered with the finely woven carpet—of spiders' webs. The windows, dedicated to "Sandkt Nitglaß", are covered with flaxen or hemp cloth. Instead of pages or lackeys he had sheep, goats and swine—"each neatly dressed in its own livery". In the armoury there were ploughshares, axes, shovels, forks, etc. In brief, the narrator adds, I was born in the Spessart, "where the wolves bid one another goodnight".

Grimmelshausen's fondness for ironical circumlocution is also reflected in his use of dialect for comic effect and particularly in his fondness for "Fremdwörter" i.e. foreign words, even where a simple German alternative would be normal and expected. These "Fremdwörter" give his style a peculiar rhetorical flavour and vigour which is not easy to define. The opposition of the linguistic purists to "Fremdwörter" in the seventeenth century was based on the double argument that foreign words deprived the German language of its native power and that they were too often used to gloss over unpalatable realities, giving a spurious air of innocence to what was dangerous or evil. There is in fact some evidence that the German language was in danger of being debased in this way during the later stages of the Thirty Years' War. The widespread currency of the innocuous word "Contribution" to describe the oppressive war-levy could no doubt be paralleled by the use of "security" or "mission" in our own day. But the interesting feature of the "Fremdwörter" in *Simplicissimus* is that they are always used deliberately, *not* to gloss over hard facts but in order to engage the reader's attention or to provoke him to reflection.

> Moreover you must ensure that there is no shortage of money, ammunition, rations and men at their posts, so you have to levy "Contribution" throughout the whole country with continual assessments and extortions. And if you send out your men for this purpose the best work they do is robbing, plundering, stealing, burning and murder . . .[12]

Occasionally Grimmelshausen first uses a "Fremdwort" and then gives a German equivalent, e.g. "I said that the name 'Mummelsee' indicated clearly enough that it was like a 'masquerade' or a thing in 'mummery'."[13] Or there is a sly comment hidden in the "definition" added by the author: "It was three whole hours before the *Praeludium Veneris* (I should have said the 'honourable dance') came to an end".[14] Such stylistic irony is merely one indicator of the characteristic pattern of Grimmelshausen's thought. His substitution of one concept for another, periphrasis for straightforward statement, his use of ironical hyperbole and understatement—all these are evidence of his impatience with stereotyped concepts and of his readiness to consider a matter from more than one point of view. This style compels the reader to ask himself at every turn whether or not the author has his tongue in his cheek. It is a style which comes close to the old definition of irony, i.e. a style by which a man "says one thing and gives to understand the contrary".

Besides Grimmelshausen's irony of style, however, there is another irony, akin to it, but much wider in scope since it pervades the whole novel. This irony, which encompasses the parts and the whole of *Simplicissimus,* also springs from the author's double perspective—his view of a person, an episode or a whole period of time from two vantage points. The result is a subtle ambiguity which reflects Grimmelshausen's preoccupation with the double aspect of human experience. It is significant that Grimmelshausen's first work—*The Satyrical Pilgrim*,[15] published two years before *Simplicissimus*—deals with a series of twenty themes, each of which is considered from two sides. The pattern followed in each chapter is "Satz—Gegensatz"—corresponding approximately to "thesis and antithesis". A third section, called "Nachklang", or conclusion, is an attempt, if not to synthesize the "Satz" and "Gegensatz", at least to bring them into harmony. Since many of the themes of *The Satyrical Pilgrim* also recur in *Simplicissimus* we are enabled to discover how Grimmelshausen approached some of the varied problems which interested him, e.g. Money, Peasants, Priests, Women, Love, Doctors, Beggars, etc. The final chapter on War is especially revealing, for it is here that Grimmelshausen gave advance notice of the publication of *Simplicissimus*. After describing the assumed advantages and utility of war—to *rulers and generals* and certain countries like Switzerland and Holland—Grimmelshausen deals at length and in terms of heartfelt experience with the harrowing life of a soldier who must march, stand guard or take part, whatever the weather, in the grim and bloody battles fought between so-called Christians, the sufferings of the civilian population, the destruction and breakdown of law. He concludes in the "Nachklang":

> I freely admit that I have not related the hundredth part of what a dreadful and cruel monster war is, for this would require enough paper for a book and could not therefore be included in this brief work. But the gracious reader will find many details of the war related in my *Simplicissimus* in an entertaining manner. My own opinion is that there is nothing less befitting to us Christians than the war which we wage against one another.[16]

The other chapter which is conspicuously relevant to *Simplicissimus* is "The Peasants and their Advantages". Here Grimmelshausen examines the dual aspect of the peasant's life. On the one hand his life is an admirable one, as the poets have often declared. All men depend upon the peasant for food. He is independent and does not yearn for a sceptre, crown or high honours:

> I might say that a peasant lives better than a prince and has no reason for changing places. For although a prince is provided with food, drink, clothing, servants and, in short, everything which serves his physical pleasure, yet on the other hand he must bear a great burden of cares, concerns and desires, as well as the heavy responsibility of his own actions.[17]

On the other hand the peasant is the first to suffer from the effects of bad weather, plagues or the ravages of thieving

Landsknechte. His existence is rough and primitive and he is often sly and dishonest by nature. It is not surprising that the only conclusion reached is "that a peasant and his condition may be either praised or criticized". It will be immediately apparent that the same "Satz" of the peasants good fortune is developed at length in the passage at the beginning of *Simplicissimus* already referred to. A few pages later there is an illustration of the "Gegensatz" when the "idyll" of the peasant's life is brutally interrupted by the arrival of mounted marauders who pillage the farmstead and torture the occupants. This is only one of many examples of themes from *The Satyrical Pilgrim* which are taken up again *in Simplicissimus* and worked into the narrative.

Grimmelshausen's habitual consideration of two opposing points of view indicates that we should be rash to draw any conclusion as to his philosophy of life from isolated quotations. The subtitle of *The Satyrical Pilgrim* is as follows :

Cold and Warm, White and Black, Glory and Shame, concerning Good and Evil, Virtue and Vice and the Advantage and Disadvantage of many Stations of Life and Things of the Visible and Invisible, of the Temporal and Eternal World. To be read with Profit and Amusement.[18]

The juxtaposition of opposites is revealing. Grimmelshausen was no less aware than other thinking men of his time of the contradictoriness of human experience : the contrasts between outer appearance and inner reality, Time and Eternity, the moral principle of constancy and the inconstancy of the world. In *The Satyrical Pilgrim* he seeks to reconcile the opposites where possible or to choose a middle point of view, but (except in the first section dealing with God) he always takes it for granted that there is a "Gegensatz" to every "Satz" and that each contains some truth. This is very relevant to our appreciation of *Simplicissimus*. It would be easy for instance to miss the irony in the passage praising money in Book III, which appears to represent the author's own point of view : "Those who appreciate the value of money and therefore make a god of it have no small reason for doing so." But after praising the power of money in all of life's situations he concludes : "In short one cannot describe what money can do, and in my 'Black and White' I have written something on the power that money has, if only one knows how to use and apply it properly."[19] Here Grimmelshausen actually refers us back to *The Satyrical Pilgrim*, Section V of which is a discussion "Concerning Money, its Utility and Necessity". The "Satz" is very similar to the passage in *Simplicissimus* already referred to above. Here, however, there is a much longer "Gegensatz" which deals with

"Frau Pecunia . . . an infernal goddess", the corrupting effects
of greed and usury, the many evils of which money is the root
cause : "War, blasphemy, perjury, murder, brawling, feuding,
adultery" etc. The "Nachklang" states that money may be harmful
or profitable according to the use we make of it.

The assumption that Grimmelshausen's picture of the world is
fundamentally ironical—in the sense that he often says one thing
but implies the opposite—can be confirmed if we examine other
themes which recur in *Simplicissimus*. There is for instance the
theme of folly or "Narrheit"—a word which occurs many times
in the novel, especially in the early pages. After Simplicius has
made himself socially unacceptable as a page boy he is forcibly
dressed in a calf's skin and treated as a fool, i.e. jester. But,
although he humours his master by "playing the fool" he also
enjoys a fool's licence and is now able to tell home-truths to the
Governor of Hanau and his entourage. The so-called fool shows
remarkable insight, especially in his analysis of the governor's
true position—that of a man possessing power, but surrounded
by enemies and hypocrites and always fearful of the future. We
are not surprised to find the Governor asking "Who has taught
you to preach? . . . I don't know what to make of you. You
seem to me to be too clever for a calf".[20] When the "fool" Simplicius in calf-skin prays devoutly, as he had been taught by the
old hermit, the Governor and the other onlookers are moved to
tears. What began as a prank in which Simplicius was intended to
lose his wits has ended as a sermon and a prayer which brings the
fool's master back to his senses.

Much has been written about Grimmelshausen's religious convictions, especially his Catholicism. Here again, however, it would
be misleading to identify the author with any one of the different
views expressed in Simplicius. It could be argued that Simplicius'
pilgrimage to Einsiedeln—albeit with boiled peas in his sandals—
and his subsequent conversion after the exorcism scene in church
reflect the author's own conversion to Catholicism. Yet a few pages
later we are reminded of the breadth of his sympathies by a long
passage devoted to the heretical sect of Anabaptists in Hungary
who led a quiet godly community life. It is hard to avoid the
conclusion that Grimmelshausen, even after his conversion, held
beliefs not far removed from Simplicius' own : "Neither like Peter
nor like Paul but merely *simpliciter*."[21]

Irony also colours the pattern of Simplicius' life. This can be
seen best if we examine that section of *Simplicissimus* which is
furthest removed in spirit from the austere moral with which the
novel concludes (Book II, 29–end of Book III). It is here that the
young Jäger von Soest becomes well-known for his bravery,

ingenuity, good looks and his amorous exploits. Taken out of its context and with slight abridgement this part of *Simplicissimus* could easily pass for a success story, for, as we are reminded more than once, this was the period when Fortune smiled upon him— to such an extent that the idea of *mis*fortune (III, 19) became unthinkable. It is true that he experiences one or two setbacks : his conflict with the rival "Jäger von Werle" who tries to impersonate him (III, 2), his arrest following a duel (III, 9) and his capture by the Swedes (III, 14). But these are exceptional short-term reverses which seem merely to confirm his progress from one bright prospect to the next. Far from rejecting the world at this stage in his career young Simplicius reaches out with both hands to embrace it. He seeks, and for a time finds, ample scope for enjoyment, adventure and advancement. The agreeable prospects which beckon to him are foreshadowed at the end of Book II where he is billeted in a comfortable convent called "Paradise". Here he thrives physically on the rich diet,

> so that in a short time I acquired a smooth skin, for there was set out the strongest beer, the best Westphalian ham and sausage, tasty and very tender beef which we used to cook in salt water and eat cold; there I learnt to spread salted butter as thick as my finger on black bread and to put cheese on top so that it went down better; and when I got a leg of lamb spiced with garlic and a good mug of beer beside it, then I refreshed my body and soul and forgot all the sufferings which I had endured.[22]

Besides food and shelter he acquires fine clothing and the opportunity to hunt small game. Most important of all he gains considerable wealth in the form of loot. This is supplemented by the discovery of a horde of treasure which he discovers in a reputedly haunted ruin. An interesting inventory is given of the jewels, precious stones and coins which came into his possession and which prompted him to reflect on the power of riches.

Fortune, however, provides more than a cornucopia. She gives the opportunity to show initiative which Simplicius is not slow to grasp. Filled with youthful ambition he distinguishes himself in the fighting by his cleverness and courage. Characteristically he is generous in the disposal of his gains and wins the popularity of most of his comrades and officers. His bravery is matched by ingenuity. The most memorable example of the latter is undoubtedly the carefully planned theft of the parson's hams through the chimney and his subsequent escape from the house by impersonating the Devil. This exploit temporarily brings the narrative down almost to the level of "Till Eulenspiegel's Merry Pranks". But his ingenuity also finds more subtle forms of expression, e.g. in his construction of dummy mortars designed to force a besieged town into surrender, or in the invention of a device for detecting the sound of the enemy from a great distance. In passing it may be noted that Simplicius' inventive skill does not desert him in later life. His resourcefulness stands him in good stead on his return from Paris when he sells a worthless tincture to gullible peasants, and later still when he is virtually the prisoner of the Czar and wins favour by manufacturing gunpowder, and finally when he is cast away on a desert island and survives by baking crude earthenware vessels or making clothes from leaves.

Carried away on the tide of his good luck the young Simplicius forgets only one thing—that Fortune is a blind, fickle and deceptive lady who cannot be relied on. Baroque poetry contains many references to the inconstancy of Fortune and the folly of the man who trusts her. Grimmelshausen echoes this view :

> I did not know (as I found out later) that artful Fortune is similar to the Sirens who are most ill-disposed to those whom they appear to favour most. Fortune raises a man up all the higher simply so that she may cast him down all the further.[23]

This is only one of several comments interpolated by the narrator, *old* Simplicissimus, which remind us of the true situation of the young hero. For far from making his way in the world, as he imagined, he had simply become a hostage of fortune :

> Fool that I was, I did not consider that the jug only goes to the well until it breaks. But that is what happens when a young reckless soldier has money, fortune and courage, for they bring after them pride and arrogance.
>
> So I gradually became aware that there is nothing more constant in the world than inconstancy itself. Therefore I was afraid that if Fortune should vent her spite on me this would cancel out my present well-being.[24]

The critic J. H. Scholte saw significant parallels between the structure of *Simplicissimus* and that of a five-act classical drama, Book I corresponding to an exposition and Book III to a dramatic climax.[25] Although some details of this comparison are open to question, there is no doubt that as the Jäger von Soest the hero reaches the height of his career in terms of worldly fortune and that, as Scholte rightly argues, he also attains a *"Tiefstand"*—the nadir of his relationship to God. And this, after all, is the true theme of the novel. Here too there is irony in that Simplicius in Book III is unaware that his good fortune is illusory. It is not unlike that "dramatic irony" by which playwrights, from Sophocles onwards, have permitted the audience to see the springs of the dramatic action, or to recognize the fate of the hero in advance, without his sharing their knowledge. Dramatic irony has been defined as "the sense of contradiction felt by the spectators of a drama who see a character acting in ignorance of his condition".[26] This is precisely the situation of Simplicius.

Simplicissimus, no less than *The Satyrical Pilgrim,* is concerned with "things of the visible and invisible worlds". If there were any doubt about this it would surely be dispelled by those three "visionary" passages, so skilfully inserted into Books I, III and V, in which the hero is temporarily transported away from the world of everyday experience. The first of these passages is a dream; the second is the vision of a madman and the third involves Simplicius in a somewhat incredible journey to the centre of the earth. Each passage provides an indirect commentary on the main action of the novel.

The first vision is the Dream of the Tree (I, 15). Cold and hungry, the boy Simplicius falls asleep in the hut of his dead mentor, the hermit. He dreams that all the trees around him gradually merge into one tree of which the foliage has been replaced by soldiers. The roots on which the whole weight of the tree rests are composed of workers, craftsmen and peasants. Above the soldiers are the non-commissioned officers and above these in turn, but separated by a slippery branch, sit the officers. At rare intervals money is poured down on to the tree, most of which is caught in the upper branches. All the figures on the tree are striving to make their way upwards, but many fall to the ground and rise no more. The tree is a compelling image of a rigidly hierarchial society at war. At the top the officers are separated from their inferiors by their noble birth. At the bottom the peasants suffer most, since they have constantly to provide the tree with new strength by money from their purses or by sending fresh recruits to sit on the lower branches. Such is the image of a world in conflict where Simplicius' life is to be played out. It is significant that he experiences this dream immediately after witnessing a series of atrocities in the forest near his retreat. His dream marks the final end of the first period of idyllic seclusion and protection afforded by the hermit in the forest. It also prefigures the world of greed, ambition and suffering which Simplicius is about to enter.

The second "visionary" section occurs at that point in the story where Simplicius has come to terms with the world and has apparently won success in it as the Huntsman of Soest (III, 3–6). While making preparations to ambush a convoy of wagons he captures a strange man who is erudite but deranged. The man imagines that he is the god Jupiter who has returned to the world in order to reform it. Here again Grimmelshausen's irony is unmistakable, since Jupiter, despite his insanity, gives an accurate account of the evils besetting Germany : the irreconcilability of the various Christian churches and the disastrous long civil war carried on in the name of religion. In contrast to this diagnosis, the cure which Jupiter proposes is fantastic nonsense. He promises to send forth a strong man—"a German hero"—who will bring peace to Germany and give her that dominant place among the nations which is properly hers. The various Christian churches will be united, if possible by persuasion, otherwise by force, and heretics who do not accept the new "Model" will simply be put to death. These dreams of a German "Utopia"—some sections of which read strangely in the light of more recent German nationalism—are put into proper perspective when Simplicius discovers that Jupiter can hardly deal with the fleas on his own person, let alone current political and religious problems. Jupiter is revealed for what he is, a dreamer whose fantasies are grandiose in scale but utterly unrealistic.

The third vision (V, 10) takes us away from the actualities of the Thirty Years' War to the larger problem of man's position in the universe. The Mummelsee episode—Simplicius' journey through the water of the lake, his exploration of a submarine realm and his interview with the king of the sylphs—represents one of the rare incursions into the novel of the supernatural. The details of the elaborate and fanciful cosmogony described in these chapters need not detain us here, for they must have strained the credulity of many a seventeenth-century reader. As in *Gulliver's Travels* the journey provides a convenient and readable framework for the authors' reflections on the human condition. The sermon given by the king of the sylphs is short and to the point. It might *seem*, he says, that the sylphs, being free from disease and equally at home in fire, water, air and earth, are more fortunate than man. But in fact they are inferior to him in the order of creation since they have no immortal soul and no hope of eternal life. Nothing surprises the king more than men's folly in frittering away this precious gift by their addiction to worldly sins and pleasure, forgetting that life on earth is not the real life but merely a testing time for the human soul : "For this reason we consider the world to be a touchstone of God by which the Almighty tests men, just as the rich man tests gold and silver."[27] There follows an interrogation of Simplicius by the king concerning the state of the world which is reminiscent of Gulliver's cross-examination by the King of Brobdingnag on the state of England. But whereas Gulliver's answers are equivocal those of Simplicius are false. He pretends that the world is inhabited by godly tolerant clerics, just rulers, honest tradesmen and artisans and that the deadly sins have virtually disappeared. As a reward for this information the king gives Simplicius a magic stone with the assurance that it "may profit and benefit you in the same measure as you have put yourself in our debt by revealing the truth".[28] Accordingly, when the magical powers of the stone later become effective, they bring Simplicius no advantage.

The visionary sections in *Simplicissimus* may be regarded as giving answers to three questions which are touched on repeatedly in the novel but never made explicit. The Dream of the Tree deals with the question "What is the state of human society?" and answers that society is evil, based as it is on ambition, privilege, conflict and the oppression of the lower orders. The utopian vision of Jupiter is an oblique reply to the question "What hope is there of reforming the world?", namely that only a lunatic could find grounds for hope. The final question in the Mummelsee episode properly belongs to a catechism : "What can man hope for as his final goal?" The answer is the orthodox Christian one that if he renounces this world he may gain salvation in the next.

The words of the sylph-king mark the final stage in Simplicius' career and anticipate closely his final "Adieu Welt"—almost the only example of Baroque rhetoric contained in the novel (V, 24). The adventures which are recounted briefly in the intervening chapters—his experiences in Russia and his journey round the world back to Rome (V, 20–22)—are diverting enough in picaresque fashion, but they cannot be considered as more than light relief—the additional sugar with which the Baroque satirist coats the pill of the moral. Simplicius has now passed through the three stages of Innocence, Experience and Repentance and is ready to return to the forest-retreat where the old hermit tended him as a child.

This ascetic conclusion makes little immediate appeal to the modern reader. An effort of imagination must be made to recall that the ideal of the devout recluse was not unfamiliar to the seventeenth century, that there were, as a matter of historical fact, hermits in Germany and elsewhere who inspired popular reverence,[29] and that Simplicius' valediction to the world was taken from the work of the Spanish moralist Guevara, the father-confessor of Charles V who himself abdicated to end his days in a monastic retreat. For Grimmelshausen the idea of such a retreat was not merely an acceptable solution; it was exemplary. No doubt he was influenced by the biographies of saints and anchorites which he, and many Catholics and Protestants of the time, had read. Such "exemplary" works appear to have offered one kind of solution to the intellectual and spiritual crisis which so many thinking men of the Baroque age underwent. Grimmelshausen, like Silesius or Gryphius, was deeply disturbed by the apparent duality of a world which was externally attractive but corrupt within, by the conflict between the demands of the passing moment and thoughts of eternity, by the problem of preserving a constant faith in a world which seemed to be governed by fickle fortune. In the hermit Grimmelshausen saw a figure who had overcome these discords and who embodied an ideal which was both attainable and supremely valid for the time in which he lived. It is unimportant that he himself did not find a similar solution in his own life or that in the sequel to *Simplicissimus* (Book VI) his hero again sets out on his travels before finding a final retreat on a remote island. Grimmelshausen's vocation was that of a moral satirist. He likened himself to the ironically smiling satyr depicted in one of his works who recognizes the crooked path followed by the world and sees through the various masks which men put on. His purpose was to ridicule what was wrong with the world and to indicate an ideal for his age. It may be claimed that in his greatest novel Grimmelshausen achieved this end and established himself as a satirist of the same order as Cervantes and Swift.

NOTES

1. Three English translations of *Simplicissimus* have appeared in recent years: *The Adventures of a Simpleton* by W. Wallich (London, 1962); *Simplicius Simplicissimus* by H. Weissenborn and L. Macdonald (London, 1964); *Simplicius Simplicissimus* by G. Schulz-Behrend (Indianapolis, New York and Kansas City, 1965). Despite the Americanisms which it contains the last-mentioned is probably the one to be recommended to English readers because it is accurate, only slightly abridged and contains a good introduction

   The edition to which the present article refers is *Grimmelshausens Simplicissimus Teutsch* (abbreviated below to *ST*), ed. J. H. Scholte, Halle 1949, and for the purpose of quotation I have made my own translations. References other than quotations are made to the number of the book and chapter, thus: III, 7.

   There is no recent full-length study of Grimmelshausen in English, but K. C. Hayens, *Grimmelshausen* (St. Andrews, 1933), is still readable and informative, though details require revision. A more easily accessible and reliable study in German of *Simplicissimus* is C. Heselhaus, "Der Abenteuerliche Simplicissimus" in *Der deutsche Roman,* ed. Benno von Wiese, Vol. I, 1963, pp. 15–63.

2. See R. Alewyn, *Johann Beer,* Leipzig 1932, and Gisela Herbst, *Die Entwicklung des Grimmelshausenbildes in der wissenschaftlichen Literatur,* Bonn, 1957, pp. 18–33.

3. See J. H. Scholte, *Der Simplicissimus und sein Dichter,* Tübingen, 1950, p. 6 ff. and Herbst, p. 35 ff.

4. Scholte, pp. 129–59. See also G. Weydt, *Nachahmung und Schöpfung im Barock*, Bern, 1968, pp. 20–43, where Grimmelshausen's reputation as a "learned man" at the time of his death in 1676 is discussed.
5. Erika Vogt, *Die gegenhöfische Strömung in der deutschen Barockliteratur*, Leipzig, 1932.
6. See H. Singer, *Der deutsche Roman zwischen Barock und Rokoko*, Cologne, 1963.
7. What grieved me often and seldom pleased me? What was it? I have put it in this book so that the reader may follow my example putting folly behind him and living in peace.
8. See A. Albertinus, *Der Landstörtzer*, Munich, 1615. On *Guzman de Alfarache* see A. Parker, *Literature and the Delinquent*, Edinburgh, 1967, pp. 33–45 and 78 ff.
9. Parker, p. 36.
10. Alewyn, *op. cit.*, p. 197 ff.
11. *ST*, p. 9 f.
12. *ST*, p. 124.
13. *ST*, p. 408.
14. *ST*, p. 96.
15. *Der Satyrische Pilgram* (1667).
16. *Der Satyrische Pilgram* in: *Des Simplicissimi Abentheuerlicher Lebenswandel*, Vol. 1, 1713, p. 116.
17. *Sat. Pilgram*, p. 18.
18. "Satyrische Pilgram, Das ist: Kalt und Warm, Weiß und Schwartz, Lob und Schand . . . Beydes lustig und nützlich zu lesen".
19. *ST*, p. 243.
21. *ST*, p. 268.
22. *ST*, p. 182.
23. *ST*, p. 255.
24. *ST*, p. 188; *ST*, p. 224.
25. Scholte, *op. cit.*, p. 12 f. See also G. Weydt, pp. 14–19 and 243–79.
26. G. G. Sedgewick quoted by J. M. Bullitt in *J. Swift and the Anatomy of Satire*, 1953.
27. *ST*, p. 423.
28. *ST*, p. 432.
29. See W. Welzig, *Beispielhafte Figuren* (Graz, 1963), pp. 143–77.

BIBLIOGRAPHY

Alewyn, R., *Johann Beer. Studien zum Roman des 17. Jahrhunderts*, Leipzig, 1932.

Bechtold, A., *J. J. C. von Grimmelshausen und seine Zeit*, Heidelberg, 1914.

Bloedau, C. A., *Grimmelshausens Simplicissimus und seine Vorgänger*, Berlin, 1908.

Gutzwiller, P., *Der Narr bei Grimmelshausen*, Bern, 1959.

Hayens, K. C., *Grimmelshausen*, St. Andrews, 1932.

Herbst, G., *Die Entwicklung des Grimmelshausenbildes in der wissenschaftlichen Literatur*, Bonn, 1967.

Heselhaus, C., "Grimmelshausen, Der abenteuerliche Simplicissimus" in *Der deutsche Roman*, ed. Benno v. Wiese, Vol. I, Düsseldorf, 1963, pp. 15–63.

Hirsch, A., *Bürgertum und Barock im deutschen Roman*, Cologne, 1957.

Konopatzki, I-L: *Grimmelshausens Legendenvorlagen*, Berlin, 1965.

Parker, A., *Literature and the Delinquent*, Edinburgh, 1967.

Scholte, J. H., *Der Simplicissimus und sein Dichter*, Tübingen, 1950.

Singer, H., *Der deutsche Roman zwischen Barock und Rokoko*, Cologne, 1963

Welzig, W., *Beispielhafte Figuren*, Graz, 1963.

Weydt, G., *Nachahmung und Schöpfung im Barock. Studien um Grimmelshausen*, Bern, 1968.

Wieland's *Musarion* and the Rococo verse narrative

Wieland's *Musarion* and the Rococo verse narrative

ELIZABETH BOA

IN many ways we are still living in a post-Romantic and post-realist age. A work based on quite different literary conventions, such as Wieland's *Musarion*, may seem rather alien to the modern reader. For this reason alone, it is useful to look at *Musarion* not in isolation, but as a work written within a particular mode. A true judgement of the poem becomes possible if we realize the Rococo conventions within which it moves.

Any discussion of a work as typical of a literary mode raises problems of method. A too rigid definition of the mode may lead us to split the unity of the individual work into what conforms to our definition and what does not. On the other hand, without any preliminary hypothesis we run the risk of not recognizing the typical, or of not appreciating the individual, way in which an author may use a convention. In Rococo further difficulties arise. Rococo is not primarily a literary term at all, but one borrowed from architecture and the visual arts. Further, as a literary term, it is associated initially with the court literature of France under the *ancien régime*. If the term is to have any useful application to German literature, it is necessary to avoid definitions based too rigidly on the visual arts or on French literature, as such definitions inevitably force the conclusion that few or no German works conform to them. On the other hand, if no common features can be found in the multifarious works to which the term is applied, it ceases to be of much critical use and leads only to confusion. On all counts, it seems reasonable to attempt a fairly general characterization of Rococo, without aiming at an exact definition. We can then consider *Musarion* not only in order to determine why it is Rococo, but also to deepen and widen our understanding of the mode through detailed consideration of one work. The general term is after all abstracted from individual works.

The attributes which spring to mind when one thinks of Rococo works—elegance, charm, grace, lightness—all suggest aesthetic rather than emotional or intellectual qualities. More than many other literary terms, Rococo refers simply to a certain style. While this is true, it is perhaps misleading, since in literature this par-

23

ticular style becomes an end in itself. Rococo implies not just a style, but a mode in which all else is subordinate to style, or more generally to aesthetic considerations.

It must also be asked what the "all else" of Rococo is. Here perhaps three elements from which this style is compounded can be distinguished—an emotional, an intellectual and a sensual appeal. The intellectual and emotional qualities of Rococo are closely connected with the social background against which it flourished. It is essentially a secular mode of social rather than religious inspiration. It addresses itself to a fairly limited public, be it the aristocracy of the court of Louis XV or, in Germany, the small courts and the cultivated bourgeoisie of a few towns such as Dresden and Leipzig. The assumption of a cultivated, urbane public leads to a familiar tone of irony and humour dependent on mutual understanding between author and public. From one point of view, this worldly, frivolous mode could be considered an effete aristocracy's flight from the approaching deluge. More positively, it may be seen as the product of a society at last far enough removed from the upheavals of religious wars to turn from religious preoccupations and fanaticisms to social and secular themes. Compared with the baroque mode, Rococo tends to look at man in purely human terms. Human life is accepted as it is, rather than judged by religious categories. Pessimistic emphasis on the transience of life gives way to optimism and acceptance of man's sensual nature. Frivolity perhaps, but also common sense and realistic psychological insight are the marks of the mode. Here a certain difference is noticeable between France and Germany. A greater predominance of the frivolous and highly sensual in France, in Germany of a more didactic and emotional tendency, point to the great difference between the final flourish of the *ancien régime,* and the awakening consciousness of a German bourgeoisie still partially dependent on borrowed aristocratic modes, but adding to these its own ethos and preoccupations.

This is the background also of the Enlightenment with which Rococo has much in common. The distinctive feature of Rococo might be sought in its emotional appeal. Both have a humanistic rather than a religious approach to man. Both are optimistic. But where the Enlightenment emphasizes more typically the dignity and the self-sufficiency of man as a rational creature, Rococo is more concerned with the pleasures of earthly life and with man as a sensual being. As such, the predominant note is anti-heroic and common-sensical, gay and lighthearted. To sing the joys of life—"And learn a style from a delight" (with apologies to Empson), such are the aims of Rococo.

The third, perhaps most essential element of Rococo, is a strong sensuous appeal, the logical outcome of a view of man as a rational, but also as a sensual, being. It is here that the analogy between literature and the visual arts is clearest. Bosoms and buttocks abound. The curving shape of the *rocaille,* from which the term Rococo is probably derived, is echoed in the curving shape of the female form, whether a Boucher nude or a Dresden shepherdess. It is a sensuality expressed through graceful formalism rather than harsh realism : *Fanny Hill,* not *Tropic of Cancer.* Colour, movement and decorative detail replace the grandeur and massiveness of the baroque style. The fluid rhythms of free verse replace stricter metres. The frozen flourish of a porcelain hunting group, the swirling movement and shifting colour of a Rococo interior, the all-pervasive decorative detail of a Mozart opera or an anacreontic poem : all these are manifestations of the sensuous and sensual appeal which is the hallmark of Rococo in whatever medium.

Rococo style, then, is the blending of an intellectual, an emotional and a sensual element into a unified elegant form. Where intellectuality becomes too strong, the mode approaches the rationalism of the Enlightenment; where emotion is untempered by wit and sensuous beauty, the mode tends towards *Empfindsamkeit* or the cult of sentiment; where sensuality runs riot, unbounded by formal control and unlightened by humour, Rococo will tend to degenerate into overdecorative *Kitsch* or pornography. (Could one imagine, with a bit more humour and elegance, a Rococo de Sade?) Everything must be subject to elegant form which is the product of a balanced mingling of appeal to the senses, the mind and the emotions.

In its literary manifestations, Rococo is very much a "bookish" mode drawing heavily on the classical heritage. However, it is not a classicism in the heroic mould, but one inspired by *late* Greek literature, particularly Anacreon, and by the Roman poets Catullus and Horace. Several translations of Anacreon appeared in German in the 1740s, indeed the dominant form in Rococo literature, along with the verse tale, is the anacreontic poem with its Arcadian setting and hedonistic praise of love and wine. The German poets not only adopted anacreontic motifs, current since the sixteenth century, but were concerned to introduce into German the simplicity of tone and flexibility of language associated with Anacreon and Catullus. Other literary influences were mainly French and English. In the Rococo *Verserzählung* Lafontaine's fables were a major influence from 1738 onwards, when Hagedorn published a selection of translations into German. In 1744 a translation of Pope's *Rape of the Lock* appeared and was widely read. The English combination of wit and frivolity with ethical concern, as in Pope, Prior, Gay or Fielding, was if anything more important in the development of German Rococo than the more highly sensual and anti-moralistic tendency of the French Rococo proper. The main German poets to adopt the *Verserzählung* as a form were Hagedorn, Gellert, Rost and Lessing. B. A. Sørensen distinguishes two main types, the pastoral and the farce.[2] To these Alfred Anger adds a third category based on mythological motifs and used by Gerstenberg, J. G. Jacobi and Wieland.[3] Sørensen gives an excellent brief summary of the changes in style from Baroque to Rococo. *"Vers libre* instead of Alexandrines; chatty irony instead of rhetorical pathos; epicurean enjoyment of love instead of petrarchan lament; subtly sketched psychological states instead of unpsychological exaggerations resulting from a tendency to flamboyant gestures."[4] In Wieland's *Musarion* all these characteristics of the Rococo *Verserzählung* are present, along with a deep knowledge of classical philosophy and a unique sense of the spirit of late Greek and Roman culture.

Musarion was published in 1768 at the height of the Rococo fashion in German literature. It comes in the same period as the author's Rococo *Komische Erzählungen* and the novel *Agathon*. In the 1760s Wieland, after eight years in Switzerland, had returned to Biberach in his native Swabia. The nearby Schloß Warthausen provided a centre of intellectual and social activity under the patronage of Graf Stadion. In this atmosphere Wieland's conversion from the pietistic and sentimental tendency of his Swiss period was completed. In Swabia and in South Germany as a whole, Rococo culture found a more fertile soil than in Switzerland, and it is here that Wieland's first Rococo works were written, principal among them *Musarion*.[5]

Musarion tells of a young Athenian, Phanias, who having lost his fortune retires to the countryside to devote himself to philosophy and the simple life. His mentors are the stoic, Kleanth and the pythagorean, Theophron. The poem opens with the arrival of Musarion, an Athenian hetaira, with whom Phanias has fallen in love but whom he had alienated by his excessively love-lorn posturing. Musarion with the aid of her beautiful slave, Chloe, reveals to Phanias the folly of his philosopher friends. She shows him the way to true wisdom through her "philosophy of the Graces", which seeks a golden mean between idealism and hedonism and tempers emotion with humour, wisdom with grace.

The poem is above all striking for the harmony it achieves between aesthetic and didactic intent. The dominant formal principle of irony fulfils the double function of creating the distance necessary both for aesthetic pleasure and for critical judgement. A philosophy which teaches the unity of ethics and aesthetics is expressed in a form which combines the didactic with the beautiful. We shall see how in a variety of ways—in the treatment of setting, situation and character, narrative technique, details of style and metre—Wieland exploits to the full both the formal beauty and the ironic wit of the Rococo mode with combined didactic and aesthetic effect.

Rococo has a marked tendency towards the miniature form.[6] *Musarion* with almost fifteen hundred lines might seem rather long, but its length is mitigated by its structure. It falls into three sections, each of which forms a typically Rococo scene or tableau. In the first section, Musarion meets the melancholy Phanias who has just decided to forget the pleasures of the world and to lead a life of stoic resignation. Phanias is much disconcerted by her sudden appearance and we see that philosophy has not yet defeated sentiment. They discuss Phanias' misfortunes and their former friendship. Finally Musarion invites herself to spend the night at Phanias' cottage.

The situation and setting of this first section are a charming example of Rococo art. With a few light strokes Wieland sketches an Arcadian-setting—we could easily imagine an embarcation to Cytherea. We see a woodland slope with rough path, a glimpse of the nearby sea and close at hand a cottage with its inevitable linden tree, that archetypal symbol of all German idylls. A nightingale sings. True it is not yet night, but the nightingale is there in his formal rather than his zoological persona. We are in Arcadia, a highly formalized Arcadia robbed of all but the faintest memory of panic terror. As Musarion implies, in venturing into the wilderness, the main risk has been to her coiffure rather than her safety (451).[7] Her fear of cloven-hoofed satyrs is simply an excuse for accompanying Phanias to his cottage (552). The setting then is not so much pastoral as mock-pastoral. In Wieland's irony, however, there is no satiric intent. Nature is not being mocked by a man of urban culture. His irony serves simply to preserve the pre-eminence of the human in this natural setting. The landscape he paints is neither completely formalized, as in a baroque garden, nor yet shown to be in opposition to culture, as in a wild romantic landscape. It might be compared to the landscape gardening of a Capability Brown in which art and nature produce a gentle harmony neither dominated by, nor yet threatening to man.[8] The mythical age is remote, we are in a thinly disguised eighteenth century.

The same irony marks the treatment of the situation. The conventional meeting of nymph and hero or god suffers a comic reversal. As Musarion remarks, the old order is reversed and it is the hero, Phanias, who flees before the pursuing nymph

(192–6). The motif is ancient, but the psychology is eighteenth century. A variety of individual motifs contribute to the Rococo atmosphere, such as the nightingale, the gathering twilight,[8] the rosy cheeks and graceful movements of Musarion. The flashback to the moment of Phanias' awakening love for Musarion is a perfect Rococo miniature (285–94). He gazes with adoration at the nymph asleep in a grove after her bathe. This sensual image is lightened by the comic counter-image of what Musarion saw when she awoke : "Something half way between faun and Eros !" (295). A typical Rococo blend, then, of Arcadian motifs, sensuality and an underlying humorous appeal to common sense. The comic lack of one typical motif—the garland of roses which Phanias is *not* wearing (5)—adds another of the ironic touches which transforms the general Arcadian setting into a Rococo Arcadia.

In the second section, the stoic, Kleanth, and the pythagorean, Theophron, meet Musarion, the embodiment of the "philosophy of the Graces". During a festive evening, Musarion, a gentle Circe, transforms the stoic into a drunken satyr and draws the pythagorean from contemplation of the beauty of the spheres to more active pursuit of beauty in the spherical breasts of the slave-girl, Chloe. Phanias learns that there is more to wisdom than wise words.

The setting and situation of this second section form a second Rococo tableau, this time of a feast by candle-light. Here wine, music and love, the anacreontic themes, are united in a scene which begins with cultivated table talk, but ends as an orgy : a Rococo orgy, however, for it is only a "little Bacchanal" (1000).[6] The canvas is more richly painted than in the opening, coolly elegant, pastoral scene. Decorative motifs abound—the serving youth with his tangled hair, the bowls of fruit, the six jugs of nectar, the lyre and curling beard of Theophron, and the wreath of flowers which completes his transformation into amorous satyr. The strongly pictorial qualities of the poem, which would justify the use of the term Rococo even if it had no accepted literary usage, are splendidly exemplified in the lines describing the entrance of Chloe (965–78). Her round head, crowned by the round shape of a basket with its rounded fruits, her curving breast and shapely calves, her knee, white as wax, glimpsed through shifting veils, what could be more Rococo? The curving decorative shapes, the movement, the grace, the sensuous and sensual appeal are all there to a high degree. The comparison with Hebe and Aurora add the literary touch of classical reference. The wit of the literary Rococo is present too in the reactions of the two philosophers—Theophron immediately inflamed, Kleanth more interested in the fruit. It is in this last detail of Kleanth's indifference to all but the culinary aspect of this feast of beauty that the subtlety of Wieland's art is most evident. Though the poet directs the barb initially against the coarse greediness of the self-confessed stoic, he also achieves a certain comic deflation of what might otherwise have been too cloyingly sweet or oppressively sensual in the description of Chloe. Wieland is no eighteenth-century D. H. Lawrence. Even the taste of sensual pleasure is improved by a grain of salt. This scene, like the first, is typically Rococo in setting, situation and individual motifs, though here we see the more rumbustious side of the mode, as compared with the delicate elegance of the first scene. Both combine the conscious formalism, the wit, the decorativeness and the lightedhearted sensuality which are the general marks of the mode.

Musarion's bedroom is the setting for the third section. The orgy is over. Kleanth has been carried in a drunken stupor to the pig-sty. Where Theophron and Chloe may be is uncertain, but we can guess. Musarion is followed to her room by Phanias, where his education is completed. He learns that though the disciples may be foolish, the doctrines of the Ancients are not invalidated. Musarion teaches him to combine what is best in the stoic and pythagorean doctrines. A middle way of good sense is the lesson she teaches. They enjoy a night of love, it too an experience which teaches, since Phanias learns true love which is neither philandering nor sentimentality. The poem closes on the prospects of their idyllic life together, a life of simple pleasures and quiet wisdom.

The third scene completes the Rococo tryptich. We enter that pre-eminent Rococo setting—a moonlit bed. The situation too is very Rococo—the persistent lover and the reluctant but finally yielding mistress. Once more details of presentation transform a classical motif into eighteenth-century Rococo. This love scene is not one of pagan nakedness nor of Roman self-abandonment in physical passion. Goethe in his *Roman Elegies* is more classical in this respect than Wieland when he celebrates the naked human form, or in his third Elegy compares the speedy course of his love affair with the loves of the gods in the heroic age when— "Desire followed the first look, enjoyment the desire".[9] Wieland, in his bedroom scene, concentrates rather on the sighs and pleadings which are the preliminaries to love. It is the struggle of the nymph which we see, rather than her final abandonment, a prolonged titillation of the reader's senses rather than a frontal attack on his sensibilities. This is in line with countless anacreontic poems where lovers plead outside moonlit casements or are surprised in dalliance rather than in the act. The generally playful nature of Rococo is evident in this concentration on the preliminary play of love. Similarly Rococo offers not nakedness but indiscreet glimpses. In the preceding scene Chloe's veils and Musarions' slipped kerchief allow only momentary glimpses of knee or breast. Here too, a carnation-coloured nightgown allows Phanias to sense rather than see a youthfully swelling breast (1203). Even in the visual arts hints and glimpses are more typical than nakedness. The sensuous appeal of a Bustelli figurine lies in the curve of the whole figure, the typical coquettish backward look and perhaps the glimpse of an ankle. Much is left to the imagination as in pictures of young men watching young ladies on swings and even Boucher's most celebrated nude lies on her face.

In setting and situation this scene, like the others, makes full use of Rococo convention. Once more wit and humour prevent the convention from becoming too sweet. Wieland's ironic use of convention is perhaps most evident in his treatment of the struggling nymph motif (1164–73). This motif in Rococo art is already highly formalized. The nymph struggles because it is the convention that she should, but the lover (and the author and reader) are perfectly aware that the flailing fists and clawing nails are a literary rather than a psychological manifestation. See, for example, the comic *pointe* in Christian Felix Weiße's *The Kiss*. Chloe declares she will scream if her lover kisses her—"And did she scream? Of course she did—But not till it was all over".[10] Wieland takes this literary self-consciousness a step further. Since to scratch is the conventional preface to surrender, Musarion, therefore does not scratch since she is not going to surrender, at least until she is sure of Phanias' love. This is rather similar to the absent rose wreath in the first scene. Wieland adds an extra layer of irony to an already consciously artificial motif. He artificializes the artifice. The scene, then, is a daring combination of extreme sensual appeal with an extreme of witty distance from that very appeal.

The three sections of *Musarion* are three Rococo tableaux and in each we find the elegance, sensuality and wit characteristic of the mode. The Rococo spirit of the poem is evident also in details of style. Recurring anacreontic images and metaphors emphasize the pastoral setting. The joys and pains of love are conveyed through images of wine, dew, flowers, breezes, butterflies, bee-stings and honey. Flatterers and false friends are compared with swarms of flies (45, 435). Philosophy has true and false friends, just as the bee and the caterpillar suck honey or poison, respectively, from the same rose (810). The minor deities of Arcadia, the gods of Olympus and the heroes of classical mythology are constant points of reference. Countless allusions to classical philosophy are decorative and meaningful. They underline the Greek setting; they contribute to the urbane tone of the poem which takes for granted a cultivated public; they express in classical terms a

modern philosophy. The conventional, decorative vocabulary of
Rococo, to which R. H. Samuel refers, is all-pervasive.[11] But to
concentrate simply on the conventional vocabulary and the principle of decorative detail would be to miss the essence of the
style in *Musarion*. This is the blending of decoration and convention with a more familiar, colloquial style. As a result, we
find at the level of language the same sort of witty play with
convention as we remarked at the level of situation and setting.
The conventionality of a phrase or an image is deliberately underlined through ironic juxtaposition with more familiar language.
We are not invited to enter the convention, but are asked to contemplate it from outside, to admire artifice as artifice and to
smile at it.

Other aspects of Wieland's style and technique in *Musarion*
are the conversational tone of the narrator, his stance towards the
characters and the reader, rhythmic and syntactical effects, the
use of narrative suspense and so on. Though aphoristic and
incisive verbal wit plays a rôle in *Musarion*, the main charm of
the poem lies in a warmer overall humour produced by the chatty,
familiar tone and leisurely pace at which the poem progresses.
Wieland's main affinities in English "Rococo" are with Fielding,
not Pope. A rather long passage is therefore necessary to bring
out the peculiar quality of Wieland's narration and the following
extract may serve to illustrate most aspects of his style.

The passage comes near the beginning of the poem. Phanias
has just reached the conclusion that the truly heroic man is he
who seeks wisdom and peace of mind before worldy honours
and glory:

> In solche schimmernde Betrachtungen vertieft
> 135 Lag Phanias, schon mehr als halb entschlossen;
> Als Amor unverhofft die neue Denkart prüft,
> Die Gram, Philosophie und Noth ihm eingegossen.
> Er sah, und hätte gern den Augen nicht getraut,
> Die ein Gesicht, wovor ihm billig graut,
> 140 Zu sehn sich nicht erwehren können.
> Die Götter werden ihm den Ruhm doch nicht mißgönnen,
> Ein Xenokrat zu seyn? Was hilft Entschlossenheit?
> Im Augenblick, der uns Minerven weiht
> Kommt Cytherea selbst zur ungelegnen Zeit.
> 145 Zwar diese war es nicht : doch hätte
> Die Schöne welche kam, vielleicht sich vor der Wette,
> Die Pallas einst verlor, gleich wenig sich gescheut.
> Schön, wenn der Schleier bloß ihr schwarzes Aug entdeckte,
> Noch schöner, wenn er nichts versteckte;

150 Gefallend, wenn sie schwieg, bezaubernd, wenn sie sprach:
Dann hätt ihr Witz auch Wangen ohne Rosen
Beliebt gemacht; ein Witz, dem's nie an Reitz gebrach,
Zu stechen oder liebzukosen
Gleich aufgelegt, doch lächelnd, wenn er stach
155 Und ohne Gift. Nie sah man die Musen
Und Grazien in einem schönern Bund,
Nie scherzte die Vernunft aus einem schönern Mund;
Und Amor nie um einen schönern Busen.
So war, die ihm erschien, so war Musarion.
160 Sagt, Freunde, wenn mit einer solchen Miene
Im wildsten Hain ein Mädchen euch erschiene,
Die Hand aufs Herz! sagt, liefet ihr davon?
"So lief denn Phanias?"—Das konntet ihr errathen![12]

The Rococo vocabulary and imagery is very evident in this passage as in the frequent use of *schön* and the adjectives *gefallend* and *bezaubernd*. The combination of *Witz* and *Reitz* for which Musarion is admired are precisely the qualities sought by Rococo as a whole. The effect of beauty is compared in a typical image with a bee-sting. The decorative use of classical mythology is also there in the reference to Paris' favouring Cytherea (i.e. Aphrodite) rather than Pallas Athene. We see too an example of how Wieland clothes eighteenth-century philosophical and moral disputes in classical garb when he ironically calls Phanias a Xenokrat, that is the teacher of Zeno the stoic, and a man famous for his ability to withstand the charms of women.

The main flavour of the passage comes not so much from this decorative language in itself, as from the variety of tone with which the convention is presented. This is largely the result of the variety of sentence construction. Long periods, rhetorical questions, brief antithetical constructions are mingled with simple conversational colloquialisms. Down to line 144 we find a largely rhetorical style: complex construction, rhetorical questions, and in the couplet (143–4) a final elegant summary clothed in the terminology of classical myth. The irony behind the rhetoric is brought out by the sudden intrusion of the conversational phrase: "Of course it wasn't her" (145), and the comic insistence, also in conversational tone, on the aptness of the classical comparison which follows. Wieland suggests here that the reader might have taken the conventional language literally and supposed that Cytherea herself was approaching. He hastens to assure that this was not the case, thereby underlining ironically the conventionality of the convention, making sure that we notice that the reference to Cytherea is a poetic device. The same effect follows from his insistence that the poetic hyperbole, contained in the comparison of Musarion with the goddess of love herself, is no hyperbole. By thus deliberately making us aware of the conventionality of the language he is using, Wieland invites us to enter into an urbane conspiracy of mutual understanding, to admire a poetic creation which both he and the reader know is artificial.

The passage continues with an excellent example of Wieland's use of free rhythms (148–57). The constantly shifting caesura and frequent enjambement stand in graceful tension with the occasional symmetrical alexandrine or antithetical couplet. The resulting rhythm suggests not geometrical perfection of form, but flowing sinuosity. Emil Staiger quotes these same lines to illustrate the "inexpressible sweetness" of Wieland's verse.[13] This is as consciously poetic in its own way as the rhetorical opening and once again is followed by a change in tone to a very down-to-earth conversational note, from line 159 to the close. What is the effect of the change of tone? First, this poetic vision is rendered abruptly more earthly by our being invited to consider Musarion simply as any young man would consider any beautiful girl suddenly emerging in a lonely woodland glade. Second, the comic transposition from ideal to real makes us more aware than ever that Musarion is an ideal figure whom we are not likely to meet. We find the idea comic in the same way as the discrepancy created by the sudden appearance of an Apollo or an Aphrodite in everyday life would be comic. Musarion is a figure who hovers between the ideal and the real, her very ideality being underlined by more realistic touches.

The shifts in tone from the conventional and poetic to the familiar and down-to-earth distance us from the convention, cause us to look, admire and smile from the outside. The poet uses other techniques with a similar tendency. There is above all the ever-present voice of the narrator, pointing out to us aspects of his own art, addressing himself to the reader over the heads of his characters. There is the intrusion of a fictive reader, expressing interest in the course of events and reminding us that this is fiction, not reality. As K. H. Kausch points out, this also draws the reader into community with the author and fellow-readers, so adding to the intimate, social tone typical of the Rococo *Verserzählung*.[14] Equally ironic in effect is the use of dramatic, or rather undramatic, suspense, since it so often takes the form of the narrator inviting us to wonder what will happen next, when this is quite obvious. Metre and punctuation also create false suspense, as in the frequent use of a dash in mid-line : "He leapt up from the ground, and— stood a moment still" (166).[15] Indeed the obviousness of the plot as a whole, on which Emil Staiger comments, contributes to the predominance of form.[16] A plot is necessary, but we are not absorbed by it, we are made aware by its very obviousness that it is a formal device. We have seen how Wieland emphasises the formal quality of the Arcadian setting. This is true also of his treatment of time, as Staiger points out in his analysis of the Greek background which is really a timeless sphere. That it is intended as timeless is evident from the way anachronism takes on the force of a formal principle. The casual appearance of Hogarth, Goldoni or Cervantes in this classical world is another example of Wieland's witty play with the conventions he is using.

In a great variety of ways Wieland both exploits and ironizes the poetic conventions on which *Musarion* is based. The final effect is of a consciously beautiful, consciously artificial creation. Artificial is used here with no pejorative undertone, since Wieland's irony is in no way destructive. He ironizes without intent to invalidate, but rather to create the distance and awareness essential to aesthetic experience. The mirror of art is here very much a magic mirror enframing a world of heightened beauty and perfection. The strong aesthetic intent of Rococo as a whole is very evident in *Musarion*. This non-mimetic, formal approach points not only to an aesthetic but also to a didactic intent. We are held at a distance not only that we may admire, but also that we may learn. We have seen many incidental felicities in *Musarion,* but the success of the poem as a whole must depend on how far Wieland has succeeded in integrating didacticism and Rococo form. This question is of peculiar significance, since Wieland's "philosophy of the Graces" propounds the unity of ethics and aesthetics. A unified form, at once didactic and beautiful, will convey with all the greater conviction, indeed will exemplify, such a doctrine.

Musarion herself is intended as the very embodiment of the "philosophy of the Graces". Her attributes are a combination of physical and moral grace, the beauty of her mind being manifest in the beauty of her form. The spirits hovering round her, like cherubs round any Rococo beauty, are the Muses, the Graces, and Love himself (155–8). These deities are not merely decorative but convey the attributes of Musarion : wisdom, charm, beauty, and warmth. The Graces in particular convey the double meaning of physical and moral grace. The grace of Musarion is her essence and is manifest in her graciousness to others. This is analagous to the religious use of grace which is a gift of God to be bestowed on others. Musarion's perfection is human, however, not God-given. Yet even Musarion does not escape the veil of humour which envelops the poem since, as we saw, we are invited to regard her simultaneously as poetic ideal and ordinary desirable girl. Musarion's double nature as poetic ideal and desirable girl expresses in itself the philosophy of the poem which teaches a high ideal and yet takes account of human nature. It also allows Wieland to express his philosophy while preserving the humour and sensuous appeal of Rococo.

Phanias is treated even more ironically than Musarion. None of his feelings is taken seriously, neither his misery at the beginning, manifest in his unkempt beard and missing rose wreath, nor his illusory devotion to stoic wisdom. We do not identify with Phanias. His psychology is not presented from within, as an end in itself, to allow the reader insight into a complex individual. He serves rather as a vessel for certain *types* of emotion which we are invited to judge from a combined moral and aesthetic standpoint. This is reminiscent of the treatment of Hans Castorp in *The Magic Mountain*, as is the use of an irony which brings both enlightenment and aesthetic pleasure. There is a general affinity between formal irony to create aesthetic distance and didactic irony used as critique, and Wieland's didactic presentation of his characters in no way conflicts with the Rococo form of the poem. He merely takes the inherent comic tendencies of the mode and uses Rococo humour to a didactic end.

The grace of Musarion is bestowed on Phanias through what amounts to an educative process. Wieland, whose novels represent the first great examples of the German *Bildungsroman,* follows in this Rococo poem too the development of a young man towards maturity. Musarion's philosophy is largely expounded through her attempts to counter the extremes into which Phanias falls. By a neat irony, the last step consists of Phanias drawing Musarion away from momentary exaggeration when he finally persuades her to accept his love (1351–6). The educative process is complete and the pupil has become an equal partner in the dialogue.

In the excesses of Phanias and the doctrines of his two mentors, Wieland criticizes major tendencies of his own age. In the arguments of the stoic Kleanth, Wieland attacks the still surviving aspect of baroque thought which preaches the vanity of all life and the mortification of the flesh as the source of all evil. Musarion, and Wieland, partially accept the view that life is governed by fortune or fate, a fate which includes human nature itself. Kleanth's mistake is double : his conclusion that all is therefore vanity is too pessimistic; his belief in his own power of rational control over the "baser" side of his nature is too rationalistic and takes no account of human psychology. Wieland's strongest argument is the psychological insight that an excess of asceticism and a too blind belief in the powers of reason turn man not into sage or saint, but into beast. Kleanth ends up appropriately in the pig-sty. Wieland teaches, as does Shaftesbury, that true humanity is achieved not through the suppression but through the cultivation of human nature.

In Theophron, the poet castigates another form of contemporary excess. Theophron, unlike Kleanth, is a worshipper of beauty, but of beauty freed from the "filth of sensuality" (921).[17] His discourse is pursued in tones of high enthusiasm. He too, though in a different way, seeks to transcend the human condition and so falls into various extravagant postures, symbolized in his refusal to eat beans, a ludicrous aspect of pythagorean doctrine. Wieland is criticizing all the various excesses of emotional idealism where the overheated imagination loses all touch with reality. *Empfindsamkeit* and *Schwärmerei* or sentimentality and enthusiasm are the terms applied to the various types of irrational, at times anti-rational, cult of spirituality and feeling current in the eighteenth century.

Yet Musarion does not reject the teachings of the Ancients, only the absurdities of the disciples. In the last section of the poem, she praises the great heroes who lived out the doctrines of the sages before these doctrines were ever formulated. But these heroes were great by *nature*. They did not transcend human nature, they brought it to its fulfilment. Our nature itself is given, is an aspect of fate which we must accept. Yet even if we are not all born heroes we may still cultivate our nature as far as possible, by the very faculties bestowed on us by nature, by reason *and* imagination. Musarion herself is presented as an ideal of natural perfection, just as the opening landscape is nonetheless natural for all the elegance of form with which it is presented. In the nineteenth century Rococo was accused of artificiality, whereas Storm and Stress and Romanticism were credited with insight into nature and human nature. This is surely false. What Johan Huizinga writes of Rococo as a whole is certainly true of *Musarion* : "It [the nineteenth century] did not understand that the eighteenth century sought quite consciously in that play of motifs a way back to Nature, but, through stylish form".[18] Musarion's "philosophy of the Graces" teaches a doctrine of natural perfection. This perfection is based on what Sengle calls "the idea of balance",[19] that is on the harmony of the potentially centrifugal forces of human nature, of sentiment and sensuality, reason and emotion, wit and imagination, the good and the beautiful. This doctrine renders explicit the synthesizing tendency which Fritz Martini[20] sees as the outstanding quality of Wieland's work and which B. A. Sørensen[21] attributes to the whole Rococo mode.

Has Wieland succeeded in integrating the philosophy and the Rococo form of the poem? Occasionally a certain strain is evident. In the last section Musarion's need for reassurance concerning

Phanias' intentions seems more typical of a well-brought-up, middle-class young lady than of a Greek hetaira or a Rococo beauty. Overemphasis on humble acceptance of one's lot occasionally disturbs. For the most part, however, the wit with which the philosophy is presented, and indeed the nature of the philosophy itself, allow for perfect formal integration. This is achieved in a variety of ways. One way, as we have seen, was the presentation of the characters. Another is the parallelism of intellectual and physical, or moral and aesthetic qualities which is set up, so that physical description implies moral or intellectual judgement. A striking example of the mingling of the sensual and the philosophical is the glance of Musarion (described with Popean brilliance), to which the poet devotes no less than thirty-three lines (510-33). The effect of this glance on Phanias is to arouse his love again, but also to demolish his argument in favour of stoic asceticism by actively proving its emptiness. Similarly Phanias' wild beard and Theophron's refusal to eat beans are both signs of extravagance and do as much to discredit their intellectual attitudes as any argument. Musarion's beauty and the wrinkled ugliness of Kleanth imply a moral and intellectual judgement on their respective attitudes.

A similar mingling of the sensuous and aesthetic with the ethical and intellectual extends also into details of style. A sensuous adjective qualifies an abstract noun, a verb conveying a physical effect is used to suggest moral or emotional effects, and so on. The description of Musarion quoted above has several examples of these devices. *Scherzen,* a verb with strong sensual undertones in the eighteenth century, and unexpected even in its modern meaning of to joke, is used along with *Vernunft* (156), *Witz* with *Reitz* (151). The effect of the intellectual attribute of *Witz* is conveyed through verbs of physical sensation, e.g. to sting and to caress. Alliteration and rhyme bind together polar qualities and lend formal elegance to serious thought. Musarion's abstract arguments are lightened by the use of sensuous images, as when the ideal of the golden mean is conveyed by the image of breeze-ruffled water compared with wild storm or complete stillness (1136–40). Comically homely concretizations convey abstract thought, as when we are told that enthusiasm is as catching as a cold (310), or that it is absurd to expect the wisdom of Zenos' beard under a women's bonnet (272-3).

Above all it is the "mischievously gentle tone of irony" (685)[22] of Musarion, and of the narrator, which allows so much philosophy to be tempered with wit in Rococo form. The typical conversational tone of the Rococo *Verserzählung,* taken over from Lafontaine and first exploited in German by Hagedorn, is used by Wieland with great mastery. As Preisendanz points out, this technique owes much also to Fielding and the English novel and brings *Musarion* close to Wieland's novels.[23] It serves a similar purpose here to that in the novels. It allows the author to interpret his material, to illuminate it from as many angles as possible, so that the process of interpretation becomes more important than the action itself. As K. H. Kausch put it : "The narrative stance in Wieland is far more varied than the narrated action."[24] Preisendanz distinguishes between Wieland's ironic narrative technique with its ultimately didactic intent and the merely playful irony of the Rococo *Verserzählung* in general, where play with convention through the deliberate breaking of the poetic illusion is an end in itself. Such a distinction, however, overemphasizes the didactic aspect of *Musarion*, to the detriment of its aesthetic qualities. The French critic Michel writes of *Musarion* : "Wieland did not separate poetic form and philosophic action : that is why his genre was the moral tale."[25] The voice of the narrator in Musarion serves as much to create the poetic form as to express a philosophy and the one cannot be separated from the other. Indeed *Musarion* is valuable as a work of art rather than as a potted version of Shaftesbury's moral philosophy, because that philosophy has been transformed into eloquent and elegant Rococo form. The end of the poem provides a brilliant example of Wieland's irony (1432–41). A typical Rococo intrusion of reader and narrator breaks into the idyllic vision of Phanias' and Musarion's wise and peaceful life together. The reader, no doubt exhausted by all the philosophy, catches the poet before he closes to ask about Theophron and Kleanth. The former has learnt to eat beans, says the narrator, and the latter emerged the next day from the pig-sty and was never heard of again. Thus the poem closes on a comic anti-climax in a typical Rococo play with the convention of the pastoral idyll. Yet this comic close does not invalidate the ideal of the "philosophic idyll",[26] but simply underlines that it is an ideal. The comic twist is a humorous expression of Wieland's rueful insight into human limitation, an insight which informs his whole philosophy. Thus philosophic import and Rococo formal wit are fused here as in the poem as a whole.

Musarion is very much a central work of its age. Formally it is indebted to the literary conventions of the mid-eighteenth century. The "philosophy of the Graces" is compounded of the moral and aesthetic philosophy of Shaftesbury, the rational and optimistic humanism of the Enlightenment, and a concern with nature and the imaginative powers of man which might be called pre-romantic.[27] A final evaluation of the poem must surely rest on its nature as a complex unity. It is complex through its variety of appeal to the senses, the mind and the emotions, through the balance it holds between so many currents of thought. It is a unity by virtue of its complete integration of form and content, or rather of aesthetic and didactic intent, since both "form" and "content" combine these two elements. Is it exemplification or transcendance of the Rococo mode? Preisendanz argues that its seriousness lifts it above the frivolity of Rococo.[28] Huizinga, on the other hand, writes of Rococo as a whole words which certainly apply to *Musarion* : "Few ages in the history of art have held such a perfect balance between the serious and the playful as Rococo."[29] Does it matter in the end? A literary generalization is a step-ladder to approach the individual work and can be left behind when its purpose is accomplished.

NOTES

1. Cf. I. A. Stamm, "German Literary Rococo", in *G.R.* 36, 1961, pp. 230–41 where a definition of Rococo derived from music and the visual arts is used as an instrument of negative criticism.
2. B. A. Sørensen, "Das deutsche Rokoko und die Verserzählung im 18. Jahrhundert", in *Euphorion* 48, 1954, pp. 125–52.
3. Alfred Anger, *Literarisches Rokoko,* Metzler (Sammlung Metzler No. M25), Stuttgart, 1962, p. 78.
4. Sørensen, op. cit., p. 134.
5. See F. Sengle, *C. M. Wieland,* Metzler, Stuttgart, 1949 for a description of life at Warthausen (pp. 141–50) and for a discussion of South Germany and Rococo (pp. 171–2).
6. See Alfred Anger, op. cit., pp. 50–2, for a discussion of "Der Zug zum Kleinen" in Rococo.
7. Line references to *Musarion* are given in brackets throughout. Quotations follow the edition of Alfred Anger, Reclam, Stuttgart, 1964.
8. Cf. A. Anger, "Landschaftsstil des Rokoko", *Euphorion* 51, 1957, pp. 151–91. Though 1773 is the date of the first English garden in Germany, the landscape in *Musarion* has something of the expansiveness of the English style as well as having the enclosed grove and labyrinthine paths typical of literary Rococo settings. Anger also refers to the shadows and twilight typical of Rococo settings.
9. "Folgte Begierde dem Blick, folgte Genuß der Begier".
10. "Und schrie sie nicht? Jawohl sie schrie—/Doch lange hinterher" Ch. F. Weiße, *Scherzhafte Lieder,* Leipzig, 1758.
11. R. H. Samuel, Rococo, in *Periods in German Literature,* ed. J. M. Ritchie, Oswald Wolff, London, 1966, pp. 49–50.
12. "Deep in such shimmering meditations as these
   Lay Phanias, already half decided,
   When love at once appears and tests the novel thoughts
   Which pain, philosophy and need inspired in him.
   He saw, and fain would have misbelieved his eyes,

The one visage which he rightly fears
He cannot dare to see.
The gods will surely not begrudge to him the fame
Of being a Xenocrat? What use decision?
In the instant we are given to Minerva
Comes Cytherea herself in most untimely fashion.
Of course it wasn't she: and yet
The beauty who came perhaps had feared as little
To face the test which Pallas once lost.
Fair, when the veil uncovered only her dark eyes,
Yet fairer when all was uncovered.
Pleasing when she was silent, enchanting when she spoke;
Then would her wit have made lovely
Cheeks without roses; a wit which never failed in charm,
Ready to sting or to caress—
Yet never sting without a smile
And free of poison. Never were the Muses
And Graces in more perfect union,
Never did reason laugh from a lovelier mouth;
Nor love play round a fairer breast.
Such was she who appeared, such was Musarion.
Say, friends, if in some lonely woodland grove
A girl like this appeared before you,
Hand on heart! say, would you run away?
'Did Phanias run then?' You easily can guess".

13. Emil Staiger, "Wieland: Musarion", in *Die Kunst der Interpretation*, Atlantis, Zürich, 1955, p. 107. Also in *Wieland, vier Biberacher Vorträge*, Insel-Verlag, 1954.
14. K. H. Kausch, "Die Kunst der Grazie", in *Jb. der deutschen Schillergesellschaft* 11, 1958, pp. 12-42.
15. "Er sprang vom Boden auf, und—hielt ein wenig still".
16. Emil Staiger, op. cit.
17. "Schlamm der Sinnlichkeit".
18. Johan Huizinga, *Homo Ludens: Vom Ursprung der Kultur im Spiel*. Rowohlt, Hamburg, 1956, p. 179. c.f. English Version. Routledge & Kegan Paul (London, 1949).
19. F. Sengle, op. cit., p. 205.
20. Fritz Martini, "Wieland und das 18. Jahrhundert", in *Festschrift für Paul Kluckhohn und Hermann Schneider*, 1954, pp. 243–65.
21. B. A. Sørensen, op. cit., p. 128.
22. "Schalkhaft sanfte Ton der Ironie".
23. Wolfgang Preisendanz, "Wieland und die Verserzählung des 18. Jahrhunderts", in *G.-R. Monatschrift* 12, 1962, pp. 17–31.
24. K. H. Kausch, op. cit., p. 25.
25. Victor Michel. *C. M. Wieland, La formation et l'évolution de son esprit jusqu'en 1772*, Paris, 1938, p. 378.
26. Cf. Michel, op. cit., p. 375.
27. See Fritz Martini, op. cit., for an evaluation of Wieland's seminal position in the development of German literature.

28. Wolfgang Preisendanz, op. cit.
29. Johan Huizinga, op. cit., p. 179.

BIBLIOGRAPHY

For full bibliographical information on all aspects of Rococo see:

Alfred Anger, *Deutsche Rokoko-Dichtung*. Ein Forschungsbericht. Metzler (Stuttgart, 1963) offprint from *DVjs* 36, 1962, pp. 430–79; 614–18.

Alfred Anger, *Literarisches Rokoko*, Metzler (Sammlung Metzler No. M25) (Stuttgart, 1962), is a shorter version of the same material.

See also R. H. Samuel, "Rococo", in *Periods in German Literature*, ed. J. M. Ritchie (London, 1966), for publications since 1962.

For literature on the "Verserzählung" and Wieland's *Musarion* see works cited in the Notes and:

J. Wiegand, "Verserzählung", in *Reallexikon der deutschen Literatur*, III, 466ff.

K. H. Kausch. "Wielands Verserzählunger im Unterricht der Oberstufe", in *Der Deutschunterricht*, xl, 1959, p. 71 ff.

Lessing's *Hamburgische Dramaturgie* and the Enlightenment

III

Lessing's *Hamburgische Dramaturgie* and the Enlightenment

R.W. LAST

IN an age when the theatre was dominant, Lessing's *Hamburgische Dramaturgie* was funnier than many of the comedies, profounder than many of the tragedies of the time; yet it may seem a little suspect to select this piece of critical rather than creative literature as the representative work for the Enlightenment; and its choice might well provoke one of two reactions: either, that there are no creative works of sufficient standing to fill the part; or, more charitably, that none of them is representative enough. There is some truth in both reactions, for in Germany the Enlightenment was both a hard struggle towards literary independence and a prolonged one. It was no short-lived explosion initiated by great works, tailing gradually off into insignificance, but rather the reverse. The great works came only after extensive critical and philosophical preparation. Nor was it an harmonious gathering of like-minded spirits; indeed many men of letters of the time disputed furiously among themselves, and there was no better exponent of the literary feud than Lessing himself. The eighteenth century in Germany may have been the Age of Reason, but it was the age of a whole host of other things too.

In this confusion of literary cross-currents bearing the deceptively straightforward title Enlightenment, the *Hamburgische Dramaturgie* stands out as a unique document of the aspirations and disappointments of a man burning to raise German literature to the level at which it might stand comparison with that of its French and English neighbours; it reflects far more than the deplorable state of the German drama, the art-form at the centre of the literary revival, for it also offers a picture of the towering intellect and personality of a great rationalist who used this starting-point to produce an unequalled impact on the mental climate of his age.

In 1767, Gotthold Ephraim Lessing (1729–81) found himself faced with one of the many disappointments that beset his life. Born almost inevitably as one of the numerous children of a

45

Lutheran pastor in Kamenz, Saxony, he had shone at school both near his home and at St. Afra's in Meissen. His early years laid the solid foundation of a profound knowledge of the classics and of literature in general; a portrait of the child Lessing depicts him surrounded by learned tomes staring intently out from the canvas; and even when still a schoolboy he made his first ventures into writing—with a comedy. 1746 found him at Leipzig University, where, in accordance with the wishes of his father, he embarked on the study of theology, but he was soon drawn to more worldly disciplines, and to extra-curricular activities such as the theatre and journalism, neither of which afforded him any financial security.

He had already gained success as the author of the first important German middle-class tragedy, *Miss Sara Sampson* (1755), and of the comedy *Minna von Barnhelm* (1767), as well as of critical writings, notably *Laokoon* (1766), when, in 1767, the post of librarian at the Royal Library in Berlin fell vacant. This seemed to offer both a due reward for his labours and security in surroundings congenial to his literary interests, and Lessing was recommended on all sides to Frederick the Great. But the position was granted instead to a Frenchman (by all accounts, a totally unsuitable candidate), in a kind of symbolic statement of the lowly condition and standing of German culture in its own land; and thus, when an invitation arrived for Lessing to join the newly-formed National Theatre in Hamburg, he accepted with alacrity.

Hamburg was the leading theatrical centre of the time; and the opera house had been demolished to make way for a new theatre building—the old was cramped and inadequate—which first opened its doors at the end of July 1765. The manager, Konrad Ernst Ackermann (1710–71), had brought his own company to perform there, but fell into difficulties and was compelled to resign. A group of twelve businessmen came together to reconstitute the theatre under Johann Friedrich Löwen (1729–71), who had been instrumental in Ackermann's decline and fall. Löwen put forward the title National Theatre (*Nationaltheater*). The project bristled with good intentions: the advancement of the German theatre, the betterment of conditions for the actors, etc. No eighteenth-century German theatre being complete without a resident dramatist, the new management cast about for a suitable figure to fill the post, and lighted upon the name of Lessing, whose already established reputation would, they hoped, lend dignity and prestige to the National Theatre.

Lessing, by his own admission neither actor nor poet, and lacking within him the "living well-springs" (101–4, X, p. 209)[1] essential to the true creative writer, was reluctant to commit himself to writing plays to order. Still, his appointment was confirmed without, so it seems, his actual tasks being clarified. So it was that, instead of a resident dramatist, the National Theatre found itself with a resident critic.

According to the dates which head the 104 issues of his reviews of the National Theatre productions, which he termed the *Hamburgische Dramaturgie* (and which he just avoided calling the *Hamburgische Didaskalien* (101–4, X, p. 211)), it seems that Lessing filled this unique position with unflagging enthusiasm for fifty-two wccks, writing at a rate of two issues per week, even including one for Christmas Day, 1767. The actual dates of publication, however, reveal that he started regularly enough, but gradually fell further and further behind both the ostensible dates of publication and the performances discussed (for example, the issue dated 16 February 1768 makes reference to three plays first performed between 22–24 July of the previous year), and the last twenty or so issues did not appear until Easter 1769.[2]

The reason for this discrepancy, and for the decline of the National Theatre leading to its final collapse in March 1769, lies in the widening gulf between its aspirations and actual attainment. The repertory of the theatre shows "hardly a trace of that purpose which Löwen had emphasized . . . namely, to encourage and further the interests of German—or indeed, any other—dramatic literature . . . The plays which were performed were selected exclusively from the standpoint of theatrical expediency".[3] Of the 120 productions, the majority of which were comedies, eighty were foreign in origin. Of these, there was a scattering of English, Italian, and Dutch pieces, but by far the largest number (70) were French, a situation which speaks volumes for the condition of the German theatre at the time. And only four of the plays Lessing discussed were first performances.

As the fortunes of the National Theatre wavered, Lessing's writings became more and more removed in time and content from the performances; from reviews and polite comments upon the acting they rapidly developed to the status of an independent work with a wide range of interest, which cast only an occasional cursory glance at the stage it was supposedly furthering with its analyses.

The *Hamburgische Dramaturgie* has been tarred with so many brushes that it is difficult now to see through to its real significance. It has been damned as derivative, and excused as eclectic ; hailed as seminal, and passed off as a work of very little lasting influence on the course of German letters, but, for all that, "still interesting in itself".[4] One of the commonest complaints raised against it is that it does not hang together; and that "too much of the *Dramaturgie* is taken up with relatively worthless subjects".[5] This is rather like accusing a dictionary of lacking a plot and including much frivolous material; for the *Hamburgische Dramaturgie* is by its very nature episodic and dependent upon external stimuli. It is no carefully excogitated critical study on a single theme, which sets out to present a package of ideas already fully matured in advance; it grows rather from a series of performances of plays—which may or may not be worthless in themselves—into arguments and discussions on a whole variety of topics, and it is these latter, not the catalytic performances, that form the core of the work. Lessing is not acting, but reacting. To a large extent the National Theatre is as irrelevant to the *Hamburgische Dramaturgie* as its half-hearted and piecemeal efforts were to the advancement of the German stage; in again and again drawing general conclusions from specific points of detail, Lessing is arguing the necessity of a well-founded theoretical basis before any genuine progress can be made in practice. Hence, in spite of its apparent disjointedness, there are several threads running through the *Hamburgische Dramaturgie* which lend it some kind of unity, although it does not aspire to a tightly-knit construction; of these, four are relevant to our study of its place in the Enlightenment: (1) the concern with first principles; (2) the theory of tragedy; (3) the personality of the author; and (4) the positive aims.

(1) The concern with first principles

In his discussion of the qualities of the actor Ekhof, Lessing underlines the necessity for a confident and accurate delivery, and then issues this warning:

> When need be, even a parrot can be taught to speak with the correct inflections. How far removed is the actor who merely understands a passage from one who can at the same time feel it as well! (3, IX, p. 193).

Lessing demands of the actor not simply that he go through the motions of portraying character, he must also show a profound and genuine emotional involvement. Appearances are not enough.

All the critical sallies and theoretical soliloquies in the *Hamburgische Dramaturgie* pursue this pattern: they set the superficial against the genuine, the half-hearted against the sincere. They seek to break through the confused tangle of outward appearances in order to distil the essential principles that underlie them. Above all, in the exposure of pedantry to the harshest treatment and the constant endeavour to create a sharp distinction between what he himself termed the letter and the spirit, they show Lessing in pursuit of Truth, the Enlightenment goal.

This comes across clearly in the observations on the place of historical truth in the drama, which lie scattered about the text of the *Hamburgische Dramaturgie*. A tragedy, argues Lessing, is not, and should not be, history re-written in verse form:

> For the dramatic poet is no historian; he tells his story . . . not for the sake of mere historical exactitude, but with another, much higher, purpose; historical truth is not his goal, but only the means to his goal; his aim is to offer us an illusion, and through illusion move us. (11, IX, pp. 227–8.)

As we seldom know the whole truth about them, historical personages present many apparent contradictions of character, and we are in no position to resolve them; for this reason they are unsuitable in their raw state for drama, where intimate knowledge of the hero and his motivations is essential. Besides, Lessing argues, the dramatist does not need history just because it happened, but because it happened in such a way that it proffers the best vehicle for dramatic expression in the circumstances. The dramatist should, therefore, not concern himself with the outward pattern of events, but rather with their "inner plausibility" (19, IX, p. 261). History is useful, but only as a starting point.

> In short: tragedy is not history rendered into dialogue; history is for tragedy no more than a collection of names, which we are accustomed to associate with certain character-types. If the dramatist finds in history a large number of circumstances suited to the embellishment of his material and rendering it individual ; well and good, let him make use of them. (24, IX, pp. 282–3.)

It is not the function of the dramatist to produce a replica of the historical Cato on stage, but to use the name "Cato" as a convenient label for a central figure bearing those qualities associated in the mind with Cato. The choice is free; but, once made, the characters must be utterly consistent and credible.

So the superficial in drama is represented by the historical background, the essential by the characters. For it is the characters, not the events or milieu, that lie at the heart of the dramatic form.

The same concern for first principles can be seen in Lessing's crucial discussion of the attitude of the French towards the rules that govern drama, and hence their suitability as models for the German stage ; here, in a caustic comment on Voltaire's *Mérope*, Lessing concedes that its author does indeed conform to the unity of time, but he has been true to the letter of this rule, but not to its spirit. For what he causes to take place in *one* day can indeed be accomplished in *one* day, but no man in his right mind would do it in *one* day. (45, IX, p. 375.)

It is fortunately not our purpose to engage in the controversy surrounding this attack by Lessing, in which various claims are made that he misunderstood the French.[6] From his statements in the *Hamburgische Dramaturgie,* however, it seems clear that he understood them only too well; besides, the real point at issue is not whether he comprehended their principles and intentions in absolute terms, but how he interpreted them and what his attitude towards them was.

It should be made clear, not only in regard to his francophobia, but to all the attacks he makes, that, although Lessing's onslaughts are pitiless, they are not vindictive. He is not engaged in personal bickering ; he attacks with a higher purpose. Voltaire may be pilloried for his vanity in allowing himself to be adulated by his audiences, but he is also praised in the *Hamburgische Dramaturgie* for his intelligence and creative thinking. A cornerstone of Lessing the rationalist's convictions, as both man and critic, is his insistence upon intellectual honesty and integrity, and on these grounds too some very harsh words are meted out to Voltaire : he accuses him of dubious critical practices in that he crept behind the pseudonym of Lindelle in order to attack an Italian version of *Mérope* by Maffei.

Lessing's main target, however, is neither vanity nor duplicity, but rather the weaknesses he finds in the arguments of Lindelle/ Voltaire :

> Lindelle accuses Maffei of frequently not linking his scenes together, of frequently leaving the stage empty, of frequently letting his characters come on and go off without motivation; all these fundamental errors, which one would nowadays no longer pardon in the work of the most wretched hack.—And these are fundamental errors? That is the French critic all over. (44, IX, p. 370.)

The key word is "fundamental". Lessing asks if such secondary considerations really matter, in the same way as he demands else-where, when discussing the merits and demerits of a play's title, if it is not preferable to have a good comedy with a poor title, rather than the reverse.

The French, in Lessing's view, have tied themselves down to regulations to which they pay lip service without examining their validity. And this is the burden of his confrontation with Corneille :

Corneille had already written all his plays when he sat himself down to compose a commentary on Aristotle's *Poetics*. For fifty years he had worked for the theatre : and this experience would doubtless have allowed him to make invaluable statements about the old dramatic codex, if only he had consulted it more keenly in his work as a dramatist. But he only seems to have done this with regard to the mechanical rules of art. In the more fundamental aspects he did not bother himself with them, and when in the end he found that he had transgressed against them, although it was not his intention to have done so, he sought to excuse himself through his interpretations and put things into the mouth of his supposed master which the latter had clearly not the least intention of saying. (75, X, pp. 104–5.)

Lessing accuses Corneille of having done immeasurable harm to French drama, partly because of this manipulation of the precepts of Aristotle, partly also through his vanity—and that of the French nation as a whole—in believing that to take the drama one step away from barbarity was tantamount to bringing it to the threshold of perfection (81, X, p. 128).

He enumerates Corneille's most blatant distortions of Aristotelian tragic theory : tragedy, says Aristotle, demands both pity and fear, but Corneille says one or the other alone will suffice; this pity and/or fear should be generated by one single character, but this is not, in Corneille's eyes, necessary; Corneille misunderstands the nature of pity and fear and their cathartic effect; he distorts the statement that no wholly good man should suffer misfortune, because, maintains Lessing, more than one of Corneille's "tragic" heroes would otherwise be in grave danger of being nothing of the sort; he distorts the reverse, that no wholly bad character can fill the central rôle of a tragedy; and, finally, Corneille manipulates the concept of moral goodness in the tragic figure.[7] No wonder Lessing states that he prefers a Spanish play which breaks every rule in the book, because it possesses qualities that far outweigh a mechanical subservience to standing orders :

A highly individual plot; a very inventive intrigue; a large number of extraordinary coups de théâtre, all original; the tensest situations; characters that are for the most part well motivated and consistent throughout; and the whole expressed in dignified and powerful language. (68, X, p. 75.)

The essentials are present; the rest does not matter. Better break the rules well than keep them badly.

To the Ancients, the rules of drama were simply the inevitable consequence of the total situation in which their works were written and performed. All other rules flowed naturally from that of unity of action. When the French took over the rules, they found them something of an embarrassment, to say the least. Instead of having the courage of their convictions, like the Spanish playwright, they twisted them to the point of meaninglessness. They circumvented the inconvenience of the unity of place by making the setting "an undefined locality" (46, IX, p. 378); and the unity of time by stretching it to allow the characters to go to their several beds not more than once within the course of the action. Lessing's reaction to these tortuosities speaks for itself :

> What a fuss they make about sticking to the rules which they have made so immensely simple for themselves!—But I cannot endure to discuss these rudiments any longer.
>
> For all I care Voltaire's *Mérope* and Maffei's can last a week and be located in seven different places in Greece! But let them only be endowed with qualities such as will make me forget these pedantries!
>
> The strictest adherence to the rules cannot compensate for the least error in characterization. (46, IX, p. 379.)

But if the French tragedians represent merely the letter of the rules, and are thus unsuitable as models, what reflects the true Aristotelian spirit? If Lessing is seeking to rid the German stage of these pseudo-tragedies from beyond the Rhine, what does he want to put in their place?

The answer is a little obscure, partly because, in the *Hamburgische Dramaturgie,* Lessing tends to accentuate the negative, but also because the German theatre-going public was not ready for the kind of reforms he would like to institute. The fate of the grandiose National Theatre enterprise is itself justification enough for Lessing's only sketchy setting up of Shakespeare as a counter model to the French.

This is yet another favourite battleground for the academic critic, for the *Hamburgische Dramaturgie* contains relatively infrequent references to the bard, and those that are there do not make it clear whether Lessing intends Shakespeare to fill the part of an Aristotelian tragic dramatist or not. Lessing accuses Christian Weiße, for example, of showing a thoroughly bad Richard III, but Shakespeare's King is equally lacking in the essential admixture of qualities and defects. It is possible that Lessing either totally misunderstood Shakespeare or that he considered his plays not to be tragedies in the Aristotelian sense, and therefore not covered by the rules.[8] This would either render him a fool, or inconsistent in putting Aristotle at the head of an empire which he does not govern. And Lessing is neither a fool nor inconsistent. The most reasonable interpretation of Lessing's advocacy of Shakespeare is surely that he intended it firstly to form part of his general campaign for a greater English influence on the German stage; and, secondly, that he *did* "understand" Shakespeare in his own eighteenth-century terms; that is, that he "understood" and used what he saw in Shakespeare in the same way that Wieland's translations put Shakespeare across in a manner understandable to the audiences of the day in the light of their attitudes to life. There are two further important considerations : the first is the kind of praise which Lessing bestows upon Shakespeare :

> All things in Shakespeare, even down to the smallest details, are fashioned according to the grand scale of the historical drama, and this bears roughly the same relationship to the tragedy in the French taste as a vast fresco to a miniature painted for a ring. (73, X, pp. 95–6.)

Shakespeare is not working to rule, but according to his own powerful natural inspiration; he embraces all life, not just the narrow confines of court society. And the other consideration is that Shakespeare grasps the essence of drama in his superlative characterization. Lessing may have found himself unable to reconcile these qualities of Shakespeare and their natural laws with his own—and Germany's—need for an authoritative basis for drama, but even so he is at least able to recognize that the central virtues of Shakespearean drama are of greater validity for the German theatre than the superficial restrictions and artificiality of French classical tragedy.

(2) *The theory of tragedy*

The character-centred drama which Lessing propounds is to be founded upon Aristotelian principles; Lessing, however, always aware of the realities of a situation, does not work from theory to practice, but rather asks himself first the essential question :

> Why the tiresome drudgery of the dramatic form, why build a theatre, dress up men and women, torture their powers of memory, invite the whole town to one spot, if all I intend to do with a work and its performance is to excite some of the emotions which a good story read by anyone in his comfortable nook at home would also arouse in roughly the same way? (80, X, p. 123.)

His answer is that the drama is the sole art medium that can exercise an immediate, powerful, and direct impact upon its audience, and for this reason the principles upon which it is founded should be the soundest possible, in order to render that impact most unambiguous and beneficial.

Life, argues Lessing, is contradictory, filled with tragic and comic elements juxtaposed in a random pattern; why should dramatic art not be similar? For, after all, art is, in the view of the Enlightenment, supposed to be an imitation of nature. But, he continues, some kind of limitation of viewpoint is essential— and this is no more than we do all the time in real life, for we are too restricted creatures to be able to see the workings of Providence in all things simultaneously; therefore we select. Only thus can we learn the lessons of life. Lessing uses the same argument to discourage the creation of characters with inner contradictions, "for they lack educative force" (34, IX, p. 327). The other element of art—beauty—is also brought to light by selectivity. (It is curious—and something of a relief when dealing with a man of such incisive clarity of mind—to note, however, that Lessing had no objection to the highly suspect contemporary practice of having a comic epilogue to round off the evening at the theatre, imme- diately following upon high tragedy.)

Having established the validity and purpose of theatre, namely to please and instruct, Lessing continues by exploring its workings, based upon Aristotle's rules. Tragedy should move and educate; and the means towards this end is the exploitation of the emotions of pity and fear.

Pity is experienced for a character in a tragic situation only if he or she is neither wholly good nor wholly bad. In the first case, a wholly good character suffering is inconsonant with an ordered, meaningful universe (for example, Corneille's Polyeucte); and in the second, we should have no pity for a thoroughly bad character (Weiße's Richard III). Fear is pity turned in on ourselves, which grows from a sympathy for the suffering character. We fear that we might by some lapse or other become enmeshed in a similar unpleasant web of circumstances. When the dénouement comes, the result is catharsis, purging of the emotions; and after the curtain has fallen at the end of the drama, our pity has now been fully worked out, and only fear remains as an educative force.

It is too much to expect that the theatre should be a kind of clinic for spiritual healing; in both tragedy and comedy (where laughter replaces pity), it reinforces good rather than curing bad:

Granted that Molière's L'Avare never cured a miser, that Regnard's Joueur never cured a gambler; admitted, that laughter is incapable of curing these fools: so much the worse for them, but not for comedy. It is sufficient, although it cannot heal hopeless sicknesses, that it strengthens the health of the sound in mind. A miser can be instructive even to the generous man; even the non-gambler can learn from the man who gambles; the follies which they do not have are to be found in others with whom they have to live; it is beneficial to know such follies as one can meet with; beneficial to protect oneself against being favourably impressed by their example. Positive medicine too has its value. (29, IX, pp. 303–4.)

And, reducing tragedy to its basic essentials, Lessing states that

in a word tragedy is a work of literature that arouses pity. By nature it is the imitation of a sequence of actions, like the epic and the comedy : but by genre it is the imitation of a sequence of actions that merit pity. From these two concepts every single one of its rules can be adduced; and even its dramatic form should be determined by them. (77, X, p. 111.)

This is the true spirit of tragedy; and any other "rules" are—or should be—but a natural consequence.

(3) The personality of the author

The *Hamburgische Dramaturgie* reveals much of what Lessing was like, particularly so because in this loose critical newsletter form, when reacting to external challenges, he is in his element. In the *Hamburgische Dramaturgie* he is completely in command, relaxed, and unpretentious. At one point, for example, he feels no qualms about telling his readers that he would like to quote something, but unfortunately cannot lay his hands on the book in question. Only occasionally is he caught off his guard with a misquotation, or with a passage like the one on theatrical music, in which he tediously states the obvious at great length (26–7, IX, pp. 290–8).

For the most part, however, whatever the merits of the subject-matter, the *Hamburgische Dramaturgie* is a delight to read. Lessing has an infectious enthusiasm for ideas : at times he is even carried away by them to the extent that he seems more anxious to score debating points than to reach a valid conclusion. But he is mostly anxious to get to the bottom of a problem; often he expresses it in terms of a paradox, and worries away at it until it is solved to his satisfaction.

At the heart of the *Hamburgische Dramaturgie* lies this Enlightenment delight in exercising the mind, and in involving and carrying the reader with him on his polemical path. Nowhere is he shown to better advantage in this respect than in the matter of Voltaire's ghost in *Semiramis,* which he compares unfavourably with Hamlet's father, and questions the advisability of a spectre appearing before a large gathering :

In Shakespeare it is with Hamlet alone that the ghost has dealings; in the scene where the mother is present, it is neither seen nor heard by her . . . The ghost calls forth a response in us more through Hamlet than of itself. The impression it makes upon him is transferred on to ourselves and the effect is too evident and too strong for us to cast doubt upon its extraordinary cause. How little Voltaire has understood this technique! A great deal of people are frightened by his ghost; but not a great deal. Once Semiramis cries out : "Heavens! I die!" and the others pay about as much attention to him as one would to a friend thought to be some way off, who suddenly enters the room. (11, IX, p. 230.)

As soon as one problem is resolved, Lessing is off to tackle another. The hunt gives him more real pleasure than the kill.

To this approach the form of the *Hamburgische Dramaturgie* is ideally suited. The style, in the best Enlightenment manner, is straightforward, always lucid and appropriate to the subject-matter :

Dialogue (with or without the other person's reply) is Lessing's fundamental form of expression. Not only in the drama but in the critical writings. Someone is being addressed nearly all the time. It is a vivid style punctuated by accents of arraignment or appeal. An orator pleading a case, ridiculing an enemy, tickling the responses of the public. It is a persuasive style and therefore rhetorical devices are in place in it. We note the use of interjections, apostrophes (sometimes to the reader), intensification by repetition or variation or enumeration, the anaphoric taking-up of an idea and spinning it further, the casting of a word into unusual relief by unusual word-order and the brilliant use of punctuation in which the very dots and dashes speak.[9]

Lessing's intellectual standards are rigorous. He relentlessly seeks out factual errors; and is particularly savage with bad ideas, notably when demolishing Corneille's rehash of Aristotle. Corneille, it will be recalled, suggests that it is not necessary to have both pity and fear together in tragedy, and Lessing retorts :

If, for example, we say of a lady that she has neither wit nor beauty : what we are trying to express is that we should be content if she had just the one or the other; for not only can one think separately of wit and beauty, the two are truly separate concepts. But if we say : "This man believes in neither heaven nor hell", are we trying to say in this case too : that we should be content if he only believed in one of them, if he only believed in heaven and not in hell, or only in hell and not in heaven? Of course not : for he who believes in the one cannot help but believe in the other; heaven and hell, punishment and reward are interrelated; if one exists, so must the other. (76, X, pp. 106–7.)

Lessing's touch is supremely confident, and with justification, although some of his lesser opponents must have found it a little galling to be described as grasshoppers :

But why am I wasting my time with these gossipers? I shall continue on my way and pay no attention to the grasshoppers chirping by the wayside. It is too much trouble even to take one step off the path in order to crush them. Their brief summer is so quickly over! (96, X, p. 191.)

There was nothing Lessing liked better than a dispute with a man such as Voltaire, whom he considered to be his intellectual equal; and it annoyed him that so many people were meddling in the arts whom it was not worth the ink and paper dismissing, and so few of the calibre of Voltaire.

But let this not give the impression that Lessing was a mere intellectual machine : as a true *Aufklärer* his concern is for man above all things, and his insight into human nature is acute and penetrating. He is not without awareness of his own limitations; he belittles his own talents as a dramatist, saying that he does not feel within him the compelling urge to write that makes the true dramatist, but that his proper function is that of the critic, not just in a negative, but in a positive, educative sense too.

(4) The positive aims

To understand the nature of Lessing's aspirations with regard to the advancement of the German theatre, and, through it, literature in general, it is necessary to consider them, not simply *vis-à-vis* the Hamburg venture, but in the wider context of the cultural and social background of the day.

"Germany" is a term which only in two relatively brief periods of history has been descriptive of a single united country under a central leadership. In the eighteenth century it was little more than a muddle of virtually autonomous autocratic states, a few large, the majority very small, with a rigid class structure and an outdated economy. There was, in contrast to France and England, no cultural focal point, indeed no true centre of any kind, no standard language, no sense of nationhood. It is therefore not surprising that in such a climate the German stage was at a low ebb.

There were two principal kinds of theatrical entertainment in the first decades of the century : for the exclusive delight of the nobility there were performances of grand opera, "an entertainment on which quite disproportionate sums were lavished in Germany because it was the habit of German princes to try to make up in external pomp for what they lacked in real power";[10] and for the common people wandering troupes of players, whose crude offerings—crude in every sense of the word—sought only to please the lowest common denominator. A nineteenth-century critic describes the plays they put on in this outburst of outraged rhetoric :

> Like a weed the wildest kind of impromptu theatre grew and blossomed in the most harmful manner. History books, tales from the Bible, fashionable novels, even the latest happenings of state were exploited for the acting texts they threw together, but their performance was at the mercy of the first whim of the moment, the mood of the performer, and the blindest chance. Political events, astounding deeds of bravery by renowned or fabulous heroes or kings, the bloodiest outrages rubbing shoulders with the most genteel speechifying of princes and princesses and the most impertinent pranks of the buffoons, magical tricks and transformations, dreams and apparitions, heaven and hell all jumbled together in the most fantastical fashion with solemn allegorical didactic figures, entr'actes, ballets, choruses, arias, illuminations and fireworks, such were the constituents of these *Haupt- und Statsaktionen*. With every day their degeneration grew more terrible![11]

For the growing respectable middle class, however, there was no suitable theatrical entertainment. As far as drama was concerned, Germany was a culture with a hole in the middle.

And it was the intention of the Leipzig professor, Johann Christoph Gottsched (1700–66), to fill this yawning chasm in his collaboration with the Neuber troupe, whose leader was anxious to provide dramatic fare more suited to a decent audience. Gottsched's reforming zeal, which directed itself also at poetics and the German language, fell short of his abilities. Not that the difficulties confronting him were small. Almost everything conducive to a stable, regular, and well-filled theatre was lacking. The prospective audiences were unsophisticated and indiscriminate; knowing no better, "they accept what the dramatist puts before them" (13, IX, p. 237). The actors lacked training, a regular income and place of work, and a proper position in society. They were numbered among those outcasts whom even the poorest peasants could look down upon :

Among [these groups] were illegitimate children, shepherds, millers, bath-keepers, linen weavers, hangmen, knackers; many public employees of low rank, such as beadles, summoners, night-watchmen, customs men, gravediggers, etc. But also comedians, gleemen, and certain musicians were not considered honour-able.[12]

In contrast to his French neighbours, the dramatist was accorded very little esteem and poorly rewarded for his labours. The repertoire of plays was also of an extremely low quality, and such versions of classical themes as existed were debased to a considerable degree. An Englishwoman abroad, Lady Wortley Montague, describes a performance in Vienna (where, in spite of some vicissitudes, there was a stronger and more vital theatrical tradition)[13] of a version of *Amphytrion* :

I never laughed so much in my life . . . But I could not easily pardon the liberty the poet has taken of larding his play with, not only indecent expressions, but such gross words as I don't think our mob would suffer from a mountebank. Besides, the two Sosia's very fairly let down their breeches in the direct view of the boxes, which were full of people of the first rank that seemed very well pleased with their entertainment, and assured me this was a celebrated piece.[14]

And even when the actors found themselves having to learn their lines instead of extemporising, the plays were still far behind those of France and England. Gottsched's own alexandrine tragedy, *Sterbender Cato* (1732), would have been hooted off the Paris or London stage, but its author, in his preface to the work, was able to express his pleasure "that this play's performance has found favour among both learned and ordinary men and brought many of both groups to tears".[15] This is an indication both of grateful relief on the part of audiences at the advent of a regular theatre, and their failure—for want of comparisons—to recognize the work's weaknesses.

Gottsched leaned heavily on French models—most of *Sterbender Cato* is virtually a straight translation of a French play—and sought through their example to provide a drama which both pleased and educated and which was suitable for a middle class audience. Unfortunately Gottsched regarded the making of a play as a purely mechanical intellectual procedure which can be analyzed and taught to others. His *Critische Dichtkunst* (1730) seeks to do just this, and his recipe for penning a tragedy omits all references to intuitive, creative processes and the rôle of the artistic imagination. To him as to his French antecedents these are suspect, and should be kept well in check.

The dramatist selects for himself a moral object-lesson which he wishes to impress upon his audience by enacting it before their eyes. For this purpose he works out a general plot which illustrates the truth of the lesson. Next he seeks out from history persons of renown to whom something similar has occurred; and from them he borrows their names for the characters in his plot, in order to accord the latter some dignity. Then he thinks out all the circumstances, to lend credibility to the main plot; and they are given the name episodes . . . These he then divides into five parts of about equal length, and organizes them in such a way that the end flows naturally from the beginning; but does not worry himself any further as to whether everything actually happened thus in history, or whether all the secondary characters really bore the names he has given them.[16]

This initial preoccupation with rules is not the result of a strange obtuseness of intellect that beset contemporary figures, nor is it due to the fact that many of them were academics; it is rather a reflection of the desire to inject order and a clear pattern into a chaotic situation, into a retarded and dispirited society that could see no way out of the impasse in which it found itself. Hence the constant emphasis in the early Enlightenment in Germany upon the moral purpose of art and the necessity for the inculcation of good taste. Hence too the distrust of the arbitrary workings of the individual imagination in literature, which parallels the fear of the effects of violence and passion on society at large; and respects for the civilizing processes of education, with its parallel scorn for the untutored mob (Pöbel). Such was the gulf between the ambition of order and reality that Schnabel, in his novel *Insel Felsenburg* (1731), set his ideal state on a remote and impregnable island, far from the corruption of European society; and even Gellert's novel *Schwedische Gräfin* (1746), although located in Europe, creates in its sentimental togetherness a closed circle—a more bourgeois and down-to-earth version of the equally unworldly grace of Rococo—against the noxious and uncertain world outside, where men are at the peril either of the unruly elements, or the equally unpredictable whim of those set in power above them. Miller's novel *Siegwart,* which, although published in 1776, belongs in its attitudes more properly to the fifties, is haunted by this sense of helplessness in the face of the world, and nowhere more forcibly than in this incident involving Veit, father of the hero's closest friend and the local landowner:

On the way Veit's brutal temperament came right out into the open and caused him to do a terrible thing. A poor peasant woman from his village was going into the fields to hoe with her two children, a lad of four, and a girl of six years. One of Veit's hounds sprang at the children who set up a piteous wailing. The poor woman struck back, seeking to beat off the dogs. Veit, observing this, spurred the rest of the dogs on to them as well, and a terrible outcry arose. Siegwart, whom this scene touched to the quick, and Kronhelm both leapt at the dogs and fought them back. Scarce was the woman out of danger than her affronted maternal tenderness transformed itself into wrath; she began to curse and cry: "A fine way that to treat folk! It would shame me to set dogs on to children! I've never heard the like. If you want to beat children, have a cane to hand. That's you fine lords all over! You grudge us the very ground we tread, and now you seek to torture innocent children : but just wait, your turn will come in Hell! The Devil will have a fine time setting about you!"—As she spoke these words, Veit aimed his gun to fire upon the woman. But his gamekeeper grasped his arm from the rear and the shot went off in the air. He flew into a terrible rage, and began foaming at the mouth : "Hell and damnation! Unhand me, that I might trample her down, the dog!"[17]

In spite of the protestations of Siegwart and Kronhelm, the woman is cast into prison, and the children left to fend for themselves. Such was the contemporary social background.

Through Gottsched's efforts, original works and translations of plays were written and performed, corresponding more or less to his "rules", and many of these he collected in the six volumes of his *Deutsche Schaubühne* (1740–5); although, particularly in the comedy, despite the solemn banishment in 1737 of Hanswurst, the central figure of the coarse popular theatre, many concessions to public taste were made. This was in large measure due to the impossibly restrictive rules Gottsched imposed upon comedy.

Gottsched's reign over the German stage lasted roughly from 1724–40, but even at the time of the Hamburg National Theatre at the end of the 1760s broadly the same situation prevailed as before his pioneering efforts commenced : a stranglehold of French classicism, few original German dramas of merit, hardly any sign of native talent. Translations may well serve as a stop-gap, but "the progress of the theatre is in fact, as might be expected, intimately bound up with the question of the number and quality of original plays that could be performed".[18] And both were conspicuous by their absence.

But, as Lessing seems tacitly to recognize in the *Hamburgische Dramaturgie*, the situation held within it an unresolvable paradox :

on the one hand, there was the need for authority in the shape of Aristotelian poetics, and on the other the need for a more potent influence than the insipid politeness of French classical tragedy, namely Shakespeare. The crux of this conflict between external and internal law lay in the fact that no real progress was possible until a genius, a genuine inspired creative artist, emerged, and within the context of the Enlightenment this was simply not possible. It was not until the rejection of the concept of an ordered society, and the revolt of the individual against mute subordination to an absolute code, which came with Storm and Stress in the 1770s and 1780s, that new life came to the German stage, with performances of works by Goethe, Lenz, the other *Stürmer und Dränger,* and translations of Shakespeare. The *Hamburgische Dramaturgie* affords a penetrating insight into the growing dilemma of a rationalist age needing inspiration, yet afraid to unleash the power of the individual imagination lest it challenge and ultimately destroy the ordered universe in whose necessity, if not actual existence, it believed.

Thus these four aspects of the *Hamburgische Dramaturgie* illustrate the temper of the Enlightenment. Lessing's search for essentials and his relentless pursuit of truth and knowledge indicate his response to the clarion cry *sapere aude.* His is a lucid and independent spirit questioning, analyzing, reducing all experience —including religion—to terms amenable to logic.

This disciplined, authoritarian world demands a brilliant and lively mind. In Lessing, one sees this at its best; but all too often, notably at the hands of Gottsched, intellectual activity seems to have degenerated into mere pedantry, although Gottsched in particular has been oversimplified as a fool and figure of fun, the embodiment of the popular concept of the stuffy University professor. Not only did Gottsched contribute much of the groundwork without which Lessing's brilliance would not have shone so brightly nor the Storm and Stress advanced so vigorously; but also the less laudable aspects of his character are due to tensions occasioned by the conditions of the age : his far-sighted dream for German literature was restrained by a timid acquiescence in authority; his burning enthusiasm was tempered by his fear of the imagination; and, as he has said himself, he was forced into the rôle of dramatist, to which he knew he was not suited, because he recognized the urgency of reform but could find none other better equipped for the task.

Signs of talent, or even genius, among others, are also frequently expressed in terms of a conflict between reason and the imagination : Gottsched's first wife, Luise, betrays in the scene-structures of her comedy *Das Testament* (1745) the struggle between orthodoxy and individual talent; J. E. Schlegel's personification of evil in Ulfo, in his tragedy *Canut* (1746), has much of the relentless individualism of the Storm and Stress hero, yet confronts the incredible passive Enlightenment integrity of Canut; Haller's poem *Die Alpen* (1729) both pleases and educates, but its moral attacks, rather than reinforces, established society.

So Lessing represents the highest peak of the Enlightenment, rather than a figure pointing forward to the breakthrough of the 1770s. Yet his achievements, like those lesser heights scaled by Gottsched before him, paved the way for what was to follow. Even then, however, Germany was never to attain a period of literary stability such as France had known in the *siècle d'or*. There the tradition built up was so strong that even a minor dramatist like Deschamps, on whose *Caton d'Utique* (1715) Gottsched based most of his *Sterbender Cato,* was able to write sound and polished verses. Gottsched's flatfooted alexandrines certainly demonstrated that French *civilization* could not be superimposed upon German *Kultur;* and only the recognition of genius and the native tradition, through the agency of Herder and others, was to allow the liberation of the individual talent and the full flowering of the German theatre in particular, and literature in general.

NOTES

1. The first figure in brackets refers to the *Stück* number; volume and page references are to Lachmann-Muncker (eds.), *Gotthold Ephraim Lessings sämtliche Schriften* (3rd. ed.), vols. 9–10 (Stuttgart, 1893–4).
2. See J. G. Robertson, *Lessing's dramatic theory* (Cambridge, 1939), pp. 127–9.
3. Robertson, p. 40.
4. R. R. Heitner, "The effect of the *Hamburgische Dramaturgie*", *Germ Rev*, XXXI (1956), p. 33.
5. Heitner, pp. 28–9.
6. See K. S. Guthke, "Lessing-Forschung 1932 bis 1962", *DVjs,* XXXVIII (1964), Sonderheft, pp. 140*–2*.
7. To be fair to Corneille, it must be stressed that he was not aspiring to a full implementation of Aristotelian principles.
   See D. W. Charlton, "Corneille's dramatic theories and the 'didacticism' of *Horace*", *French Studies,* XV (1961), pp. 1-11: "What is Corneille's principal aim if it is not didactic? It is to please, at a level of dignity appropriate to tragedy, by deeply stirring the feelings of his audience . . . Hence the unity of [*Horace*] lies in the dangers through which the hero passes" (p. 9). And to be fair to Aristotle, Lessing is to some extent imposing his own interpretation, if not actually misinterpreting. See H. Mayer, "Lessing und Aristoteles", in E. Schwarz et. al. (eds.) *Festschrift für Bernhard Blume* (Göttingen, 1967), pp. 61–75. A similar approach, which, like that of Mayer,

stresses the differences in relation to catharsis, is made by K. A. Dickson, "Lessing's creative misinterpretation of Aristotle", *Greece and Rome*, XIV (1967), pp. 53–60.

8. See L. M. Price, *The reception of English literature in Germany* (Berkeley, Calif., 1932), p. 277.

9. E. A. Blackall, *The emergence of German as a literary language 1700–1775* (Cambridge, 1959), p. 366.

10. W. H. Bruford, *Theatre drama and audience in Goethe's Germany* (London, 1950), p. 7.

11. F. J. Freiherr von Reden-Esbeck, *Caroline Neuber und ihre Zeitgenossen* (Leipzig, 1881), p. 37.

12. F. Hertz, *The development of the German public mind* (London, 1962), vol. 2, p. 76.

13. See C. P. Magill, "Austrian comedy", *GLL, N.S.* IV (1950–1), pp. 31–41.

14. Quoted from her letters by B. Aikin-Sneath, *Comedy in Germany in the first half of the eighteenth century* (Oxford, 1936), p. 42.

15. J. C. Gottsched, *Sterbender Cato* (Stuttgart, 1964), p. 17.

16. J. C. Gottsched, *Critische Dichtkunst* (Darmstadt, 1962), p. 611.

17. J. M. Miller, *Siegwart* (Leipzig, 1776), pp. 228–9.

18. E. Purdie, *Studies in German literature of the eighteenth century* (London, 1965), p. 105.

BIBLIOGRAPHY

H. E. Allison, *Lessing and the Enlightenment* (Michigan, 1966).

F. Gundolf, *Shakespeare und der deutsche Geist* (Berlin, 1927).

K. S. Guthke, "Lessing-Forschung 1932 bis 1962", *DVjs,* XXXVIII (1964), Sonderband, pp. 68*–169*.

R. R. Heitner, "The effect of the *Hamburgische Dramaturgie*", *Germ Rev XXXI* (1956), pp. 23–34.

P. Michelsen, "Die Erregung des Mitleids durch die Tragödie", *DVjs,* XL (1966), pp. 548–66.

E. Purdie, *Studies in German literature of the eighteenth century* (London, 1965).

J. G. Robertson, *Lessing's dramatic theory* (Cambridge, 1939).

E. Schmidt, *Lessing* (2 vols.) (Berlin, 1923).

H. Schrimpf, *Lessing und Brecht* (Pfullingen, 1965).

H. Steinmetz, "Der Kritiker Lessing. Zu Form und Methode der *Hamburgischen Dramaturgie*", *Neoph,* LII, pp. 30–48.

B. v. Wiese, *Lessing* (Leipzig, 1931).

Lenz's *Hofmeister* and the drama of Storm and Stress

IV

Lenz's *Hofmeister* and the drama of Storm and Stress

M. A. L. BROWN

THE choice of a drama to represent the Storm and Stress in a work of this kind is not surprising. Despite the undoubted affinity which existed between the Storm and Stress conception of creative genius and the poetic form of the lyric, an affinity reflected in the finest poems written by Goethe between 1770 and 1775, drama was the most popular mode of literary expression with this generation of young writers. It was the field, as they saw it, on which their revolutionary battles could be best fought and won. It enabled them, in the words of one critic, to present "a microcosm of the world" which would be both "immediate and active, combining speech and gesture".[1] But why choose a play by Lenz? Or perhaps one should ask, expanding the implications of the question, has the drama of this brief period sufficient artistic merit or even interest to justify such a choice on any other than purely historical or representative grounds? Until about fifteen years ago the answer from the critics might well have been a heartfelt "No!" An unholy alliance of quite separate factors made a serious critical study of Storm and Stress drama, as distinct from a historical one, a remote possibility and Lenz was the particular victim of this situation, as of so many others in his lifetime.

Mature, balanced critics always feel an instinctive revulsion from the immature extravagance of emotion and form such as Goethe, Schiller and Klinger but not Lenz were lucky enough to outgrow: Hettner finds in Lenz's works "unruly impertinence in place of depth of emotion and passion".[2] Gundolf describes him as a "crazy dreamer, the usual case-history of the outsider with illusions of genius"[3] and a standard modern history comments: "with him [Lenz] freedom becomes unbridled behaviour".[4] The lofty self-assurance of these comments also demonstrates a further difficulty in any critical approach to Lenz: in his case even more than in Goethe's, it is difficult to prevent biographical fact from colouring one's whole interpretation of the works and to stop oneself finding "internal lack of system" coupled with "the ruins of external unity" everywhere in his dramas because they were present in his life.[5] A critical difficulty of a different kind altogether arose because German critical discussion of drama has tended to see it strictly in terms of "tragedy" or "comedy" (seeing German drama itself as tragedy) and to be embarrassed by the existence of plays in an "impure" mixed form. The concentration on tragedy extended also, naturally enough, to the discussion of dramatic structure : there existed a highly sophisticated critical vocabulary which was well-adapted to analyse or describe a "classical" drama by Lessing, Schiller, or even Kleist, but its emphasis on "ordered structure" made it inadequate to describe a characteristic Storm and Stress drama except by negatives, e.g. as "a polymorphic dramatic event".[6] Lenz's two best known plays, *Der Hofmeister* and *Die Soldaten,* are not only structurally at variance with the strict canon—even Brecht writes of *Der Hofmeister* that "the contents unfold in all directions in natural disorder"[7]—they defy straightforward categorization as tragedies or comedies altogether. By 1968, however, this no longer counts as an immediate disqualification on aesthetic grounds. Prompted partly, perhaps, by developments in the contemporary theatre in Germany and elsewhere, a new and productive interest has been shown by critics not only in Storm and Stress and in Lenz but also in the broader questions of tragicomedy as a genre and its tradition in Germany and of "open form in drama". The important critical studies that have appeared since 1958 by Guthke,[8] Hinck,[9] Klotz,[10] Höllerer,[11] Schöne[12] and Titel[13] constitute a revaluation of Lenz's work in particular and have produced immediate results—a collected edition has appeared,[14] a complete one is under way[15] and a reprint of the correspondence is promised (though a theatrical revival has yet to be announced). The respectability of Storm and Stress no longer has to be established by referring to its close association with the Enlightenment.

Der Hofmeister appeared anonymously in the spring of 1774, not quite a year after the first publication of Goethe's *Götz von Berlichingen* and while the Storm and Stress movement was in full spate. It was hailed rapturously in the *Frankfurter Gelehrte Anzeigen,* the organ of the writers of Storm and Stress, as an exciting new contribution to the wave of works which was sweeping away the last desiccated remnants of pseudo-classicism.[16] One contemporary at least was seriously convinced that, after *Götz von Berlichingen* and *Der Hofmeister,* German literature could compete with Shakespeare.[17] Lenz had possibly worked on an early version of the play even before he left Königsberg for Straßburg in 1771; the earliest version of which a manuscript exists, however, dates from 1772 and the play in its final form was completed between that year and 1774. It was also during the years 1771–4 that Lenz's most important theoretical work was written, in particular his major contribution to the dramatic theory of Storm and Stress, namely, his *Anmerkungen übers Theater*. These were probably originally delivered in the form of lectures to the literary-philosophical society in Straßburg of which Lenz was still a member (as Goethe had been earlier) and they were then revised for publication in 1774. During these years Lenz's activities centred on Straßburg and Alsace, the region which almost seems to form part of all early Storm and Stress activities as a result of the happy chance which brought Goethe and Herder together there and provided them with an ideal combination of scenery, folk-poetry and architecture as a stimulus to ideas, an illustration of theories, and an inspiration to poetry. Lenz had arrived in Straßburg just in time to meet Goethe before the latter's departure for Frankfurt, immediately wished to model himself on him and was soon in regular correspondence with Goethe himself and with members of his circle such as Herder and Lavater, meeting them as frequently as possible when they travelled through Straßburg.

It is easy to make *Der Hofmeister* sound like the worst kind of Storm and Stress product in the bad old sense—a farrago of fantastic and confusing invention with no recognizable shape. The action moves rapidly by means of a large number of mostly short scenes from one setting to another, and from one type of setting to another—indoors, outdoors, in town, or country, in manor or hovel; the characters and also the plots proliferate; shots are fired in anger and a suicide attempt is made on stage; off-stage one character castrates himself and another goes to the dogs in a more than usually literal manner; the passing of two years here and nine months there in intervals of the action is referred to casually; the dialogue abounds in oaths and imprecations but also alludes explicitly to Shakespeare, Rousseau and Lessing; true emotion verges on incoherence or inarticulateness; three favourite Storm and Stress themes are all included : the seduction of a girl who then has to flee her parents and live wretchedly ; the artificiality, cynicism and emptiness of upper-class life ; and the antagonism between children and parents. But all of this, though true, misrepresents a play in which the basic situations are surprisingly "normal" and continuity from one scene to the next is in fact very carefully maintained, though not by means of any "closed action".

The action of *Der Hofmeister* in outline is as follows : a new tutor is appointed to an aristocratic household; shortly afterwards the daughter of the house has to part from her childhood sweetheart who is leaving to spend three years at university; once there he takes up his new life and is soon involved in the exploits of his student friends while at home the girl is involved with the new tutor; when she becomes pregnant she and the tutor leave her home, separately, and they do not subsequently meet; much later her father finds her on the very point of committing suicide, he saves her and she is reunited with her family, eventually also with her old sweetheart who takes her back along with his infant son; one of his student friends is also happily reunited by the end with a girl whose honour he had earlier compromised *and* with his own father from whom as a student ne'er-do-well he had been estranged; by this time the tutor, aghast at the consequences of his own sexuality has castrated himself, but nevertheless he can find a peasant girl who will be happy to marry him. Essentially these happenings are domestic, arising out of one initial family situation and culminating in a happy family reunion from which the outsider who had joined the family at the beginning is finally excluded, but they are also concerned with the social issue of class, as the outsider is of a lower class than the others. With the exception of the act of self-mutilation, however, are the situations and the action remote from experience? The structure of the drama largely follows the pattern of the events themselves; it is only in the last act that one is conscious of the sequence of events being forcibly arranged to produce a well-timed grand finale. In almost the full Storm and Stress sense of the term the play is "Shakespearean" : it is a long story spread over a number of years, full of incident and emotion, with the action dividing and proceeding simultaneously in different places before being reunited; a large number of characters drawn from different social backgrounds are involved; comedy and tragedy are mingled. However, the Storm and Stress characters par excellence, the "grosser Kerl" or the "Kraftweib", are missing, along with the vast historical scale of events within which they usually operate and which also forms part of the "Shakespearean" manner.

His irreverent polemic with Aristotle in the *Anmerkungen übers Theater*[18] might lead us to expect that Lenz would totally disregard the unities of time and place and the action of *Der Hofmeister* clearly requires that characters become separated from each other over a long period of time. It is from this separation and the resultant isolation that the emotional crises flow. At the same time, however gleefully he cocks a snook at authority in the *Anmerkungen* (e.g. in the phrase "the ever so ghastly, sickeningly famous Bull of the Three Unities"),[19] he expresses his admiration of Shakespeare elsewhere[20] for throwing aside the two unities of time and place only where the third one, that of action, demands it; the unity of action or at least of dramatic interest he does not

wish to see destroyed. In *Der Hofmeister* there is no suggestion
that he is trying to stretch the new freedom as far as it will go,
no sense of leaping from place to place out of sheer youthful
exuberance to the detriment of dramatic unity or probability.
Instead the distances covered result naturally from the situations
(e.g. son leaving home for university, then moving to another one,
pregnant daughter leaving home in panic, disgraced tutor likewise,
distracted father pursuing both) and the situations are essentially
domestic and firmly rooted in the social reality of Germany in
Lenz's own lifetime. The wish to convey a sense of political, historical or geographical scale by moving the action from place to
place, which is important for example in *Götz von Berlichingen,*
plays no part in *Der Hofmeister.* As a good follower of Storm and
Stress, Lenz views the miniature portraiture of "regular" drama
with distaste—too much of experience is squeezed out for his
requirement of a "picture of human society" to be met. The
choice of a contemporary setting in Germany for *Der Hofmeister*
and *Der neue Menoza,* and one in Flanders for *Die Soldaten,*
gives him sufficient freedom to do this; the more remote and less
substantial Storm and Stress settings, whether Italianate, pseudo-
American or historical, are rejected.

The Storm and Stress writers as a whole preferred the "open"
form of dramatic structure to that of "closed action" for a number
of reasons. No doubt the combined power of Shakespeare's histories
and tragedies and the native product *Götz von Berlichungen* out-
weighed even the emotional force of *Ugolino* and demonstrated
that the dramatic power of a whole drama does not have to be
in direct ratio to the "concentration" of the action. But more
significantly, this new generation of writers was attracted by and
responded wholeheartedly to the sheer diversity of reality, to the
possible range of human experience (in spite of the limits set),
and to the characteristically individual quality whether of human
beings, historical periods, nations, regions, social classes. Lenz's personal enjoyment of the "multiplicity of natural phenomena" comes
out strongly in his critical writings, especially in the *Anmerkungen,*
and he uses the term "Raritätenkasten" (casket of curiosities), as
Goethe had done, to convey the sense of a constantly moving,
excitingly coloured panorama passing in front of our eyes which
may be provided by historical events themselves but can also be
created by the dramatist in imitation of reality. The idea of showing
an individual standing against the "inevitable course of the whole"[21]
would clearly also require dramatic action on the broadest possible
scale, but this is not relevant to Lenz's dramas.

A further important characteristic of the "open form", as Klotz
has emphasized in general and Titel shown in relation to Lenz,

is that the action unfolds in time as a "Geschehen" (happening) rather than a "Handlung" (plot), as a chronological sequence of which the drama itself can show only a part or parts and which will necessarily be discontinuous—the action of the play is presumed to "continue" in the lapses of time between scenes or acts—and which may lead eventually to a conclusion. If so, however, this will not have been suggested earlier in the drama as inevitable or implicit in the situation, background and character of the opening. The effect produced in *Der Hofmeister* is one of at times almost casual chronological continuity rather than of concentrated, one-directional causality—even once the action of the play is well advanced a number of possibilities or directions remain open at any given moment for further development. The opening scene of the drama is a simple early example : it takes the form of a monologue, a traditional opening or so it seems, except that here the speaker, Läuffer, instead of recapitulating past events for the benefit of the reader, past events on which the action of the drama will largely depend, is running through his personal employment prospects for the immediate future. He lists the range of possibilities and rules them all out on one count or another; presumably the situation must be resolved soon or he would not be anxious, but he is not desperately anxious and the insistent "by today at the very latest" of *Wallenstein, Der zerbrochene Krug,* or *Maria Magdalene* is quite absent. The next scene follows on directly as two more characters appear in the same street and we realize that the issue is more nearly decided than Läuffer realized; by the third scene his new position is established fact—events have moved in a particular direction quite quickly after all. Much later in the action Läuffer seeks refuge with the village schoolmaster (a completely new character, but the reasons for Läuffer's choice of host, if only implied, are obvious enough); he is given shelter and protected in his immediate danger, but then he stays on and on till he comes to expect to remain there to the end of his days; from this gloomy prospect he is saved by the totally unexpected appearance and intervention of Lisa. In a rather similar way, we have Fritz and Gustchen at a moment of extreme emotional anguish and uncertainty at the very end of Act I and we may well expect, if we mistake the structure of the play, to be shown at the beginning of Act II what has happened to them, but by then two whole years have elapsed during which, as we soon learn, Läuffer has stayed on as tutor and Gustchen and Fritz have stayed apart, but Fritz has formed no new attachment and neither, yet, have Gustchen and Läuffer though their state of unhappiness, has steadily intensified over the period. Fritz has grown up, "you're not a child any more" (II, 3) and Gustchen has presumably taken her first communion, but nothing else has "happened'. It is only when Gustchen is about to commit suicide and her father must arrive in time to prevent her that the time factor is crucial to the action. When Gustchen's father looks for her lost child, he is successful eventually; Fritz races home in the end not, say, in time to prevent her marrying someone else, but because (as he believes) she is dead—how soon or late he arrives matters to him but not to the action. A number, though not all, of the scenes have a consciously inconclusive ending which emphasizes this absence of plot tension still more e.g. they finish on the phrase "we'll know eventually" (IV, 6) or "we'll see" (IV, 4).

It may perhaps still be felt that this structure, if not chaotic or fragmented, is shapeless and serves no useful purpose in relation to subject or theme, especially as the act divisions do not correspond to natural breaks in the action or to regular or symmetrically spaced divisions of time. The result, however, is not confusion and if one accepts Schöne's general statement of the theme of the play it can be seen that the apparently shapeless time sequence is the mould which contains the repetition, with a large number of variants, of an exemplary event or situation.[22] One could go further and suggest that it is also the means by which Lenz can create, within a relatively limited, realistic framework, emotional extremes of characteristic Storm and Stress violence. In his most convincing analysis, Schöne sees the play as a series of variations on the theme of the Prodigal Son, a parable which might have been designed to be a Storm and Stress archetype as it illustrates not only the difficult relationship of father to son, but also jealousy between brothers. According to Schöne this is the thematic link between the different sets of characters and the apparently straying strands of the action. The action has a well-defined general outline in that at the beginning (from Act I, 3 to the end of the act) all the main characters are together. It is the dramatic function of Act I to show them grouped together in this way before the first imminent departure, that of the son, Fritz. From the beginning of Act II until Act V the characters are dispersed, separated and estranged, seldom communicating with each other and suffering constantly from loneliness, poverty and remorse. In the final two scenes (V, 11 and 12) the family is together again and is even extended to include Gustchen's infant and Pätus along with his father, grandmother and bride. Läuffer is now excluded from the group, but has already, in the immediately preceding scene, found himself a wife. Schöne argues that the key relationships in the drama are those of parents to children and not, for example, those of friends or lovers. Läuffer's father misjudges his son's interests, makes an ill-advised choice of education for him, and encourages him to submit to indignity and humiliation in his employment. He is concerned at his son's suffering—but helpless; and there is every reason to agree with the Privy Councillor that he himself is largely to blame for his son's situation. The Major treats his son with brutal contempt; he dotes on his pretty daughter who deceives him. The Major then goes nearly mad with grief, more at losing her than at what she has done; without her the very idea of family is meaningless and he would rather go and fight with the Russian army against the Turks than stay at home, bereft of her, with his wife. He finds his daughter about to commit suicide from grief at the suffering she has caused him, not out of hopeless love for Fritz. The latter in the meantime has got into difficulties because of a friend's financial escapades and his father, the Privy Councillor, abandons him to his fate. The friend in question, Pätus, has been cast off by his father for over-extravagance and dissolute living and his substitute mother, the landlady, Frau Blitzer, has lost all patience and had him thrown into jail for debt. Wenzeslaus becomes a substitute father for Läuffer and even expresses hopes of turning him into a father of the church, after his terrible deed has removed all further hopes of physical paternity. The musician, Rehaar, out of paternal affection and a proper concern for his daughter's honour, has to send her away, to separate her deliberately from her family. The emotional heights of the final protracted reunion depend only partly on the skilfully contrived cumulative effect which is spread over two scenes and scarcely at all on the conventional unmasking and recognition of a host of long lost or even unsuspected relatives. The full emotional effect is produced because parents and children have to beg forgiveness of each other, as Gustchen and the Major did earlier, and to admit to the terrible wrong they have done. When all consciences are clear again and all debts from the past, emotional and otherwise, are paid, Fritz can solemnly adopt Läuffer's son as his own—an appropriately extravagant gesture of magnanimous fatherhood which rounds off the two scenes perfectly. Interestingly, the model morality of Fritz's act was lost on the contemporary critics at the time of the play's first appearance. The fact that it is clearly intended to excel his earlier acts of self-sacrifice and loyalty could not make the critics overlook the other moral implications of his deed, namely that he is foolish enough to marry a woman who has earlier been seduced and whose disgrace was publicly known.

Because the language in which the characters express themselves and describe their situations is less violent, less prone to rhetorical exaggeration than that to be found in Klinger's dramas or those of the young Schiller, and because the only two acts of destruction or aggression in *Der Hofmeister* are self-inflicted rather than directed at other characters, and perhaps also because of Lenz's preference for short speeches and short scenes, it is easy to underestimate or overlook the emotional intensity with which many moments in the play are charged and to conclude that in this respect *Der Hofmeister* is moderate enough to be untypical of Storm and Stress. In an article on *Die Zwillinge*, K. May wrote:[28]

> The passion of man's drive for expansion catches fire and spreads, flares up and fades away, then roars up again filling the work from beginning to end. This inner process is the only real action, ringing the rhythmical changes of tension and counter-tension up to the crescendo when it finally explodes into external action when the brother is murdered.

And he sees as the most characteristic feature of Storm and Stress drama the way in which this "inner process" forms the only real action and determines the dramatic structure. It is something very close to this which Lenz is aiming at in *Der Hofmeister,* but true to his own principles and conscience he wished at the same time to portray and comment on contemporary social reality. The story of the Prodigal Son enabled him to do this not merely by supplying a model of a family conflict situation which could be given a social setting of the author's choice; it is also part of the New Testament story that the son plunges from a position of material comfort, to one of extreme poverty, hardship and misery, which lasts until his return home, when quite abruptly the pendulum swings to the other extreme and he is surrounded by feasting and rejoicing. The father sums up the extremes of his son's experience in the memorable comment "This my son was dead and is come alive again". Obviously the "internal action" of *Der Hofmeister* is not the course of a passionate "drive for expansion" leading to murder, but rather one of anxiety or unhappiness breaking in on a character and being intensified, degree by degree, over a considerable period of time to a point of hopeless suffering, of "wretchedness" (Elend) which is not tempered by any hope, however precarious, of a solution, but at best by the thought of an escape into death. The progression takes the form of material hardship and social descent as well as emotional loss and deprivation and it leads into such depths that the ultimate horror of suicide can be contemplated. At the beginning Läuffer is uncertain about the future, the uncertainty is then removed and the first blow delivered to his conceit, but then his salary is pegged down and down long past the point where only his conceit suffers; the mockery and insults of his employers, both shown in the action and reported, mount by Act II to such an extent that he says with literal directness,

"I'll have to find some way to put an end to this wretched existence, seeing that I'm not allowed to kill myself" (II, 2); three scenes later things have got still worse—"How can I stand it any longer? I must quit" (II, 5). His only escape is to the humble and ill-fed post of Wenzeslaus' scribe, where he actually has to do some work and where he can soon say of his new master, "He'll schoolmaster me to death" (III, 4), and indeed Wenzeslaus promises that soon he will not know himself. After this the shock of recognizing his new-born son stuns him completely: his response is to castrate himself.

At Gustchen's first appearance she is already desperate or at least thinks she is, but in fact she is still half a child and playing at passion as her solemn vow of constancy to Fritz demonstrates: "I give you my oath that as long as I live I shall be no other man's wife, even if the Czar of Russia himself were to ask me" (I, 5). Two years later she is a capricious young lady whose only pleasure in life, as she says half in tears, is her drawing. Three scenes later, when she is presumably already pregnant, she feels ill and totally isolated, her family show no interest or affection, and she fears that Läuffer too may leave her; half in a dream she falls back into the Romeo and Juliet fantasy she had shared with Fritz and describes her situation in the heightened language of tragedy, "Can't you see your Juliet is dying for you—hated, despised, rejected by the whole world, by her own family even" (II, 5). At her next appearance she is brutally changed, much more so than her father had suggested in describing the deterioration of her looks and health before she left home: now she lives in a hovel in the forest where she wears a rough smock and has food enough for only two days; she has given birth to a child, but fears that to add to her suffering she might have her father's suicide on her conscience as well; her own suicide is the next logical step when her strength is at an end and she still has no news of him.

Pätus begins as a penniless student, penniless as the direct result of his own pleasure-seeking extravagance. In one quickly-moving scene his situation deteriorates rapidly. He has no outdoor clothes, so, as a simple solution to the dramatic situation, he chooses not to go out; the landlady's remark that even his dressing-gown looks "as if it had been strung up on the gallows and then fallen off and landed in a heap underneath" (II, 3) is not so easily shrugged off; then comes the serious threat of the debtor's prison; when in desperation he decides to go to the theatre in August wearing a wolfskin, he is chased in terror through the streets of the town by dogs, as he believes mad dogs, to the great amusement of the respectable citizenry. The heartless practical joke which leads to this is played by his friends, but it anticipates the later more

malicious comment that he is "the last word in loose living, a man
I wouldn't give twopence for even if he were dying on a dung-heap"
(III, 3). Fritz voluntarily accepts imprisonment on Pätus' behalf
to let his friend travel home to beg for money, but Pätus returns
empty-handed and helpless, with no solution to the situation.

The Major is increasingly anxious and worried as he sees the
progressive change in his daughter; he gives way to strange fancies
and thoughts of destruction and violence; this melancholy becomes
desperate when he discovers the reason for his daughter's changed
behaviour and then when he loses her he becomes almost demented,
determined to die if he cannot find her, or even to die in order to
rejoin her beyond the grave : "I must have my daughter again,
if not in this world then in the next" (IV, 3).

It is this downward progress to despair, wretchedness and
thoughts of death which gives the drama a many-stranded pattern
of emotional tension despite the absence of superficial suspense
in the movement of the action. The multiple strands of this tension
extend over most of the action—the depths of Läuffer's agony are
reached only at the beginning of Act V. The tension is broken
in a way which for Gustchen and the Major is highly charged with
emotion, but it need not be—it is reported that Fritz and Pätus
have evaded their responsibilities; they then simply change their
universities and continue happily enough. Läuffer recognizes his
drastic act as a turning point, even supposing that it will not lead
to his death : since the loss of his innocence, he says :

I progressed step by step in passion and ended up in despair.
If he were not going to lead me to my death perhaps I could
begin to live again and be reborn as Wenzeslaus. (V, 3.)

After the turning point there follows for all the characters a lull,
a definite slackening of the tension, an *Entspannung,* to use May's
term, e.g. Gustchen's situation between IV, 5 and V, 11; Läuffer's
in V, 9; Fritz's from IV, 1 where his escape from prison is reported
to V, 6; the Major's from IV, 5 to the discovery of the infant in
V, 12; Pätus' in the scenes with Rehaar. During this lull the
characters need to appear very seldom and do or say very little
and again, as at the end of Act I, one wonders what will cause
events to turn definitely in a new direction. The answer is a
series of surprises which occur when the characters least expect
them and transform the earlier near-tragic end and the period of
uncertainty and aimlessness following it into delirious happiness
and rejoicing : the now sexless Läuffer is meditating gloomily on a
theological future when Lise walks in on him; Pätus resolves the
duel with Rehaar and undertakes to marry his daughter, where-
upon the money he and Fritz both need to get home falls into his

lap; Fritz gets the deceitful letter telling him of Gustchen's death (first shock!) and Pätus wins the money needed to travel home, so they do this and Fritz is reconciled with his father, but decides that he must follow Gustchen to her supposed, watery grave when all the time (second shock!) she is in the next room; the Major's wish of finding his grandson is granted. Lenz ensures that the period of lull does not coincide for the different characters apart from Gustchen and her father, although at the same time he has to contrive to keep the final unions and reunions to the very end. Paradoxically, one is most aware of the separation of the strands of the action at the point where each disappears from the stage for a long period. The progression from a fairly normal situation at the outset, with little suggestion of serious underlying tensions, to an extreme of despair in which suicide or castration is seriously considered or even effected, and thence to heights of elation in which it is not inappropriate to speak of being "wiedergeboren" (born again), is swift and overwhelming, and, as we have seen, many times repeated.

The character who reacts to the upward and downward swings of emotion with the maximum of unhibited spontaneity is, of course, the Major whose completely unreflected choleric or melancholic outbursts, violent language, abrupt exclamations and at times almost demented ravings have all the emotional turbulence expected of a Storm and Stress hero. Two reactions reveal this aspect of him with particular clarity : the first when he shoots at the man whom he knows to be the seducer of his daughter but who he also hopes may know her present whereabouts; and the second when he has just saved Gustchen's life. After the shot he exclaims :

> God! Is he dead? (*Slaps his own face*). What have I done? Can you really not give me any more news of my daughter? (IV, 3.)

On saving Gustchen he is simultaneously aware that she deserved to die for her immorality, that she had disgraced her family and that he is overjoyed to have her back. The contradictions are expressed with heartfelt immediacy in the words :

> Oh my darling, my one and only treasure. To be able to hold you in my arms again, godless wretch! (IV, 5.)

Obviously the Major lacks the full amoral "drive for expansion" and power of a Storm and Stress hero, but interestingly it is he who sets the action moving by his first ill-considered act of employing the tutor, and he sustains part of it at least by looking for and finding Gustchen and subsequently her infant son. Without the missing "power", the "grosser Kerl" is in some danger of becoming comic or ridiculous and indeed the Major's behaviour is often criticized, notably by his wife, who describes the comic extravagances of his eccentric behaviour as judged by conventional standards of upper-class good taste, and by his brother, the Privy Councillor, who is an enlightened rationalist. From the second scene of the play onwards, the Privy Councillor tries to demonstrate to the Major by argument and persuasion the folly of his actions— much later in the action when all else fails he inevitably has to restrain him by force. It is usual to consider the Major as wild and ineffectual, lacking the insight which his brother shows most clearly in his admirable enunciation of the meaning of freedom at the beginning of Act II. It is in the name of Enlightenment principles (and in its vocabulary), that the Geheimrat launches this lucid, full-scale rationalist attack on many faults of contemporary German society and its attitudes, an attack which completely overwhelms the wretched pastor who has prompted it by voicing his own acceptance of the *status quo*. It may be that this eloquent Enlightenment defence of freedom and the right of the individual to it shows the common ground that existed between Enlightened "Humanität" and Storm and Stress "Natur", and that Lenz shows considerable magnanimity by portraying the Enlightened Councillor as far and away the most admirable character in the play.[24] However, judged by actions rather than words in the crucial test of who is the better father, the Major does better and the Privy Councillor less well than might be expected—the latter's fine principles and analytical intelligence fail him (and his son) later in the action when he accepts an account of his son's bad behaviour and extreme misfortune with calm resignation as divine punishment for his own earlier misdeeds and does nothing to help him. He takes this callousness further when Gustchen later tries to intercede for Fritz ; he tells her that his son does not deserve special consideration because he has not reached the point of trying to kill himself : he has not earned paternal forgiveness hard enough. The Major, by contrast, brushes aside the perfectly reasonable protests at the futility of his endeavours and the suggestion that his daughter is probably already dead and simply forges ahead to find her. The Major is a comic figure, not because his impulses are so exaggerated but because this so often makes them self-defeating, yet he is in no sense a ridiculous one, and on one occasion at least he has sufficient self-awareness as a Storm and Stress figure to utter the words "even though I cannot give it a name, I can feel it and comprehend it" (III, 1). By the end of the play the Privy Councillor is once again the more sympathetic figure he had appeared at the end of Act I, where his lecture to the "foolish children" on the theme of their irresponsibility is qualified by his genuine fondness for them and his appreciation that their sense of panic on Fritz's departure, if not their grand passion, is quite genuine.

In Storm and Stress drama in general, moderation of feeling and the physical restraint of passionate feelings are equally deplored and verbal expression as a means of conveying emotional states to the reader or the audience is supplemented by a whole language of physical gesture and movement which evidently has the function of "expressing" even more immediately than is possible in words. Hinck has analyzed this aspect of Der neue Menoza[25] in his edition of that play and the frequency and precision of the indications of physical movement and gesture in the plays of the young Schiller have often been commented on. In Der Hofmeister the gestures may replace words entirely or add something not contained in the words, or they may reinforce words, or they may take over in a form of "Steigerung" where words are no longer adequate. Only occasionally do the stage directions themselves suggest the same absolute correspondence of gesture and feeling as those in the early Schiller dramas commonly do, e.g. "he pushes him angrily" (IV, 3). The gestures in Der Hofmeister are often conventional, e.g. throwing oneself at someone's feet to beg forgiveness; they are always clear and precise, and usually uncomplicated by any conflict of feelings, the outstanding exception to this being the love "pantomime" sequence in Act II, 5 where the words, the feelings and the gestures are operating on different levels.

The following examples chosen from the many scattered over every page of the play will illustrate this technique. In Act V, 11 when Fritz and his father meet after their long separation their inevitable greeting is simply, "Father!" "Son!"—but the meaning of the words comes out only in the accompanying gesture : Fritz (falls on his knees before him), Privy Councillor (raises him up and embraces him). The step by step intensification of feeling is demonstrated very simply in Act II, 5, V, 10 and V, 12 (Fritz embracing the infant) as in the graduation from "takes her by the hand" to "rushes to embrace her" and finally "kisses her" in Act I, 5. Gesture reinforcing speech when the feeling has already been given forceful verbal expression is clearest in the many instances where anger leads to abusive language, then threats, and finally to physical intervention, e.g. simply and conventionally "gives him a clout on the ear" (IV, 6), or more "characteristically" "drags his wife from the theatre unconscious" (III, 1). The emotional states most commonly conveyed by gesture are anger, affection and shock, but pleas for forgiveness and general excitement (e.g. "rushes in", "leaps out", etc.) are also commonly uttered in this way. Extreme, instantaneous shock is a characteristic Storm and Stress emotional state shown by instant loss of consciousness, e.g. at the opening of Act III (Major's wife) and Act V (Läuffer) and in Act V, 6 (Fritz). The last case is interesting as Fritz does not quite pass out, perhaps because he is prepared for a shock inwardly and outwardly—the latter by throwing himself in a chair before the fateful letter is read to him; that he is visibly overcome is then shown by his friend's gesture of sprinkling him with lavender water; subsequently Fritz stands up but sits down again to cover his face in anguish at the thought of his own guilt, and then finally leaps to his feet presumably from frustration at his wish to take some action where none is possible. All the dramatis personæ use this gestural language—the infant even becoming an object for others to gesture with (Act V, 1 and 12)—but it is differentiated to express individual characteristics. Pätus expends more physical energy on gestures of joy or despair than any other character, and the Privy Councillor predictably least of all. His normal calm is broken usually to correct or restrain the gestures of others, e.g. by raising Gustchen from the ground when she has thrown herself at his feet (Act I, 6) or by holding back his brother (Act III, 1 and IV, 3—here he is forced finally to fire off a pistol in the air to prevent the Major from injuring someone). However, the nature of the final reunion scene moves even this restrained rationalist : as the scene opens (V, 11) the Privy Councillor and Fritz run into each other's arms, and as it closes, the Privy Councillor wipes away a tear.

It has already been remarked that this play combines two different kinds of thematic material, both of which were popular with the Storm and Stress artists—the father-children relationship and the attack on social injustice. The former is exploited here for its emotional and moral potential, as we have seen, but not because of its social (or metaphysical) implications. What is remarkable about the social criticism in *Der Hofmeister* is not the towering passions and colourful denunciation it employs, but the concreteness and precision with which injustice is defined and illustrated. The difference between the life led by the aristocratic characters and the others is repeatedly measured with candid realism in terms of money and food and drink, and to a lesser extent clothes and housing. The Privy Councillor himself is not content with a theoretical definition of freedom, freedom as a principle, but translates this immediately into the details of day-to-day social experience (II, 1). In that section of society which prides itself on its refinement of taste one may spend some thirty thousand gilders on learning to dance, consume six hundred oysters and twenty bottles of champagne with only one companion (and suffer no after-effects) and pass one's time otherwise with card-playing, hunting, serenades, country-walks and other entertainments, moving from town to country as appropriate. Swimming is no doubt too practical and inelegant to be an aristocratic pastime, so the elegant Graf Wermuth declines to jump in to help the drowning Gustchen. A privileged servant, such as a private tutor, may receive roast beef for lunch every day and punch every evening and permission to be seated on the sofa beside a lady, but, quite apart from the insults he has to endure, his salary is screwed down year by year to the point where he can no longer live on it. The village schoolmaster is well aware of the extreme simplicity of his own regime and points out its advantages to Läuffer, but the facts remain : he drinks wine two or three times per week and coffee, tea and chocolate not at all, and although he has a cooked meal at mid-day he goes without breakfast and eats a simple cold supper such as Knackwurst and salad from a table without a cloth. Like the schoolmaster, the student Pätus smokes a lot, but having a wealthy father he can afford coffee and gorgeous clothes till his money runs out and he has to live on credit : then his problem is how to find the fare home in order to ask for more money. Once Gustchen descends to living in a hovel she and Marthe have to rely on begging for charity to support themselves and the infant which is raised somehow on a diet of "cabbage and root vegetables". The details of this documentation, some of them provided in lengthy descriptions by individuals of their own or other people's way of life, others mentioned in passing, a few referred to in stage directions, form an eloquent statement of some of the major faults in contemporary German society. Their irrefutable authenticity makes them much more telling and exact as social criticism than any possible symbolic interpretation of Wenzeslaus' crabbedness and Läuffer's mutilation as wounds inflicted by society.

An acute awareness of faults in their own society and a sense of bitterness at their own sufferings in consequence frequently activated Storm and Stress writers, but they usually made their point more obliquely by choosing a historical or foreign setting and the aim of their attack was seldom as sharply in focus as in Die Soldaten and Der Hofmeister. Lenz had his own experience of soldiers and of being a private tutor, the latter being a common fate of well-educated sons of burgher families who had to earn a living at that period. He also had a clearly defined intention as a dramatist which he formulated in a letter to the Gräfin de la

Roche : to write about the social classes as he knew them to be and not "as some persons from a higher social sphere imagine them".[26] His proposals for a cure in both plays, though of a practical nature, are less convincing than the diagnosis of the disease and indeed, despite the abundance of teachers and pupils in *Der Hofmeister,* an ideal teacher is not shown. The figure of Wenzeslaus with his spectacles on his nose, his rule in his hand, and his pipe in his mouth is a magnificent grotesque which allows Lenz to indulge his taste for caricature, but he accepts his situation and has adjusted himself to it. He may treat aristocratic trespassers roughly and money-grabbing doctors satirically but he is not a reformer. It is the Privy Councillor who really argues for social upheaval and, by an ambiguous irony which brings the social criticism of *Der Hofmeister* neatly into line with other Storm and Stress dramas after all, he is an aristocrat.

NOTES

References are to the following editions:

J. M. R. Lenz, *Werke und Schriften,* Vols. I & II, ed. B. Titel and H. Haug (Stuttgart, 1966, 1967)
Briefe von und an J. M. R. Lenz, Vols. I & II, ed. K. Freye and W. Stammler (Leipzig, 1918).

1. J. D. Stowell, in *Periods in German Literature,* ed. J. M. Ritchie (London, 1966), p. 90.
2. H. Hettner, *Geschichte der deutschen Literatur im 18. Jahrhundert* (Leipzig, 1928), p. 140.
3. F. Gundolf, *Shakespeare und der deutsche Geist* (Berlin, 1922), p. 256.
4. H. de Boor and R. Newald, *Geschichte der deutschen Literatur,* Bd.6/I, *Von Klopstock bis zu Goethes Tod* (Munich, 1957), p. 259.
5. F. J. Schneider, *Die deutsche Dichtung der Geniezeit* (Stuttgart, 1942), p. 201.
6. H. Schauer's article on *Das Drama* in P. Merker, W. Stammler, *Reallexikon der deutschen Literaturgeschichte,* I, p. 247.
7. B. Brecht, *Werkausgabe* (Frankfurt am Main, 1967), Bd. 17, p. 1221.
8. K. S. Guthke, *Geschichte und Poetik der deutschen Tragikomödie* (Göttingen, 1961); and K. S. Guthke, "Lenzens 'Hofmeister' und 'Soldaten'. Ein neuer Formtypus in der Geschichte des deutschen Dramas", in *Wirkendes Wort,* 1959, Vol. V, p. 274–86.
9. W. Hinck ed., *J. M. R. Lenz, Der neue Menoza* (Berlin, 1965).
10. V. Klotz, *Geschlossene und offene Form im Drama* (Munich, 1960).
11. W. Höllerer, Interpretation of *Die Soldaten* in *Das deutsche Drama. Interpretationen.* Vol. I, ed. B. v. Wiese (Düsseldorf, 1958).
12. A. Schöne, *Säkularisation als sprachbildende Kraft* (Göttingen, 1958).
13. B. Titel, *"Nachahmung der Natur" als Prinzip dramatischer Gestaltung bei J. M. R. Lenz* (Diss. Frankfurt am Main, 1962).

14. *Werke und Schriften,* ed. Titel und Haug (Stuttgart, 1966/67).
15. J. M. R. Lenz, *Gesammelte Werke in vier Bänden,* ed. R. Daunicht. So far appeared *Dramen I* (Munich, 1967).
16. "Despite some reservations the *Frankfurter Gelehrte Anzeigen* of 16 July 1774 welcomed this as one of those refreshing works, like life-giving rain over land suffering from a long drought. More precisely this drama was felt to open up new paths for an art languishing in the chains of a desiccating pseudo-classicism". "Nachwort" to the Reclam *Hofmeister,* ed. K. S. Guthke (Stuttgart, 1966), p. 85.
17. "I could never bring myself to believe that a German would ever seriously compete with Shakespeare, wrote Johann Georg Scherff on 27 September 1774 . . . but first *Goetz von Berlichingen* and now *Der Hofmeister* have conquered my fears". Ibid, p.85.
18. *Werke I,* pp. 329–62.
19. Ibid, p. 344.
20. *Werke I,* pp. 363–8, "Über die Veränderung des Theaters im Shakespear".
21. "Rede zum Shakespeares Tag", in Goethe's *Werke,* Vol. 12, Hamburger-Ausgabe, 1953, p. 226.
22. A. Schöne, op. cit., pp. 92–139.
23. K. May, "Die Struktur des Dramas im Sturm und Drang" in *Form und Bedeutung* (Stuttgart, 1957), p. 45.
24. Interpretation of *Der Hofmeister* by H. O. Burger in: *Das deutsche Lustspiel,* ed. H. Steffens (Göttingen, 1968).
25. *Der neue Menoza,* ed. W. Hinck, pp. 84–92.
26. *Briefe, I,* p. 115.
27. Cf. R. Pascal, *The German Sturm und Drang* (Manchester, 1953), especially the chapter entitled, Sturm und Drang and the Social Classes, pp. 56–86.

BIBLIOGRAPHY

Most of the important recent critical writings referring in detail to Lenz are named above; some additional titles are as follows:

B. Markwardt, *Geschichte der deutschen Poetik,* Vol. II, Part II, Sturm und Drang (Berlin, 1956).

L. Schneider and R. Loewenthal (eds.), *Sturm und Drang. Kritische Schriften* (Heidelberg, 1949).

H. B. Garland, *Storm and Stress* (London, 1952).

E. Genton, *J. M. R. Lenz et la scène allemande* (Paris, 1966).

W. H. Bruford, *Theatre, Drama and Audience in Goethe's Germany* (London, 1950).

Wilhelm Meister's Apprenticeship and
German Classicism

V

Wilhelm Meister's Apprenticeship and German Classicism

DAVID TURNER

A WORK set uncompromisingly in contemporary German society, without noticeable reference to the world of classical antiquity; a work using not a form of long-established tradition, but that of the modern novel; a novel, moreover, of such comprehensive structure that the Romantic, Friedrich Schlegel, could see it in terms of his ideal of "Universalpoesie". Reasons for not choosing *Wilhelm Meister's Apprenticeship* as a representative work of German Classicism are both numerous and obvious. Of course the date fits—the novel was completed in 1796 —and the work owes much to that period of close collaboration between Goethe and Schiller. But these facts in themselves prove nothing. If the novel is indeed to emerge as a classical work, more substantial and essential qualities will have to be adduced to demonstrate the fact.

I

From an early date, and not always to the benefit of its proper understanding, *Wilhelm Meister's Apprenticeship* has been regarded as a model of what goes by the name of "Bildungsroman", that peculiarly German production, which takes its hero through a great variety of experiences until he achieves a maturity of wisdom and insight into life and can meet the moral and spiritual demands which contemporary society makes on him. The word "Bildung" itself, however, immediately brings us face to face with one of the central concepts of Weimar Classicism. Professor Bruford has already mapped out in great detail the rôle it played in the thinking of many of the leading literary figures of the age, who in a quite remarkable way became associated with one small German court towards the end of the eighteenth century.[1] This is not the place to cover the same ground again, but it may be appropriate to recall—in admittedly crude summary—some of their noble ideals of personal cultivation, for it is against this background that *Wilhelm Meister's Apprenticeship* must inevitably be seen. For Wieland, an earlier arrival in Weimar, it was a question of

87

achieving a harmonious balance between the instinctive and the spiritual man. Thus formal education should not seek to produce scholars or—still worse—pedants, but prepare those receiving it for life itself, developing their moral awareness so that they might do what is good for its own sake and from taste. In Herder's case, as seen chiefly in his *Ideas towards a Philosophy of Human History* (1784–91) and his *Letters on Humanity* (1793–7), it was a matter of self-education or self-improvement towards the ideal of humanity divinely planted in man as a germ to be developed, an ideal principally ethical in nature, which should bring out especially those qualities, such as reason and justice, which raise man above the level of the animals. For Fichte, lecturing a few miles away at Jena on *The Mission of the Scholar* (1794), the demands of true humanity were still higher; they required that all man's powers be developed equally, all his capacities cultivated to the peak of perfection. With Schiller, finally, the starting point was a picture of modern man as a being whose essential self had not been allowed to develop properly because of the inevitable specialization in contemporary society. In his letters *On the Aesthetic Education of Man* (1795) in particular he discussed the important rôle to be played by art and the artist in bringing man to inner freedom, the necessary precondition for his development to full humanity. And the ideal of humanity that inspired him was of a totality, of a balance between the senses and the mind, sensibility and reason, inclination and duty.[2]

It would be wrong to talk of a unity of thought among these writers, and even more so to suggest that they were all equally "classical". Nevertheless one cannot fail to perceive a certain similarity not only in their general concern for true humanity and the means of fostering this, but also in some of the specific qualities—notably harmony and balance—which they attached to their ideal.

In Book V of *Wilhelm Meister's Apprenticeship* the hero, confirmed in his determination to remain with the theatre by his friend Werner's eulogy on the virtues of commerce, writes some of the most frequently-quoted words of the whole work:

> to cultivate myself, just as I am, was my obscure wish and intention from my youth (p. 290).[3]

And only a page or so later he mentions his irresistible inclination towards "that harmonious cultivation" of his nature. Such aims are clearly in line with the general interest in "Bildung" shown by other leading literary figures of the age. The temptation is to read too much into them or to accept them simply at their face value. An example of the former is provided by the commentary

in the "Hamburg" edition of the novel, which refers in this connection to a letter of Goethe's to Lavater in September 1780. In
it he speaks of his own overwhelming desire to elevate the "pyramid
of his life to the highest possible peak" (p. 615). This reference
might easily lead one to suppose that Wilhelm attains some
absolute perfection at the end of the novel, that he reaches a point
of ideal humanity which allows no further development. The novel
itself, however, does not support such an interpretation. In the first
place, the goal of cultivation Wilhelm has in mind still has something superficial about it : he wants to be socially agreeable.
Furthermore, it should be remembered that, although he regards
the stage as the only path to true personal cultivation open to a
member of the middle-class such as himself, it is not long before
he is bidding a final farewell to the theatre.

After leaving the theatre, Wilhelm finally comes into the orbit
of the "Turmgesellschaft", a society reminiscent of a masonic lodge
and very much concerned with his development. For if blind
chance seems to affect the course of the hero's life at certain
points, at others it is the Society of the Tower, consciously applying
its educational principles. And in fact some of the wisest and
noblest views on personal development are expressed by its members
or embodied in the certificate of apprenticeship handed over to
the hero near the end of the novel. It is here we read of that ideal
of balance between thought and activity, for example, since
thought on its own is an enlarging but also a crippling experience,
while activity is enlivening but also restricting (p. 550). And it is
here also that we find that ideal of the universal development of
all man's faculties, not within one individual, but in a community,
where each member restricts himself and so contributes to the
whole (p. 552). Yet once again we must beware of assuming that
the Society of the Tower represents an unambiguous key to the
understanding of Wilhelm's development or that he fulfils its
demands and intentions in every respect. It is of course true that
he ultimately decides to make surgery his profession, a choice
which of necessity rules out other possibilities. But this acceptance
of his one-sided function in the organization of the whole comes
only in the *Travels* (completed 1828-1829) and cannot fairly be
used as evidence here. More important is the way in which Goethe
has so arranged things in the earlier novel that we are induced,
not to reject, but at least to take with a pinch of salt the wisdom
of the Tower. When Jarno reads out extracts from Wilhelm's certificate of apprenticeship and the latter repeatedly interrupts with
cries of impatience, confusion or bitterness—the scene occurs very
shortly after the death of Mignon—the reader must surely find
himself more in sympathy with the hero than the insensitive Jarno.

Again, for all the utopian aura that sometimes seems to surround the "Tower" and its ideals, Goethe unmistakably makes us aware of the foibles of its individual members—the excessive claims made by the Abbé for the influence of the mind on Wilhelm's development,[4] or the activity of Lothario, so much praised by Jarno and yet expressing itself most memorably in love-affairs![5]

An honest examination of the novel, then, reveals that Wilhelm attains neither that ideal of full development of all his faculties nor that opposite ideal, embodied in the Society of the Tower, of self-limitation in the service of a community. This does not mean, however, that Goethe had no room for such ideals. In Italy he was himself talking quite earnestly of wanting to "cultivate himself fully".[6] And as late as 1829 he could still write that his sole aim was to "cultivate himself as much as possible, after his own fashion, so as to partake with greater and greater purity and joy of the infinite in which we are placed" (letter to K. E. Schubart on 10.5.1829). In both cases, moreover, he used the same verb to denote his aim ("sich ausbilden") as does Wilhelm Meister. But here in the novel he is concerned not so much with an ideal as with a real venture in human self-cultivation in a contemporary setting. Leaving Wieland aside, it is interesting to note that the other great exponents of classical "Bildung" developed their ideas in theoretical, philosophical form—even poems like Schiller's "The Gods of Greece" and "The Ideal and Life" are not real exceptions to this—while Goethe's novel deals with a living hero in concrete situations. This must inevitably lead to a different approach and, ultimately, to different results. For him the novel was essentially concerned with real life,[7] and so the writing of *Wilhelm Meister's Apprenticeship* may be said to have involved the reconciliation of the real with the ideal, the working out of what an enthusiastic, idealistic, even impetuous young man like Wilhelm might reasonably be expected to become with the help available to him and under the conditions imposed on him by his circumstances. Not only do the results carry more conviction and interest than abstract speculation, but they may also be said to represent one aspect of Classicism. In viewing the drama of Manzoni Goethe once observed its aim of reconciling moral and aesthetic demands with the real, inescapable facts. And this in itself, remarks Professor Killy, is classical.[8]

If Wilhelm neither attains the heights of universal self-cultivation nor, in the present novel at least, commits himself to a one-sided activity within the community of the Tower—the *Apprenticeship* leaves us with the prospect of a further journey for the hero— what, then, does he achieve? And is there anything "classical" about it? In the first place, it must be stressed that he reaches not the end of his life, but only a stage in it. That he receives a certificate of apprenticeship cannot be taken to signify that, having gone through all the manufacturing processes, he has now come to the end of the human assembly line as a finished product. Wilhelm is an organism, for whom finality can come only with death, an individual always open to development and always therefore liable to mistakes and temporary aberrations.[9] As if to remind us of this, Goethe makes his hero come very close to entering on a wrong marriage (to Therese) even after the Abbé has declared his years of apprenticeship over.

A corollary of this incomplete personal development is that the stage reached by Wilhelm at the end of the book is relatively modest; no superman has emerged. Nevertheless it is no longer the same Wilhelm; he has undergone a change, and for the better. The general direction of his development is away from extremes and one-sided enthusiasms towards a balance of those opposite poles of living with which he is faced. At the beginning of Book II he is depicted in all his bitter sorrow at the supposed infidelity of Mariane. The excess of this emotion is brought home to us not only by the way in which the narrator ironically plays along with his hero in a veritable profusion of similes, but also by the extension Wilhelm gives to his grief. Since his love for Mariane is bound up in his mind with his theatrical activities, his disappointment in the one leads him to the extreme of denying his talent as a poet and actor completely and violently and then of seeking to devote all his energies to business, the sphere which he has already inwardly left behind. This is Wilhelm at his most immature, swinging suddenly from great enthusiasm to deep dejection in a manner more reminiscent of Werther and Tasso. But here we are in the world of the "Bildungsroman", and where the violent swings of the emotional pendulum spell disaster for Werther and are never properly resolved even at the end of *Torquato Tasso*, the course of *Wilhelm Meister's Apprenticeship* brings an increasing, though never complete, equilibrium between the extremes to which the hero is prone or at any rate exposed.

This important aspect of balance expresses itself at different levels and in different spheres, of which only a few can be discussed here. In the first place, it is a question of thought and feeling on the one hand and activity on the other. When Wilhelm is faced with the task of writing a detailed journal of his doings, as he earlier promised his father he would, he finds that the only experiences he can recall are those of the heart and mind (p. 266). And this highlights a special danger in his way of life : an excessive concentration on his inner development. For even what he does, in connection with the theatre, for example, has something provisional, dilettante, or even foolish about it; it is more of an excuse for true activity. This latter, however, is what Wilhelm learns to devote himself to at the end of the novel, preparing to consolidate his estates for the future good of his newly found son and admitting to himself the folly of his life hitherto :

> The time is past for you to waste away your own and other people's years; pull yourself together and think of what you have to do for yourself and for the good creatures whom nature and inclination have bound so firmly to you. (p. 504.)

Thought and feeling have not of course been eradicated from his life—and one might add : fortunately. They have simply found a counter-balance in purposeful activity.

The same development also expresses itself as a balance between concern for self and concern for the world, between looking inward and looking outward. For is this not a further consequence of the new life Wilhelm has to build on finding his son? The necessity to try and educate his son imposes a new approach to life on the hero too :

> . . . his child's curiosity and thirst for knowledge made him realize for the first time what little interest he had taken in things outside himself, how little he recognized and knew. On this day, the happiest in his life, even his own education ["Bildung"] seemed only to be beginning. (p. 498.)

In saying this, he is in effect echoing one of the major points of development that crystallized for Goethe himself in Italy. Although his administrative duties and scientific concerns during the early years at Weimar were already beginning to direct his attention outside himself, it was the experience of Italy which completed the process and brought the full personal gain, as Professor Staiger has shown with great clarity and in great detail.[10]

Or again, the balance can be seen as one between the ideal and the real. Thus what is true of the author's treatment of his whole subject, "Bildung", applies also to the life of his hero. And although the theatre is only a stage through which the latter passes, it provides one of the best opportunities for him to test his ideals in real situations. Consider, for example, the production of *Hamlet* in Serlo's theatrical company. Wilhelm, who has rather idealistic views of the play as an untouchable masterpiece, is brought up against the practical concerns of Serlo, who has a public to please and only limited financial and personal resources. The interesting point about this episode is not simply that Wilhelm agrees to compromise by providing a cut version of the play, but more particularly that the world of the theatre emerges from the novel as a sort of microcosm of life itself (pp. 293–8. Cf. also pp. 343–50 and 434). The hero is learning already to reconcile the desirable with the possible—a process which is of course aided by his simultaneous growth in insight, as he overcomes his utopian view of the theatre and awakens to its petty squabblings, rivalry, and so on. The meaning of the whole novel has been interpreted as the "curing of the enthusiast", who comes to accept the attraction of modesty.[11] But this could be misleading, suggesting that Wilhelm comes to lose all his ideals and dreams, when the truth is rather that he now has greater experience in complementing them with an appraisal of the real possibilities. In this respect Schiller was nearer the mark when he summed up the goal reached by Wilhelm as follows:

> He steps out of an empty and vague ideal into a definite, active life, but without thereby forfeiting his power of idealization. (Letter of 8 July 1796.)

Indeed it is to be noted in connection with all the pairs of opposites considered here that, in moving away from one pole, Wilhelm does not ultimately go to the opposite pole, but achieves something of a golden mean.

One could go on talking in terms of such reconciled opposites—of head and heart, innocence and experience, and so forth—but it would perhaps be more appropriate to do something closer to what the novel itself does and follow some of the most important personal encounters and relationships in the hero's life. For the functional significance of these characters in the economy of the narrative derives as much as anything from the possible modes of existence they hold out for him. By and large they each have something positive, though different, to offer him, but it is principally because he does *not* become like them, because he avoids the dangers inherent in the bias of their lives, that they are so important for him. Thus it is, for example, with Werner, his friend from back home and, subsequently, his brother-in-law. It is Werner who works so hard and so long in the background of the novel, looking after the hero's finances so successfully. And it seems a little unjust that he should be made to suffer the indignity the author keeps in store for him (for we probably all have a sneaking sympathy with the Marthas of this world). Nevertheless the lean, pale face, the balding head, the hollow chest and drooping shoulders, with which he appears towards the end, are comment enough on the folly of his ways, which resides in his exclusive concern for material values, for what is useful financially. In his eyes the salvation of the world depends on book-keeping by double entry, and even his marriage to Wilhelm's sister is undertaken for sound business reasons. As far as the hero is concerned, the world which Werner represents has already been left behind spiritually when the novel opens, although it remains in the background as a recurrent reminder and at one point, as mentioned earlier, is even the object of a temporary relapse in his development.

After taking his leave of home, Wilhelm joins up with a group of what seem to be unemployed theatrical folk, or even loungers, one of whom is to prove particularly important for him. This is the playful, sensual beauty, Philine, who might easily have skipped straight out of the world of rococo—name and all. Indeed her positive function for the hero is not so very different from that of the title-figure of Wieland's *Musarion* (1768), a work long cherished by Goethe. Just as the avowed misanthrope (or should it more properly be misogynist?) Phanias is cured of his ways by the playful, sensual charms of Musarion, so also Wilhelm Meister is diverted from his self-indulgent grief at the loss of Mariane by Philine. Although he renounces colourful clothes in favour of a shadowy grey (p. 117) and for some time keeps to his rather exaggerated oath never to embrace a member of the faithless sex, it is not long before he is giving in to Philine's saucy, feminine attractions and even feeling pangs of jealousy at the thought that she might be making love to another man. On the whole, then, Philine is able to cure Wilhelm of some of his gloom and grief and turn his thoughts to more pleasurable pursuits, but at the same time even her approach to life has its dangers, if pursued unrestrainedly. For light-heartedness can easily become flippancy; it can mean lack of commitment to any values and ultimately lack of sympathy. It is not just a question of Philine's insensitive mockery at the unhappy plight of Aurelie, left behind, as she supposes, with an illegitimate son, but more particularly the way in which she seems to symbolize some of the worst features of theatrical life, its hollowness, its slovenliness, its unconcern. This comes out particularly in the unfortunate episode with the count and countess. For it is by her flirtatious behaviour that Philine first persuades Wilhelm to take part in a game of disguise, in which he impersonates the count, and then almost brings him to the point of embracing the countess (Book III, Chapters 10 and 12). The game has the most serious consequences, converting both count and countess for no very valid reason to a pathetic life as religious recluses. The importance of this for the hero is that it proves a cause of guilty feelings, which ultimately become a lesson to him, while the reader is left to draw his own conclusions about the dangers implicit in Philine's way of life. Towards the end of the novel, as if to pronounce judgment on her as he did on Werner, Goethe re-introduces her in what is for her a situation of the greatest indignity. Having earlier scoffed at Frau Melina's pregnant contours, Philine now finds herself in the same position and dare not show herself in public (p. 559). Not only has her graceful figure gone, but she who refused to be tied down by any commitment is here facing the most demanding commitment of all—motherhood!

From the world of Philine and the theatre to the "Confessions of a beautiful Soul", the hero's next important encounter to be considered here, seems a mighty step. And yet in essence the step is made for us by the "Confessions" themselves, for one of the important impulses in the religious life of the "beautiful soul" is a recoiling from the superficiality, the vanity, the licence of court life, from a world, that is, which has much in common with that of Philine. The personality who confronts Wilhelm here—not in the flesh of course, but only through her written disclosures, which occupy the whole of Book VI—is a woman of great sensibility who, aware of man's potential for evil, renounces earthly pleasures and the happiness of marriage and devotes herself to her Christian faith, a faith moreover in the Pietist tradition and existing outside the orthodox churches or dogmas, relying instead on a personal relationship with God and trust in the crucified Christ. Like the "beautiful soul" defined by Schiller in his essay *On Grace and Dignity* (1793), the writer of the "Confessions" seems also to enjoy a harmony between duty and inclination. In the last paragraph which she writes, for example, we find the statement :

> I can scarcely recall a commandment; nothing appears to me in the guise of a law; it is an impulse which guides me and always leads me aright. (p. 420.)

The important "classical" concept of harmony also enters into the hero's judgment of the "Confessions", though in a rather different sense from that intended by Schiller. What so impresses Wilhelm and, he says, has an effect on his whole life is the purity of the "beautiful soul", her self-reliance, and the fact that she was unable to assimilate anything not in harmony with her noble, affectionate disposition (p. 518). He himself of course has been only too ready to rely on the—often doubtful—advice of other people or to adopt ways alien to his nature. (This is true of much he does in connection with the theatre.) And the "beautiful soul" is there among other things to point the lesson.

Nevertheless she does not embody the ideal of the novel, and when Natalie suggests to the hero that such people are there not to be copied, but as models to be striven after (p. 518), one might well go further and recommend that she should not even be regarded as a model. For all her admitted virtues the "beautiful soul" lacks one thing—an active involvement in the world. Her way of life displays that inwardness which Goethe saw, especially in consequence of his Italian journey, as a "Northern" trait, opposed to the Italian's openness to the world.[12] Moreover, one may justifiably wonder whether she is not too excessively or even "selfishly" concerned with the state of her own soul. The same doubt may also arise in connection with Goethe's Iphigenie, but there it is to be noted that the concern for personal purity is linked to a wider purpose—the removal of the curse that has so long plagued the descendants of Atreus. By contrast the "beautiful soul", prompted by the example of her niece Natalie, who is always active in the service of others, openly admits that she has never been actively generous (pp. 417–18). Her religion is directed inwards not outwards. For all her positive value to the hero it is worth noting therefore that, although her confessions come at a critical point in the narrative, when he too could easily turn in on himself—he is feeling out of tune with his theatrical associates and has just been reminded of his guilt concerning the count and countess—he does not follow her extreme example of withdrawal from the world into the protective shell of inwardness.[13]

In fact the next pull in Wilhelm Meister's development is in the opposite direction, when he soon afterwards meets another of Lothario's neglected lovers, Therese. As was the case with the "beautiful soul", Therese's way of life has been influenced by contact with dissolute living. Her own mother was a woman who had given free rein to her passions, had a succession of love-affairs, and—significantly in view of the hero's own activities—shown a fanatical interest in theatricals. The result in Therese's case has been not a withdrawal from involvement in the world, but the development of competent, practical abilities. Her interest is not in semblances—even the aesthetic semblances of art—but in life itself and in activity properly directed and controlled. She is a a model of efficiency in managing her affairs and therefore seems an ideal choice for educating young girls for their future domestic rôle.[14] The essence of her nature is summed up neatly in Goethe's description of her house, with its red and white paint, and her garden, with its intensive cultivation, its neatly arranged firewood and its clean, ordered receptacles (p. 445). Thus, when the hero begins to tire of the theatre and to see some of the dangers associated with it, it is as though the "beautiful soul" and Therese successively present opposing ways out of his position. And for a time it looks as if he will finally settle for Therese's solution; finding himself in agreement with her methods and deciding that he now needs a mother for his recently discovered son, he makes Therese a proposal of marriage. It is not until the very end of the novel that he is—fortunately—released from his engagement to her, "fortunately" because, as she later points out, it was his reason that chose her, not his heart (p. 607). In other words, it was a choice made with only part of his being. One might also point out, however, how difficult it is to imagine Wilhelm completely losing his interest in the theatre and the arts in general and therefore how problematic marriage with Therese could have proved.

In examining this selection of characters from the novel in relation to the central character it has been possible to assess something important about his personal development. For part of their function is to act as a standard by which Wilhelm can be judged; belonging, as they do, to a particular stage in his life, they remind us of what he might have become, but does not. There is something either excessive or one-sided about their approach to life, and he does well to steer his more balanced, middle course avoiding such extremes.[15] Moreover, in the last analysis this middle way is the core of Wilhelm Meister's "Bildung" : this is the balance he comes to achieve; it is here that we must look for the important element of self-limitation. For in his development the influence of one way of life is eventually limited by another, often its opposite. Were this not so, he would surely submit to one or other centrifugal impulse and cease to be Wilhelm Meister. Comparisons have previously been made between the hero's development and the laws of limitation or compensation which Goethe believed to operate in the transformations of the animal kingdom and which he expressed in the poem "Metamorphosis of Animals" (1799). But the notion that a gain here is compensated for by a loss there has more in common with the complementary ideals of the Society of the Tower as a whole and with the hero's acceptance of one-sided activity that we find in *Wilhelm Meister's Travels*.[16] More appropriate to our present concern is the poem "The Metamorphosis of Plants" (1798), which describes how the bloom results from a process of concentration and contraction :

> Doch hier hält die Natur, mit mächtigen Händen, die Bildung
> An und lenket sie sanft in das Vollkommnere hin.
> Mäßiger leitet sie nun den Saft, verengt die Gefäße,
> Und gleich zeigt die Gestalt zärtere Wirkungen an.
> Stille zieht sich der Trieb der strebenden Ränder zurücke,
> Und die Rippe des Stiels bildet sich völliger aus.[17]

Again it must be stressed that no ultimate perfection is implied for Wilhelm Meister. Nevertheless the process by which he comes to avoid the pitfalls of those one-sided extremes is at the same time a process of contraction and limitation, a gradually increasing concentration on the heart of his being. To use the concepts of Goethe's later poem "Urworte. Orphisch" (1817), Wilhelm's inborn individuality (his "Dämon") remains essentially the same, although it has developed through living contact with the world around him. Fundamentally therefore his aim to "cultivate himself just as he is"[18] may be said to be realized, even if in a way different from what he intended when he spoke the words.

Perhaps because of disappointment at the result of the hero's development there have been doubts whether *Wilhelm Meister's Apprenticeship* is to be seen as a "Bildungsroman" at all.[19] But the structure of the novel, including the use of such characters as those discussed above, still points to a central principle of personal development. One must only beware of making out the results to be more grandiose than they in fact are. Even so, what is achieved embodies something of the important classical concepts of balance, harmony and limitation. And the token of Wilhelm's achievement is that he wins the hand of his beautiful Amazon, Natalie, and is allowed to extricate himself from the engagement to Therese. As Lothario puts it, Natalie is the true "beautiful soul" of the novel (p. 608), and it is not difficult to see why. For in Natalie there is perfect harmony between the demands of her own nature and those of the world at large (p. 539). As already indicated above, what distinguishes her from her aunt, the author of the "Confessions", is the way in which her attitude expresses itself in activity, for the benefit of her fellow-men. Moreover, the essence of this activity is itself balance, in that Natalie seeks always to offset a lack in one place by a superfluity from elsewhere (p. 526). But more important than all these factors as far as Wilhelm Meister is concerned, is that she is the only woman in the novel who elicits from him not a limited, but a full response and does not disappoint him. A monologue during the period when he is still officially engaged to Therese, but desiring, without much hope, to win Natalie, makes this clear:

"Yes", he said to himself on finding himself alone, "admit it. You love her, and you feel once again what it means to love with all your energies. That is how I loved Mariane and was so disappointed in her; I loved Philine and could not help despising her. I respected Aurelie and could not love her; I respected Therese, and my paternal love took on the form of an affection for her; and now that all the sentiments which ought to make a man happy meet together in your heart, you are compelled to flee!" (p. 568).

Although Goethe's intention seems fairly clear in Natalie, one cannot avoid a lingering doubt whether she will be able to fulfil all the hero's needs. This is not so much a question of the general loss of flesh and blood and the increasing abstraction which many critics have observed in the second half of *Wilhelm Meister's Apprenticeship*.[20] It concerns rather a characteristic which is deliberately given to Natalie : as Schiller was quick to perceive, she has something of the saint about her, and her love is universal, not exclusive (letter of 3 July 1796). Add to this the hero's own description of her as his "Amazon" and one cannot help wondering whether there is not too much suggestion of asexuality to satisfy the needs of a man who has experienced the physical delights of Mariane and Philine—unless, that is, one is prepared to believe he has quite lost or overcome this particular interest.[21]

II

However modest the results of Wilhelm Meister's personal development in comparison with what some would like to see in it, the development that does take place presupposes certain beliefs and attitudes of central importance to Goethe's classicism. These are sometimes evident in the hero of the novel, but more especially they are implied in the whole outlook of an author who could conceive such a thing as this "Bildungsroman". Although there is inevitably some overlap in these beliefs, the three most significant strands to be dealt with here might be termed : (i) a confident openness to life; (ii) a concern with the present; (iii) a belief in the educative value of mistakes.

Goethe himself was aware that it was not his destiny to be a tragic dramatist; he considered that he had too conciliatory a nature (letter to Zelter, 31 October 1831). George Steiner, however, is more specific, making the interesting point that this refusal of tragedy is part and parcel of Goethe's ideal of natural growth and the ordering of natural growth by education, such as we find in *Wilhelm Meister's Apprenticeship* :

Tragedy is a deliberate advance to the edge of life, where the mind must look on blackness at the risk of vertigo. Goethe was determined to proceed upward, and so he kept his eyes to the light.[22]

Put the other way round, the very concept of "Bildung" implies a basic confidence in life and the world in which man is set, a confidence which itself has been seen as one of the basic presuppositions of the "classical" view of life[23] and which also underlies that famous and most undogmatic interpretation of the novel given by Goethe to Eckermann (18 January 1825) :

For at bottom the import of the whole thing seems quite simply to be that, in spite of all his follies and entanglements, man reaches a happy goal, guided by a higher hand.

For the hero of the "Bildungsroman" this confidence is translated into terms of a very educable character. There may be disagreements whether Wilhelm Meister is basically a passive or an active character[24]—although the latter view is more tempting—but there can be no doubt that he is eminently open to new and unknown experiences, always prepared to listen to people sympathetically and submit himself to their influence. At times of course he listens too much or to the wrong people and allows himself to be influenced more than is advisable, but his openness is ultimately vindicated. After all, is it not largely the fact that a character like Werther shuts himself off from proper contact with the world and seems incapable of letting his life be shaped by other people (that is, seems incapable of development) that makes his downfall inevitable?

In the second part of *Faust*, at a point which marks the marriage of the ancient and the modern worlds, the Mediterranean and the Northern temperaments, Faust and Helena meet together in the symbolism of rhyme. The climax of the scene, which might also be said to represent a climax of classicism itself, is expressed in that famous couplet spoken by the hero himself :

> Durchgrüble nicht das einzigste Geschick!
> Dasein ist Pflicht, und wär's ein Augenblick.[25]

To speak of "living for the moment" would smack too much of the indecent haste of "carpe diem", whereas the mood is more one of calm and confidence. Nevertheless the ideal embodied here does involve living each moment fully, aware that it may not last, but not perturbed by this, looking neither backwards nor forwards, not weakening the present experience by memories of some golden age of the past or some longing for the future, neither questioning nor neglecting what the occasion offers. Now the ability to throw himself into each new experience as it came along was something that Goethe was rarely without throughout his life—it is difficult, for example, to imagine him exposing himself to the joys and dangers of so many love-affairs without this ability—but it was during his Italian journey especially that he came consciously to affirm it as a calm, confident ideal. It is characteristic that nouns like "Dasein" and "Gegenwart" or even parts of the verb "sein" came to take on such considerable meaning and occur with such frequency at this time. This was the quality of life which he observed in the Italian people, as opposed to the unnatural, brooding, stay-at-home Northerner; it was the quality he approved of in ancient tombs such as the Maffeianum in Verona and in the stone of which they were made; and it was the same quality in the molluscs and crustaceans of the Venetian lagoons that pro-

voked the famous, untranslatable outburst ". . . wie wahr! wie
seiend!"[26] The quality of "Gegenwart" is something which Goethe
also saw as a special attribute of the Ancient Greeks[27] and, not
surprisingly, it is closely akin to the "naive" life which Schiller
believed was characteristic of the classical world and which he
contrasted with modern, reflective man in his essay *On Naive and
Sentimental Poetry* (1795).

The importance of all this for the "Bildungsroman" is that it
provides a framework of belief in which the concept of personal
development can be put into practice. For man grows and matures
not by reflecting on the past or yearning towards the future—both
of which consume his energies unproductively—but by living
involvement with the here and now. In terms of Wilhelm Meister's
development it can be argued that this ability to "live the present"
is something he gradually acquires, since at first he allows himself
to ponder too much on the loss of Mariane, but reaches maturity
when he devotes himself fully to the "present" task of educating
his son, without being cramped by unhappy memories of the boy's
mother or by utopian dreams for his future. On the other hand,
is it not true that throughout the novel, as indicated earlier, he is
usually prepared to seize what the present has to offer him, whether
it be the flirtatious Philine, a chance of performing *Hamlet,* or
whatever? He may not feel that his life has always followed a
happy course, but he can hardly have his own development in
mind—with any justification at least—when he exclaims:

> Woe to any kind of education which destroys the most effective
> means of education and directs our attention to the end instead
> of making us happy on the way (p. 502).

For, in spite of mistakes and setbacks, Wilhelm finds enjoyment
and moments of happiness all along the course of his development.

The whole question of "Gegenwart" is thrown into sharp relief
in the narrative by the presence of perhaps the most problematic
character of all, who has exercised the imaginations of countless
readers and commentators. At whatever level one chooses to regard
Mignon, there can be no doubt that she, together with the harper,
embodies the romantic appeal of the novel. In her we have a
picture of the poetic and the morbid, of rootlessness and discord
with life, and above all of a sweet but consuming longing, which
finds its satisfaction only in death. At times the object of her
longing seems to be no more than the Italy of her childhood, and
it is interesting to observe how the images of her first song, "Kennst
du das Land", appear again towards the end of the novel, when
her life-story is retold by the Italian marquis. (The oranges, the
lemon-blossoms and the myrtle of the first stanza mark the spot

where she was incestuously conceived [p. 583]; the pillars, the marble statuary and the hall of the second stanza mark her foster home [p. 587]; while the mists and crags of the mountain in the third stanza seem to be memories of her favourite activity, climbing [p. 587].) At other times, however, her longing appears to have a more profound, even religious basis :

> Nur wer die Sehnsucht kennt,
> Weiß, was ich leide!
> Allein und abgetrennt
> Von aller Freude,
> Seh' ich ans Firmament
> Nach jener Seite. (pp. 240–1.)[28]

Altogether it is not difficult to see why Mignon more than any other figure should have attracted the sympathy of the German Romantics and why they should have ultimately felt so offended at the treatment meted out to her, so offended in fact that Professor Prawer can speak of the Elisabeth-Peregrina figure in Mörike's *Maler Nolten* in terms of Mignon's revenge.[29] But Mörike himself admired *Wilhelm Meister's Apprenticeship;* it is to Novalis, whose own novel, *Heinrich von Ofterdingen,* is to be regarded as the apotheosis of poetry,[30] that we must look for a more characteristically Romantic view. After his initial admiration of Goethe's novel he came to see it as a "satire on poetry", as a "pilgrimage to the patent of nobility", and as a *"Candide* aimed against poetry".[31] And clearly it is Mignon who suffers most from what Novalis saw as an assault on poetry. Making allowances for his rather drastic formulation, it must be allowed that he was largely justified in his interpretation. Where he went wrong was in *regretting* that "poetry" (Mignon) was not permitted to hold sway to the end of the novel. Mignon might represent a Romantic ideal; she is certainly not an embodiment of Classicism. Significantly, her most memorable characteristics are precisely those which Goethe himself gradually overcame, especially as a result of his Italian journey. Where her beauty has something diseased about it,[32] we find Goethe affirming the healing effect, both moral and physical, which Italy has on him.[33] Where she is repeatedly looking forward or backwards, never at home where she is, we find Goethe completely absorbed in his present situation in Italy and, for example, deliberately shunning sadness or longing for his friends back in Weimar.[34]

It is possible to interpret Mignon on a purely symbolic level, as a sort of projection of Wilhelm's own longings[35] or as a living and painful reminder of his love for Mariane, with all that implied for him.[36] At the other extreme one can regard her simply as another character, psychologically or even pathologically affected by the misfortunes of her parents' incestuous relationship.[37] Yet whichever course one follows—though for most it will be somewhere between these opposite poles—the fundamental fact remains that she is not held up as an ideal. Mignon must die : as a symbol, whether of longing or excessive emotions, she is finally overcome by Wilhelm;[38] as a character, she evokes his sympathy and practical help, but belongs ultimately to a mysterious and alien world. No, the motto of the novel—if such it can be called—is contained rather in the words that adorn the "Hall of the Past", Mignon's last resting-place : "Gedenke zu leben!" ("Remember to live!") And what the hero does is to follow in practice the final admonition of the funeral ceremony, which assigns to the past its proper rôle in life :

> The treasure, the fair creation of the past, is now well secured! Here it rests unconsumed in the marble; in your hearts also it lives on, exerts its influence still. Stride, stride back into life! Take the sacred gravity away in your hearts, for gravity, solemn gravity alone makes life eternity. (p. 578.)

It would be inadvisable, however, to say something of Mignon's function in the novel, without also referring to the harper. And that not so much because they prove in the end to be father and child as because they both belong to the same mysterious emotional climate and both help to illuminate the hero's development by means of contrast. In part it is the ideal of "Gegenwart" which is thrown into relief by the harper's life too, since he is a man still mentally shattered by what has happened in the past. But more important is the rôle which guilt or mistakes play in his outlook. Although the full story of his incest does not emerge until near the end of the novel, the effects are brought home to the hero and the reader at a much earlier stage and with great force in his songs, the first of which expresses his plight most poignantly :

> Wer nie sein Brot mit Tränen aß,
> Wer nie die kummervollen Nächte
> Auf seinem Bette weinend saß,
> Der kennt euch nicht, ihr himmlischen Mächte.
>
> Ihr führt ins Leben uns hinein,
> Ihr laßt den Armen schuldig werden,
> Dann überlaßt ihr ihn der Pein,
> Denn alle Schuld rächt sich auf Erden. (p. 136.)[39]

The consequences of this overwhelming sense of guilt are both physical and spiritual. Even his long, white beard and flowing, brown robes evoke something of the restless, homeless wanderer (p. 128). But more important is the atmosphere of doom which overshadows his life, causing him to shrink from close association with other people for fear of contaminating them with his guilt (p. 208), making him see in friendship and love only phantoms sent to torment him (pp. 436–7). Moreover, the conclusion of the novel seems to confirm his private vision of the world, his feeling that he is the victim of some relentless fate, for just when it seems that he has been cured, he discovers and reads the document that relates his previous history. It is this—rather than the subsequent confusion, in which Felix is supposed to have poisoned himself accidentally—that causes him to commit suicide. And one is left to conclude that for him fate has decreed that the guilt of the past should be allowed to wreak its final revenge.

It must be stated most emphatically, however, that this is not to be regarded as the general tendency of the novel or as its "meaning". For, although Goethe sometimes showed an awareness of certain mysterious, destructive forces at work in man's life—as in the later novel *Kindred by Choice* (1809), for example—his fundamental attitude was still one of confidence in life. And as far as the particular question of past follies and past guilt is concerned, this meant a belief that mistakes were of positive value as a means of education. Nor is the belief exclusive to his classical period. Less than six years after his move to Weimar we find him writing to his mother (letter of 11 August 1781):

How much more fortunate it was to find myself placed in circumstances for which I was in no way suited, where I had opportunity enough to get to know myself and others by means of mistakes of misunderstanding and impatience, where, left to myself and to fate, I passed through so many trials, which may not be necessary for hundreds of men, but of which I stood in great need for my personal development. [The word is "Ausbildung" again.]

Taken as a whole, *Wilhelm Meister's Apprenticeship* also gives the same reassurance about the educative value of mistakes, not simply through the words of the Abbé, whose methods are based on man's ability to learn from his mistakes rather than let them prey on his mind (p. 495), but even more through the facts of the hero's life. And the most important of these in the present context is his treatment of Mariane. Having got her with child, he lets suspicion wrongfully get the better of trust and abandons her to her fate. Had the novel been written from the point of view of the harper, this is how one might have summarized Wilhelm's past, while he himself would have been left to consume his life in grief and

despair. But this does not happen : although he does experience
sorrow to the full, Goethe does not let matters rest there. For
whereas the rediscovery of his child spells death for the harper,
it marks the beginning of a new life for the hero. And the token
that his mistakes are to be turned to positive good is given in the
name of his son : Felix.

In both the harper and Mignon there resides a strange
incongruity. Although they possess those qualities associated—by
Goethe too—with the Northern temperament, they are by birth
Italian. What degree of objectivity must it have taken for such
an avowed lover of the Mediterranean to give the most gloomy
and romantic characters this classical origin! But of course we
never see them in their native setting; and even though they
appear here in Germany, they are essentially without home in
the world altogether. It seems therefore only appropriate that they,
together with the author of the "Confessions", that other important
figure who is not at home in the real world of the novel, should
be heard most memorably, indeed almost exclusively, not in
dialogue, but in first-person forms that presuppose no reply; theirs
is self-expression rather than true communication.

III

"Noble simplicity and quiet grandeur"—Winckelmann's much-
quoted description of Greek statues, which for some represents a
description of Classicism itself, seems singularly inappropriate to
the intricate narrative web and bustling life of *Wilhelm Meister's
Apprenticeship*. Not that Goethe disavowed Winckelmann's ideal
as such;[40] but in writing a modern novel he could hardly be
expected to allow ideals based on the visual arts to dictate its
form. Are we therefore to conclude that what classical elements
there are in the work are confined to matters of content? Certainly it seems that, while working on it, Goethe had misgivings
about the poetic possibilities of the prose novel, a form not
sanctioned by any real equivalent in the ancient world.[41] On the
other hand, Victor Lange points out that he did come to believe
that the modern story and the novel should convey some of the
philosophical purposes that once sustained classical tragedy.[42] As
a serious undertaking, in other words, it might be regarded as
modern man's answer to the tragic drama of the Greeks. Yet,
to be honest, it is the later novel, *Kindred by Choice*, that approximates to the tragic atmosphere of the Ancients more than *Wilhelm
Meister's Apprenticeship*.

Even more problematic from the classical point of view, however,
is the mixed form of this novel. To see it in terms of *universal*

poetry, as Friedrich Schlegel did, is something of an exaggeration—but of course he did not have the benefit of our experience, enlarged by the reading of novels such as James Joyce's *Ulysses*. Nevertheless *Wilhelm Meister's Apprenticeship* does display a remarkable variety in its modes of presentation, combining the expected dialogue and narration of events with elements of lyrical song, personal confession and gnomic wisdom, all of which have an essential contribution to make to the meaning of the novel. But *Wilhelm Meister's Apprenticeship* is mixed in another sense too, in that it embraces matters of high seriousness and matters of everyday triviality, characters with an aura of tragic mystery and characters with a simple, earthy vitality, and moves with ease from the sublime to the ridiculous, from lofty discussions on literary topics to "operatic" happenings in the tradition of the adventure-novel (amorous intrigues, chance encounters, the discovery of long-lost relatives, and so forth). Predictably, Schiller disapproved of this sort of thing, feeling that Goethe had given his imagination too much free play and had been misled into bowing to low public taste in such unnecessary theatrical elements (letter to Goethe, 8 July 1796). In his reply Goethe conceded the point, relating it to a realistic tendency of his to deflate the importance of things :

> Thus I shall always like to travel incognito, to dress in inferior clothes rather than better ones and, in conversation with strangers or half-acquaintances, to prefer the less important topic or at least the less weighty expression, to behave more frivolously than I am, and so to interpose myself, as it were, between my real self and my appearance. (Letter to Schiller, 9 July 1796.)

And when all is said and done, would any but the most solemn and high-minded reader of *Wilhelm Meister's Apprenticeship* wish it otherwise? Are we not positively grateful to Goethe for the colourful, "popular" elements?

If this kind of mixture is not to be regretted, however, it is difficult to say the same for the stylistic split which most critics have observed between the first and second halves of the novel, between realistic presentation and typification, between characteristic individuality and symbolic concentration, or whatever terms one chooses. When Goethe came to resume work on his *Wilhelm Meister* after the Italian journey, he sought to gain a clearer picture of the characters already created by reducing their vivid but vague contours to simple formulæ.[43] In itself this was obviously valuable to the poet—as was the related habit he developed in Italy of seeking to gain an overall view, a clear concept of the towns he visited[44]—but to judge from the results, some of the later characters have become the victims rather than the bene-ficiaries of what is after all a process closely linked to Goethe's classical approach. The seriousness of the split lies in the fact that the reader begins to entertain unwanted doubts about the value of Wilhelm's personal development which, put at its worst, seems to have brought him to a limbo full of shades. To try and justify this depersonalization of the characters, as Kurt May does, by interpreting it as a necessary parallel to the hero's own develop-ment from an individual to an ideal type, would carry little conviction even if one were to agree that Wilhelm does become an ideal type.[45] For the logical conclusion of such an argument would be that to portray a bore one must become boring, to describe a half-wit one must write half-wittedly, and so on. In all honesty one must admit the weakness and simply be grateful that the hero himself escapes such abstraction.

But it is time to be more positive. For in matters of form and style *Wilhelm Meister's Apprenticeship* is not simply either un-classical or, where classical, uninteresting and lifeless. In the first place, for all the kaleidoscope of contemporary life which is presented, the novel does have unity. At its simplest this unity derives from the figure of the hero, through whom alone we encounter the world of the novel; only what he does and experi-ences is brought before our eyes. On the other hand, he is not just an apology for real unity, an arbitrary peg on which to hang an otherwise unconnected string of adventures or scenes from contemporary life. The emphasis is not on the episodes as such, but on their importance for the hero. Comparing the *Theatrical Mission* and the *Apprenticeship,* Friedrich Gundolf observed the change from an air of improvisation and a delight in story-telling to a firmer control over the material and the direction of the narrative;[46] and more recently Professor Rasch has described the same tendency, noting the elimination of digressions and of colourful though dispensable details of personal character (such as the love-affair of Wilhelm's mother and the doubtful virtue of Mariane).[47] The result is a more purposeful narrative, which relates its various elements to a central concern—the portrayal of a character in both his unalterable essence and his gradual develop-ment. Our earlier discussion of other figures in the novel was of necessity simplified, but at least it may serve to illustrate the control and purpose which Goethe brings to their character and function. Werner, Philine, the "beautiful soul", and Therese—to mention only those dealt with previously—all mark some stage in the hero's development. And yet each one highlights a possible danger which he ultimately avoids. Similarly, Mignon and the

Harper have the function, among other things, of bringing to our attention a dark, romantic world, to which the hero might easily have succumbed, but does not. It is in this sort of way that Goethe gives shape and meaning to the multifarious world of his novel; and only towards the end does the organizing purpose threaten to stifle the life.

In discussing the disputed claims of Enlightenment and Storm and Stress, Rationalism and Irrationalism, Friedrich Sengle has proposed a form of reconciliation, according to which the importance of both tendencies is acknowledged :

> We are indebted to Rationalism above all for maintaining formal discipline, clarity and universality, and to Irrationalism for impregnating the forms with spirit, bringing them to life and giving them individuality. Above both one-sided tendencies . . . German Classicism rises to a higher validity.[48]

Is it not this sort of higher validity we have in *Wilhelm Meister's Apprenticeship*, not merely in the development of the hero towards a balance between the one-sided tendencies to which he is exposed, but also in its form, which brings order and discipline to a mass of multi-coloured life? Or to use other terminology, do we not have here a demonstration of that balance between "Stofftrieb" (the sensuous drive) and "Formtrieb" (the formal drive) which Schiller saw in his letters *On the Aesthetic Education of Man* as an important goal of culture?

Again, it can be argued that the rôle and personality of the narrator are vital ingredients in the classical stamp which the novel bears. Compared with the *Theatrical Mission* the narrator here does not intrude with his own personality; he speaks as a trustworthy man of experience, who presides over the affairs of the novel with calm and composure, refining them through the clear, steady flow of his language.[49]

> In this respect the novel is characteristic of Weimar classicism; the variety of life is as it were filtered through the medium of a clear, harmonious, serene personality . . . It is not the particular historical Goethe, but an imagined, idealized (somewhat avuncular) character, a bearer of the whole meaning of the book, and ultimately, perhaps, its most important character.[50]

It is from his perspective, a mixture of involvement and detachment, that we too judge the affairs of the novel. We are allowed to hear the words and thoughts of the hero, but we are also given the comment which other characters and even the events themselves make on what he says. There is thus a marked increase in objectivity as against the earlier *Werther*, which, in a one-sided correspondence, presents only the opinions of the hero or an account of the objective world and other people's opinions from his very individual point of view. Even the fictional editor, who has little to say as it is, presents himself from the start as entirely sympathetic to the hero.

One specific element of the objectivity in *Wilhelm Meister's Apprenticeship* needs further comment. It is the irony, which so frequently cocks a snook at the pretensions of the characters and the high seriousness of their concerns. It comes out in the tone of the narrative of course, but more interestingly in Goethe's art of juxtaposition, which makes its ironic point without need of comment from the narrator. In Book IV, Chapter 8, for example, with the troupe of actors blaming Wilhelm for their losses after the robbery, the hero solemnly—and too generously—promises not to leave them until he has repayed them two and threefold. As he repeats his promise and the actors keep an embarrassed silence, Philine sits on her trunk and cracks nuts (p. 233). And with that the chapter comes to an end. Or again in Book IV, Chapter 6, when the beautiful Amazon comes to the aid of the wounded hero, he imagines he sees a halo around her head. The picture is spoilt for him, however—and once more it is this that brings the chapter to a close—when the bullet is extracted from his chest and he loses consciousness (p. 228)!

Irony of this kind characterizes the first half of the novel in particular, diminishing noticeably in the later books. Nevertheless it is worth remarking that the same spirit informs not only the opening chapters, but also the conclusion of the novel. In Book I an ironic light is repeatedly shed on the hero's passion for Mariane and the theatre, nowhere more clearly than when he is talking about his puppet-theatre, the instigator of the passion. Even Wilhelm himself is a little ironic towards his earlier plaything, while Mariane finds his whole narration of these activities so compelling that she falls asleep! Thereafter we hear the voice of the level-headed Werner, who shows up the folly of his friend's early enterprises, reminding him how many things were begun without ever being completed (cf. pp. 24–36). As to the last chapter, it persistently refuses to get caught up in the more solemn pronouncements of Lothario and the Abbé; instead it keeps returning to the more light-hearted, even frivolous Friedrich, as he claims credit for the happy outcome of Wilhelm's tangled relations with the opposite sex.

In the novels and stories of Thomas Mann the irony frequently has a rather destructive effect, making the reader wonder whether there is anything left of positive value. In *Wilhelm Meister's Apprenticeship*, however, this is not the case. As so often with

Goethe—one need think only of the *Roman Elegies* or the earlier poem, "Wandrers Sturmlied"—it is more a question of the author's refusal to take himself or his subject too seriously. Not that the matters dealt with are not of real concern to him; but he does have the ability to stand above them. In 1810 Goethe composed a drinking-song which has as its refrain—the answer to every eventuality, good or bad—the words "Ergo bibamus". In *Wilhelm Meister's Apprenticeship* is it not as though, whatever befalls, he can resort to the invitation : "Ergo subrideamus"? For the overall tone is a mixture of seriousness and humour, warmth and coolness, involvement and detachment, a mixture which makes the novel so readable.

If the Golden Age of mankind, when the human personality could develop into the classical ideal of a harmonious whole, was believed to have occurred in Ancient Greece, why not look to a work that is set in this world for a truer representation of German classicism at its best? Part of the answer is implicit in Goethe's characterization of Torquato Tasso, a man whose imagination is so fascinated by this Golden Age that he is incapable of living his present life as a member of human society. For the point is that it takes very little to turn an interest in the *classical* world into a *romantic* longing. And it is precisely this danger that *Wilhelm Meister's Apprenticeship* avoids, because it seeks to come to terms with the ancient ideal in a real, contemporary setting. Moreover, it is a work that embodies so many of those principles which crystallized in Goethe's mind as a result of his Italian journey, as a result, that is, of an open encounter between an eighteenth-century Northerner and the classical world. Could there be a more fruitful and reliable basis for German Classicism?

NOTES

1. W. H. Bruford, *Culture and Society in Classical Weimar*: *1775–1806* (Cambridge, 1962).
2. Cf. *ibid.*, pp. 36–8, 213–33, 265–7, and 271–89.
3. Page numbers quoted in the text refer to the "Hamburger Ausgabe" of Goethe's works, Vol. VII.
4. Cf. Emil Staiger, *Goethe* (Zürich, 1956), Vol. II, p. 154.
5. Cf. Hans Eichner, "Zur Deutung von *Wilhelm Meisters Lehrjahren*", *Jahrbuch des Freien Deutschen Hochstifts* (1966), pp. 181–184.
6. *Italienische Reise,* 10 November 1786. In: *H.A.,* XI, p. 135.
7. From his remarks on *Gabriele* by Johanna Schopenhauer, in: *Über Kunst und Altertum,* Vol. IV, No. 1 (1823).
8. Walther Killy, *Wandlungen des lyrischen Bildes,* second enlarged edition (Göttingen, 1967), p. 22.

9. Cf. what Goethe wrote in a rather different context: "But if we consider all formations, especially organic ones, we discover that there is nowhere an element of stasis, nowhere an element of rest, but rather that everything oscillates in constant movement". *Zur Morphologie: Die Absicht eingeleitet,* in: *H.A.,* XIII, p. 55.

10. *op. cit.,* II, pp. 13–15.

11. Eichner, p. 179.

12. Cf. Staiger, II, p. 10.

13. Cf. Georg Lukács, "Wilhelm Meisters Lehrjahre", in: *Goethe: A Collection of Critical Essays,* ed. Victor Lange (New Jersey, 1968), p. 94

14. Cf. Staiger, II, p. 151.

15. "Beauty is the middle line between extremes", writes H. A. Korff, summarizing Winckelmann's view of Greek beauty, as seen both in art and human nature, in: *Geist der Goethezeit,* Vol. II (Leipzig, 1930), p. 312.

16. Cf. Eichner, pp. 190–1.

17.

But here, with mighty hands, Nature halts the development
And guides it gently into greater perfection.
She moderates the flow of the sap, narrows the ducts,
And immediately the formation displays more delicate operations.
Silently the growth of the spreading edges recedes
And the rib on the stem develops more completely.

18. Cf. p. 88 above.

19. Cf. especially Eichner, p. 195 and Kurt May, *"Wilhelm Meisters Lehrjahre,* ein Bildungsroman?", *Deutsche Vierteljahrsschrift für Literaturwissenschaft und Geistesgeschichte,* XXXI (1957), pp. 1–37.

20. Cf. among others: Kurt May, "Weltbild und innere Form der Klassik und Romantik im *Wilhelm Meister* und *Heinrich von Ofterdingen",* in: *Romantik-Forschung, Buchreihe der Deutschen Vierteljahrsschrift,* Vol. XVI (Halle, 1929), pp. 189–190; Karl Vietor, "Goethe: *Wilhelm Meisters Lehrjahre",* in: *Interpretationen: Deutsche Romane von Grimmelshausen bis Musil,* ed. Jost Schillemeit (Frankfurt/Main, 1966), p. 47; Roy Pascal, *The German Novel* (Manchester, 1956), p. 27.

21. Cf. Staiger, II, pp. 162–166.

22. George Steiner, *The Death of Tragedy* (London, 1961), pp. 168–169.

23. Cf. J. M. Ritchie, *Periods in German Literature* (London, 1966), p. 104.

24. Cf. Staiger, II, p. 178 and Bruford, p. 256.

25.

Do not brood over this unique fortune!
To live is duty, even if it were only for a moment!

26. *Italienische Reise,* 9 October 1786, in: *H.A.,* XI, p. 93. For a fuller treatment of these ideas see Staiger, II, pp. 19–32.

27. See the section "Antikes" from Goethe's essay on *Wincklemann und sein Jahrhundert* (1805).

28.
Only the man who experiences longing
Knows what I suffer!
Alone and shut off
From all joy,
I look at the firmament
Towards the beyond.

Mignon sings this song as a duet with the Harper.

29. S. S. Prawer, "Mignon's Revenge: A Study of Mörike's *Maler Nolten*", *Publications of the English Goethe Society*, New Series, XXV (1955–6), pp. 63–85.

30. Cf. Rudof Haym, "Novalis: *Heinrich von Ofterdingen*", in: *Interpretationen, loc. cit.*, p. 118.

31. "Fragmente der letzten Jahre (1799–1800)", in: Novalis, *Schriften*, ed. Paul Kluckhohn and Richard Samuel (Leipzig, n.d.), Vol. III, p. 314.

32. Cf. Pascal, p. 19.

33. Cf. Staiger, II, p. 10 and Barker Fairley, *A Study of Goethe* (Oxford, 1961), pp. 121–2.

34. Cf. Staiger, II, p. 11. It is interesting to note that this last point is made at Vicenza, which was at one time a possible choice for the home of Mignon.

35. Cf. Prawer, *loc. cit.*, p. 77.

36. Cf. Hellmut Ammerlahn, "Wilhelm Meisters Mignon—ein offenbares Rätsel: Name, Gestalt, Symbol, Wesen und Werden", *Deutsche Vierteljahrsschrift*, XLII (1968), pp. 111–12 and 113–14.

37. Cf. Paul Krauß, "Mignon, der Harfner, Sperata: Die Psychopathologie einer Sippe in *Wilhelm Meisters Lehrjahren*", *Deutsche Vierteljahrsschrift*, XXII (1944), pp. 327–54.

38. Cf. Ammerlahn, *loc. cit.*, p. 112.

39.
He who never ate his bread with tears,
Who never spent his sorrowful nights
Sitting weeping on his bed,
He does not know you, heavenly powers.

You lead us into life,
You cause the poor man to become guilty,
Then you leave him to his torment,
For all guilt receives its punishment on earth.

There is a curious echo of this second stanza in something Thomas Mann puts into the mouth of Schiller in his imaginative sketch, *Schwere Stunde*: "And if they [the excesses of his youthful temperament] did take their revenge, he would defy the gods who sent guilt and then inflicted punishment".

40. Cf. Staiger, II, pp. 29–30.

41. Cf. Wolfdietrich Rasch, "Die klassische Erzählkunst Goethes", in: *Formkräfte der deutschen Dichtung vom Barock bis zur Gegenwart*, ed. Hans Steffen (Göttingen, 1967), p. 83.

42. Cf. Victor Lange, "Goethe's Craft of Fiction", in: *Goethe: A Collection of Critical Essays,* p. 77.
43. Cf. "Weimarer Ausgabe" of Goethe's works, Section I, Vol. 21, p. 332.
44. Cf. Staiger, II, pp. 15–16.
45. Cf. May, "Weltbild und innere Form", p. 189.
46. Friedrich Gundolf, *Goethe* (Berlin, 1915), pp. 519–20.
47. Cf. Rasch, *loc. cit.,* pp. 90–1.
48. Cf. Friedrich Sengle, "Die Grundlagen der deutschen Klassik: Vermittlungsvorschlag in einem deutsch-französischen Mißverständnis", in: *Arbeiten zur deutschen Literatur 1750–1850* (Stuttgart, 1965), p. 93.
49. Cf. Rasch, *loc. cit.,* pp. 85–6.
50. Pascal, *op. cit.,* p. 26.

BIBLIOGRAPHY

W. H. Bruford, *Culture and Society in Classical Weimar: 1775–1806* (Cambridge, 1962).

H. A. Korff, *Geist der Goethezeit,* Vol. II (Leipzig, 1930).

Friedrich Sengle, "Die Grundlagen der deutschen Klassik: Vermittlungsvorschlag in einem deutsch-französischen Mißverständnis", in: *Arbeiten zur deutschen Literatur 1750–1850* (Stuttgart, 1965), pp. 88–93.

Klaus Gysi and others (ed.) *Erläuterungen zur deutschen Literatur: Klassik* (Berlin, 1967).

Barker Fairley, *A Study of Goethe* (Oxford, 1961).

Richard Friedenthal, *Goethe: His Life and Times* (London, 1965).

Emil Staiger, *Goethe* (Zürich, 1952–1959).

Hans Eichner, "Zur Deutung von *Wilhelm Meisters Lehrjahren",* *Jahrbuch des Freien Deutschen Hochstifts* (1966), pp. 165–96.

Melitta Gerhard, "Goethes *Wilhelm Meister* und der moderne Bildungsroman", in: *Der deutsche Entwicklungsroman bis zu Goethes "Wilhelm Meister", Deutsche Vierteljahrsschrift für Literaturwissenschaft und Geistesgeschichte, Buchreihe,* Vol. IX (Halle, 1926), pp. 121–60.

Hans-Egon Hass, "Wilhelm Meisters Lehrjahre', in: *Der deutsche Roman vom Barock bis zur Gegenwart: Struktur und Geschichte,* ed. Benno von Wiese, Vol. I (Düsseldorf, 1963), pp. 132–210.

Georg Lukács, "Wilhelm Meisters Lehrjahre", in: *Goethe: A Collection of Critical Essays,* ed. Victor Lange (New Jersey, 1968), pp. 86–98.

Kurt May, "Weltbild und innere Form der Klassik und Romantik im *Wilhelm Meister* und *Heinrich von Ofterdingen",* in: *Romantik-Forschung, Buchreihe der deutschen Vierteljahrsschrift für Literaturwissenschaft und Geistesgeschichte,* Vol. XVI (Halle, 1929), pp. 185–203. Reprinted in Kurt May, *Form und Bedeutung: Interpretationen deutscher Dichtung des 18. und 19. Jahrhunderts* (Stuttgart, 1957), pp. 161–77.

Roy Pascal, "Johann Wolfgang von Goethe: *Wilhelm Meister",* in: *The German Novel* (Manchester, 1956), pp. 3–29.

Wolfdietrich Rasch, "Die klassische Erzählkunst Goethes", in: *Form-*

kräfte der deutschen Dichtung vom Barock bis zur Gegenwart, ed. Hans Steffen (Göttingen, 1967), pp. 81–99.

Hans Reiss, *Goethe's Novels* (London, 1969).

Eduard Spranger, "Goethe und die Metamorphose des Menschen", in: *Goethe: seine geistige Welt* (Tübingen, 1967), pp. 160–91.

Jacob Steiner, *Goethes Wilhelm Meister: Sprache und Stilwandel* (Stuttgart, 1966).

Karl Vietor, "Goethe: *Wilhelm Meisters Lehrjahre*", in: *Interpretationen: Deutsche Romane von Grimmelshausen bis Musil,* ed. Jost Schillemeit (Frankfurt/Main, 1966), pp. 30–48. Reprinted from Karl Vietor, *Goethe: Dichtung, Wissenschaft, Weltbild* (Bern, 1949).

Novalis' *Heinrich von Ofterdingen* and the Romantic novel

VI

Novalis' *Heinrich von Ofterdingen* and the Romantic novel

J. M. RITCHIE

NOVALIS has never been widely known outside Germany, and even inside Germany the acclaim that he enjoys often seems to come from specialists, while the wider public knows only the cliché of "blue flower" Romanticism and little else. Indeed specialists have so often pointed out how different Novalis was from his contemporaries that one might well ask why he has been chosen as the representative Romantic author for this chapter. While other Romantics were becoming converts to Catholicism he was preaching a strange inter-confessional Christianity; while others were abandoning the present for a more "romantic" past he was conjuring up images of a Golden Age of the future; while it was "romantic" to attack the philistinism of regular employment, Novalis was a hard-working engineer and devoted civil servant. He also differed markedly from the accepted image of Romantic, being both a first-class mathematician and a trained geologist. On the other hand, it has been argued with equal force that Novalis remains the key to the German Romantic School, the poet in whom the psychology of the Romantic Movement can best be studied.[1] There has been a tendency to find in Novalis a typology of *the* Romantic poet who dies after a short life in which love and death are inextricably linked. Even when it is known that Novalis' life was in fact no shorter than that of any of his many brothers and sisters, his famous attempt to will himself to death in order to follow his beloved Sophie still captures the imagination of his readers, who then tend to treat all of his work as directly personal and confessional. As far as *Heinrich von Ofterdingen* is concerned this has resulted in its being read as a love-story expressing the author's "romantic" death-wish, although for the true romantic poet, death and the longing for death are only a transitional phase, the real goal being the consecration of life.[2]

Similarly, however fascinating the personal background of the novel, and however revealing it may be for the psychology of the Romantic poet, it is entirely misleading to see Novalis' work as characterized by emotional intensity divorced from intellectual power and aesthetic control. In this context it is important to remember that we are concerned with a narrative and not a lyrical form, with *Heinrich von Ofterdingen* and not *Hymns to the Night*. Novalis consciously singled out the novel (*Roman*) to give an entirely new and far deeper significance to the whole concept of *Roman*ticism. For him, as for his contemporaries, the novel was to be the culmination of Romantic poetry and philosophy. Being so all-embracing and "universal", it was felt to be the ideal vehicle to encompass and give shape and form to all the ideas exercising the minds of the new generation. It has always been regarded as significant that Friedrich Schlegel placed *Wilhem Meister's Apprenticeship* alongside the French Revolution and Fichte's *Wissenschaftslehre* as crystallizing the greatest tendencies of the time. A novel is thereby seen as the source of the aesthetic upheavals, the French Revolution of the political upheavals, and Fichte of the philosophical upheavals which produced Romanticism.

Friedrich Schlegel's famous *Athenäum* fragment[3] has been referred to here primarily to stress the importance of the novel form for Romanticism, and the influence of Goethe's novel on *Heinrich von Ofterdingen* will be readily apparent. But without stretching the "three great tendencies of the time" too far, where, one may ask, are the other two tendencies here? It seems folly to look for the French Revolution in a novel set centuries before the Fall of the Bastille. Indeed, according to some critics, Novalis was little affected by the Revolution.

When the French Revolution broke out, Novalis was a youth of seventeen, the age when one would expect such an upheaval to have had a decisive influence on his mind and character. But it passed him by; after a short period of enthusiasm, like all other members of the Romantic School he was hardly influenced by it.[4]

This does, however, seriously underestimate the impact of the Revolution on Novalis and his awareness of its significance for the modern world. In 1799 he was writing his essay on *Christianity or Europe,* in which the Reformation is equated with the Revolution, with particular stress on the power of religion in the life of a state. The French Revolution, as Novalis saw it, was at the same time the pinnacle and the end of the Age of Enlightenment. In it the Reformation devoured itself, thereby allowing the spirit of the modern world to emerge, a spirit already visible in Robespierre who made religion into the "centre" and the "driving force" in the state.[5] Not surprisingly, perhaps, precisely the same kind of synthesis rising out of the warring forces of reason and religion is adumbrated in the climax of *Heinrich von Ofterdingen* in

Klingsohr's famous *Märchen,* so the French Revolution may indeed be present in the novel in concealed form. Indeed far from presenting the effortless maturing of the poet in a medieval world from which all conflict has been removed, the novel makes constant references forward to Novalis' own post-revolutionary age. The three tales included in the novel all demonstrate the triadic march of time, in each case culminating in a synthesis arising out of the thesis and antithesis which have gone before. Even the "Romantic" Middle Ages which Novalis had chosen for his novel is an age of transition like Novalis' own post-revolutionary age, and as such not only peculiarly suited for revealing a superior spiritual force but also one which, while filled with awareness of the riches of the past, is equally open to the possibilities of the future.[6]

While the reader will not readily be aware of the French Revolution in *Heinrich von Ofterdingen,* he will quickly sense the presence of Fichte. Certainly he will realize that he is dealing with a typical Romantic novel in that it is supremely philosophical, though in Novalis' case there is no conflict between philosophy and poetry—for Novalis philosophy was "really homesickness—the urge to be at home everywhere", while poetry cures this same homesickness by revealing the secret path that unfailingly leads home. Romanticizing for Novalis is therefore an active process whereby the poet shows the way home to the "original meaning". *Heinrich von Ofterdingen* represents the apotheosis of poetry, culminating in the poeticization of the world and the dawn of a new Golden Age, a rebirth of the mystical past when all was poetry and man was like a wave in the womb of the eternal ocean. This is very much in line with the general trend of Idealist philosophy which attempted to present all human thought, indeed the totality of existence, as the emanation of a single universal principle which Fichte found in the process of "the self-constitution of consciousness as such". The theme of Novalis' novel thereby becomes "the awakening to consciousness, (therefore the emphasis placed on Besonnenheit) and the consequent objectivization of the implicit unity of all things".[7] What needs to be repeated over and over again is that what Novalis developed out of Fichte's *Wissenschaftslehre* is no simple escape from the so-called "real" world. On the contrary Novalis' "Realistic Idealism" shares with Friedrich Schlegel's concept of romantic poetry the active desire to reproduce the "abundance of life". Over against the "classical" ideal of art, Schlegel had conceived of an art

> sensible that the abundance and infinite interconnectedness of Nature are incompatible with any sharp cleavage of things from one another, and not more afraid of "confusion" than Nature

is; aware that the distinctiveness, the idiosyncrasy of the individual artist's vision is one of the elements in this abundance of Nature, and ought therefore not to be suppressed in art; and mindful that the task which it thus sets before itself is endless, and that no stage reached in the progress of it can be definitive.[8]

This theory of romantic art can be applied to *Heinrich von Ofterdingen*. All the ingredients are there : the apparent "confusion"; the idiosyncratic nature of the artistic vision; the eternal striving for more and more complex forms culminating in the great *Märchen* which is itself only a transition to the second (fulfilment) part of the novel; the endlessness of the task which precludes the possibility of a "finished" work of art. This is Novalis' Romantic novel, remembering always that while the goal is the revelation of "the infinite interconnectedness of Nature" the starting point is reality. The "higher sense" is found behind the commonplace. Romanticizing means for Novalis giving the *normal* a magical aura, the *familiar* the dignity of the unfamiliar, the *finite world* a suggestion of infinity.

All this would appear to make demands which even the universal form of the novel is incapable of encompassing. However, Novalis and his contemporaries did believe they had before them a masterpiece demonstrating that the ideal was attainable. Theirs was no mere generalized speculation on the nature of the *Roman* and the aesthetic qualities illustrated by it, their *Roman*ticism was associated more directly with the one great work which could be taken to inculcate the aesthetic principles they upheld : *Wilhelm Meister's Apprenticeship*. Novalis' preoccupation with *Wilhelm Meister* is well documented, especially for the period following the death of Sophie von Kühn and immediately preceding the work on his own *Heinrich von Ofterdingen*. He later turned against it when he came to realize that in the end the "marvellous" which for him was the essence of Romanticism was not upheld in the novel but instead was treated as an aberration and that Goethe in fact leads his hero out of the ideal Romantic world of art and poetry into the active world of business. But however much he was later forced to reject *Wilhelm Meister*, it was still the model to be surpassed. He even hoped to publish his own novel with the publisher of *Wilhelm Meister* in exactly the same format and using exactly the same print.[9] Even so, Novalis realized that he could not surpass Goethe in artistry or style, but at best only in content and power, in "multiplicity" and depth. His aim therefore was not to produce a Romantic counter to classical art, but, inevitably, to raise the older form of the "classical" into the

higher synthesis of Romantic art. Nor was Novalis the first
Romantic to bring out a novel following Goethe's *Wilhelm Meister*.
He was preceded by Tieck's *Sternbald,* which contributed many
details to his own novel[10] and before that by Friedrich Schlegel's
notorious apprenticeship in the art of love, *Lucinde*. In a letter to
Caroline Schlegel of 27 February 1799, Novalis wrote regarding
Lucinde :

> As far as I can see our novels will be poles apart. Mine will
> probably be finished this summer either in Toeplitz or Carlsbad.
> When I say finished—I mean the first volume only—for I feel
> like spending my whole life over one novel—which will fill a
> whole library—containing perhaps the formative years of a
> nation. The term formative years is false—it suggests a particular
> goal. With me all it should convey is—years of transition from
> the infinite to the finite. I hope it will satisfy both my historical
> and my philosophical longings.

The novel has now become a life-fulfilling task, the pinnacle of
achievement for the Romantic, the only genre capable of satisfying
both his historical and philosophical longings, that is, raising both
to a new Romantic synthesis.[11]

Samuel has summed up in what way *Wilhelm Meister* served
as a model for *Heinrich von Ofterdingen*.[12] It was, of course, full
of "romantic" situations and characters, all sorts of mysterious
strangers, extraordinary events, secret societies with strange rituals,
and, most romantic of all, the romantic fates of Mignon and the
harper as well as Sperata's story. There was the famous romantic
irony which Friedrich Schlegel had discerned in it. There was
the general philosophy in which the whole theatre of the world
was reflected through the means of poetry and the problem of existence solved, or rather, as Schlegel put it : "in the *Years of Apprenticeship*, the only thing learned is how to live". The moral was
romantic because the standard taken was not philistine convention;
on the contrary, love and temptation were seen as natural stages
in the formation of character. The form, too, of the novel was as
romantic as its contents, for the stresses came not logically but
rhythmically and melodically, with no regard apparently being
paid to order or merit, first or last, great or small. Similarly all
the characters in the novel appeared to be variations of each other,
an idea which had an enormous impact on *Heinrich von
Ofterdingen* :

> Klingsohr is the King of Atlantis. Heinrich's mother is fantasy.
> His father is sense. Schwaning is the moon and the antiquary
> is the miner and iron too. The Count of Hohenzollern has also

to reappear in different form. Not too obviously allegorical. Emperor Frederick is Arctur. The Eastern Maiden is also poetry. Three-in-one girl (342).

But most of all it was Goethe's style which left its mark on *Heinrich von Ofterdingen,* that wonderful prose which is prose yet poetry, and the "romantic" songs included in the novel, in which poetry is revealed as the natural language of beautiful souls. When Novalis set about creating his "middle-class" hero, in contrast to a Wilhelm Meister who ends up being ennobled, he strove for a style characterized by:

A certain old-fashioned tinge, careful placing and arranging of material, an unobtrusive touch of allegory; in addition a style radiating a certain strangeness, piety and wonder.

And this is a fair description of what he in fact accomplished.[13] The style of Heinrich von Ofterdingen only *seems* as simple and as natural as could be:

This is a kind of prose which apparently takes in the world of the senses, i.e. the normal finite world, but which is given back its sense of infinity by the calm regular flow of the sentences, the colourless and thereby multivalent mode of expression, the openness of much repeated everyday expression. It is a style which does show the world of external, empirical reality and yet in reality it reveals behind that the deeper unity of all things and forms, the fluid behind the static and gives visible shape to the spiritual behind the temporal. This is a form of poetic language which by the choice of simple repeated stylistic devices preserves its ambivalence and makes the concrete world presented transparent, revealing an infinite background of meaningful associations exactly in the same way that all temporal figures that Heinrich encounters are only ambassadors from an unknown higher world, and all personal and particular detail is only an embodiment of some supra-personal and general significance.[14]

Novalis' novel is a typically Romantic one in that it combines order and chaos, extreme aesthetic sophistication and naiveté; it is highly literary and intellectual, yet it preserves throughout the simplicity of the fairy-tale. It abounds not only in personal allusions but also in "lore derived from alchemy, geology, physics, the mystic writing of the Orient and of the Middle Ages, Böhme and Karl von Eckarthausen (1752–1803), Hemsterhuis and the Bible, Homer, Apuleius, Horace, Ovid, Schiller, Goethe and Tieck".[15]

The first sentence of the novel could not be simpler, more

straightforward, or more down-to-earth. This is the normal "bürgerlich" world, the "Dürer-style" :

> His parents were long since fast asleep in bed, the wall clock kept up its regular tic-toc, the howling wind kept the shutters banging (195).

But very soon the action moves into a more Romantic realm, a world of night and moonlight. A mysterious stranger has filled a young man's head with tales of strange treasures and his heart with unspeakable longings. By the second sentence of the narrative we have moved from the sights and sounds of external reality to the inner world of the young hero's thoughts and emotions. He has an obsession, an *idée fixe*. Like the narrator in Heine's famous *Lorelei* who cannot get the strange tale of ancient times out of his head, Heinrich cannot forget the blue flower, and longs to see it. The stranger seems to have been telling Heinrich something along the lines of the old Thuringian legend concerning the treasure flower of the Kyffhäuser mountain, but now it is not the story itself, nor the idea of hidden treasure that obsesses him. The concept of the flower itself has somehow lifted him out of his normal sphere. He feels he has moved into a different realm, "for who worries about flowers in the normal world". And he is the only one who has been singled out for this deep inner turmoil, this strange kind of madness, a "madness", however, which makes everything seem clearer than ever before and nothing seem foreign to him. From these small beginnings of a young man's fascination with a flower Novalis builds up a motif which was to become the supreme Romantic symbol. Indeed from the use of this leit-motif of the blue flower and of the colour blue in general it soon becomes apparent that the whole novel is a *symbolic* one in which symbols and motifs are used "to link various worlds, combine experiences and mediate between disparate realms".[16] A. L. Willson in his study of the blue flower motif associates this particular use of the Romantic flower symbolism with Friedrich Schlegel's cry for a new mythology, a longing in the heart of every Romantic poet :

> The primary concept of the blue flower is in its use as the object suggesting the unfolding of poetic growth, the development of poetic vision, the germination of poetic accomplishment. A collateral and increasingly important symbolistic function in the course of the novel is in its use as the mediator in the reconciliation of divergent religions, a motif of perfect tran-scendental love and a symbol of the merging into harmonious synthesis of the disparate qualities of man and nature.[17]

Nor must it be thought that this is reading too much into simple statements, for the world of myth is already conjured up by the young hero in the novel. He recalls another half-remembered story of ancient times when animals, trees and rocks could converse with men, and in the strange mental and emotional state in which he finds himself he feels this is about to happen any minute and that he can tell just by looking what they wish to express!

This marks another characteristic affecting the whole structure of Novalis' Romantic novel. Just as Heinrich's thoughts "tend towards music" consistent with the novel's ultimate goal of absolute harmony, so too the normal barriers of logical time are broken down leaving past, present and future to flow easily into one. The climax to the novel was to be a grand poem *The Marriage of the Seasons,* closing the never-ending cycle of the novel structure by going back to the very first lines of the novel. Six lines from this fragment indicate the ultimate harmony :[18]

> Wären die Zeiten nicht so ungesellig, verbände
> Zukunft mit Gegenwart und mit Vergangenheit sich,
> Schlösse Frühling sich an Herbst und Sommer an Winter,
> Wäre zu spielendem Ernst Jugend mit Alter gepaart :
> Dann, mein süßer Gemahl, versiegte die Quelle der Schmerzen,
> Aller Empfindungen Wunsch wäre dem Herzen gewährt. (355)

Where the novel has since the second or third sentence developed into a kind of interior monologue, now it moves deeper and deeper into the subconscious of Heinrich, who loses himself in sweet fantasies before he eventually falls asleep. What follows is a dream, and then a dream within a dream. For Heinrich's father, the realist and rationalist, "dreams are mere empty bubbles". According to him, there may have been some need for dreams once upon a time because they led to divine visions, as the Bible shows. But he denies that any such immediate exchange between heaven and earth is now possible. Hence he claims that ancient tales and sacred books are the only sources of information about any higher realm, in so far as we need any at all : now instead of direct revelations the holy spirit speaks to us through the medium of the *reason* of wise and right-thinking men. Heinrich cannot accept this realistic, rationalistic viewpoint. For him even the most confused dream is a "significant rent in the mysterious curtain falling with a thousand folds into our soul", and he continues, with a statement which is in a sense a Romantic defence of the dream as well as a pointer to the dream-like course of the narrative in *Heinrich von Ofterdingen* :

As I see it the dream is a kind of bulwark against the regular and the commonplace in life, a free recreation for the captive imagination which is given a chance to jumble up all life's images and break into the grown-up's unceasing solemnity with some merry child's play. If it weren't for dreams we should certainly age sooner. Hence even if one does not accept the dream as sent directly from heaven one can take it as a divine gift, a friendly companion on the pilgrimage to the holy sepulchre (199).

The advantages of the dream as a literary vehicle for the Romantic aesthetic can be seen here. In it all the barriers of normal existence crumble allowing Heinrich to move freely in space and time, over immeasurable distances and through wild unknown regions. He can walk across oceans, meet all manner of men, experience war and peace, and maintain what would otherwise be an unbelievably high emotional pitch. In this one dream, for example, he not only survives an infinitely varied life, he dies and is reborn, experiences the absolute limit of passion only to be eternally separated from his beloved. Clearly, as Heinrich realizes, this is not just any dream; this is his *fate*. In it he is living his own future life in extremely condensed form. And this is only the preliminary dream, for in the dream within a dream that comes to him just before dawn he penetrates even more mysteriously into the depths. After climbing upwards through the green net of a forest he finds an opening leading into a mountain. Everything he sees and experiences in his passage down the shaft into the cavern seems a symbolic revelation of the mysterious movements within his own soul—the experience is ecstasy but it is important to notice that more than mere feelings are conveyed. There is also delight for him in the countless *ideas* striving towards inner unity within him and in the new *images* which fuse together and assume visible shape. This ecstatic vision is like a small foretaste of the *visionary* quality the novel itself strives to achieve.

Nor must it be thought that these ecstatic heights leave the Romantic unaware of the erotic possibilities of dream language. Novalis' novel is in many ways far removed from the calculated eroticism of Schlegel's *Lucinde,* but it does contain some strange erotic fantasies like the passage here in which Heinrich, filled with an irresistible longing, undresses and climbs into the mysterious fountain :

Every wave of the pleasing element snuggled close to him like a soft bosom. The waves seemed like a solution of delightful maidens assuming human form against the youth from second to second (197).

As he follows the gleaming river in his dream state of ecstasy and hyper-awareness he falls into another slumber from which he awakens into yet another moment of illumination. In a strange blue light he sees the blue flower which this time is going through a mysterious transformation : in its leaves he sees a maiden's face. In this way the blue flower is early associated both with love and with his future beloved. Indeed it will be seen that when Heinrich's dream (or cycle of dreams) is studied in detail everything that is to happen to him in the novel is already foreshadowed or hinted at in them. Hence there are never any surprises for Heinrich in life : in his dreams he is offered, not only the key to his own future life, but, like his father who has experienced a similar dream, he has seen the "miracle of the world". If his father before him had kept his mind focused on the blue flower and asked God for the meaning of the dream, he too could have been the happiest man in the world and "the supreme mortal lot" could have been his.

The first chapter of the novel has revealed its inward direction and Heinrich's mother, noticing that he has become so quiet and turned in upon himself, decides on a journey to expose him to new people and new places. In other words, Novalis, who from the start has adopted the form of the historical novel, also exploits now the traditional device of the journey. His hero is to be a wanderer through the world with a girl waiting for him at the end of the journey as his prize. Later still Heinrich, when he loses this girl, becomes that even more Romantic figure, the religious wanderer—the pilgrim. It is apparent that the novel also follows the traditional German pattern of the *Bildungsroman*. Heinrich has no knowledge of the world except for what he has gathered from stories, hence his journey will be a voyage of discovery on which above all he will discover himself. At this point too it becomes clear how "romantic" is the view of the Middle Ages which the author finds so attractive, compared with the *modern* age of prosperity, uniformity and unrelated reality :

> Between the crude ages of barbarism and the aesthetic, scientific and prosperous age of the present (was) a profound and *romantic* age concealing a higher form under a simple cloak. Surely everybody likes to wander in the twilight when night fractures on light and light on night into higher shadows and colours. That's what makes us so ready to immerse ourselves in the age when Heinrich lived (204).

Revealing at this point is the significance attached to Heinrich's feelings on parting from the known world of his house on the Wartburg for the unknown world which awaits him outside. Parting means sorrow, the first awareness of the transience of all temporal things, a first premonition of death. Such experience is

seen as necessary, indeed essential, for the old world is never lost
and even at this early stage the novel's cyclical form is indicated
by the suggestion that the hero leaves only to return, his path
into the world always leads him home, following "the dialectical
principle of self-finding through self-expression".[19] This time the
miraculous blue flower which appears before him seems to mean
home.

The narrative form employed also becomes readily apparent.
There are, for example, no long or detailed descriptions of the
country through which the travelling company passes. Hence just
as it is difficult to tell exactly when in the Middle Ages this is all
taking place, so too there is no precision of geographical detail.
Instead of descriptions there are all sorts of *discussions, conversations* and *stories*. From the start the novel presents a passive
and purely receptive hero listening to various voices. The first
general conversation is essentially a hymn of praise to Suabia, the
land in the south they are journeying towards, but it soon develops
into a fundamental discussion of the true path through the
labyrinth of confusion existing in the real world. Already Heinrich,
like the boy Christ before the Elders, talks as from boyish dreams
to defend "childish untrammelled innocence" and differentiates
two paths leading to the knowledge of human society. One of
these is laborious and endless with countless twists and bends. This
is the way of experience. The other, "more like one quick leap",
is the path of inner contemplation. Heinrich's fluency in the
expression of his inner feelings, his mastery of appropriate analogies,
and his natural bent for the marvellous, reveal to the merchants
his true nature. He has the makings of a poet. Though he has no
knowledge of the art of poetry and has never seen a poem, the
seeds have been sown within him and his old teacher was obviously
correct in his prophecy that he would dedicate his whole life to
poetry once he discovered his true nature. In other words, *Heinrich
von Ofterdingen* is a Romantic novel of the artist, and the first
of many definitions of the nature of the poet then follows:

> In the old days, the story goes, poetry used to be far commoner
> and everybody had some knowledge of it, only some more than
> others. It was said to have been related to other marvellous
> lost arts. The singers were thought to be so constantly honoured
> with divine favour that inspired by this invisible communion they
> were able to proclaim divine wisdom on earth with pleasing
> song (209).

This preliminary definition is significantly expanded by the merchants who point to the difference between poetry and the arts
of music and painting. While these are mainly external in their

effect on the senses poetry is entirely internal in that the poet fills
the *inward* sanctuary of the mind with new, wonderful and
pleasing thoughts. He knows how to rouse the secret forces within
the reader and by his words reveals a marvellous unknown realm.
He can summon great ages of the past and the future, countless
beings, marvellous regions and strangest events out of the depths,
and transport us out of the everyday existence we know so well.
The words he uses are strange, yet meaningful, his utterances have
a magic power and even the most commonplace words are made
to sound so wonderful that the listener is entranced. With this
Novalis has described not any poet in any age but the creative
power of the Romantic *imagination* in particular.

At this point the merchants begin to tell stories which they have
heard on their travels. The first of these takes us back to mythical
times in ancient Greece when poets :

> were said to have been both soothsayer and priest, law-giver
> and physician, while even the higher beings, attracted to earth
> by their magic art, instructed them in the secrets of the future
> and revealed to them the symmetry and the natural order of
> all things, also the inner virtues and healing powers of cyphers,
> herbs and all creatures (211).

Here again it is significant how much power is ascribed to the
poet, for he not only brings peace into a warring universe, it is
he who brings order out of chaos and it is he who is responsible
for the peculiar traces of harmony and order still visible in nature.

The second story the merchants have to tell is taken from a
later stage in history, by which time disharmony lived on only in
the ancient tales of the poets :

> All hateful, ugly passions had been banished as discords from
> the mood of gentle harmony which prevailed in all minds. This
> wonderful age possessed the peace of soul and the blissful inward
> reflection of a contented self-created world (214).

But even this earthly paradise, in which poetry rules supreme,
is shown to be divorced from the true forces of nature and religion
and exposed to pride and socially divisive forces. The tale is a
Romantic one of a mysterious fate that disrupts a whole kingdom,
a tale of love, hope, faith and dreams, in which the difficulties that
separate lovers are overcome. Indeed love has the power to transport them out of this world :

> A higher power seemed anxious to unravel the knot more
> quickly and brought them under strange circumstances to this

romantic place. The innocence of their hearts, the magical mood of their state of mind and the irresistible force of their sweet passion and of their youth made them immediately forget the world and everything associated with it and against a background of the storm's epithalamium and the lightning's wedding torches, cradled them in the sweetest intoxication ever to have transported a mortal couple. The dawn of the clear blue day was an awakening to a new blissful world for them (221).

In a sense too the tale of Atlantis reflects the theme indicated by the title of the novel, namely the "Battle of the Poets",[26] for in the same way that Heinrich was to give birth to a new poetry incorporating but surpassing the old, so here too the young man devoted to the science of nature is inspired to poetry which far surpasses the achievements of the court poets. His voice is extraordinarily beautiful and his song displays a strange and wonderful character. It deals with the origins of the world, the stars, plants, animals and men, the almighty harmony in nature, the Golden Age of ancient times and its rulers, Love and Poetry, with the appearance of hatred and barbarism and their struggles against those benevolent goddesses, and finally the song tells of the future triumph of the latter, of the end of misery, the rejuvenation of nature and the return of an eternal Golden Age. This ecstatic poet whose eyes are filled with a vision of a secret world, whose features reveal an unnatural childlike innocence and simplicity, is more than the archetypal poet, for in this little inserted narrative, which typically seems to sum up once again the purport of the whole novel, Novalis also reveals his conception of the Romantic poet.

However, Novalis does not allow his novel to become merely a discursive novel *about* poetry and the nature of the poet. The power of poetry is demonstrated directly by the songs and Romances which he includes in the novel. These songs have also a major rôle to play in the texture and structure of the novel, recapitulating in lyrical form the essence of the action, stressing particular motifs and marking the transition to a new stage in the development. They are also great works in themselves, so that all in all the novel contains a cycle of poems and songs equal to, if not better than, the *Spiritual Songs* and the *Hymns to the Night*.[21]

Heinrich, it is clear by this time, is destined to become a poet, but though he may "inhabit a higher world" he is still "like a little bud which has not yet opened up to flower in fullest glory". He still has a growing period to go through. So the novel now

passes from the celebration at the end of Chapter Three to the
revelry of a feudal castle with talk of peace and war, a war of
religion between Christian and Muslim in the Crusades, and conversations in which once more narrative is reinforced by song.
Yet again Heinrich's whole soul is plunged into turmoil, his whole
being is excited, he is in a state of inner unrest. And once more
Heinrich's spirit is flung from one Romantic extreme to the other,
from the dark stirrings of militant Christianity to gentle compassion
with the sufferings of the captive Eastern Maiden Zulima. Once
again the narrative flow is interrupted while she then tells Heinrich
her story, starting with a kind of panegyric to nature and the
romantic beauties of this exotic paradise on earth :

> There is a special charm to living on ground long populated
> and previously given lustre by diligence, activity and affection.
> There nature seems to have grown more human and compre-
> hensible, a dark memory under the transparent present reflects
> the images of the world with sharply defined edges, and so one
> enjoys a twofold world which thereby loses everything heavy
> and insistent and becomes the magical fiction and fantasy of our
> senses (237).

The interesting point here is the *romantic* vision of nature presented through the characteristic imagery of a magic mirror.
Surface reality becomes transparent and the awareness of a twofold world stressed, the normal world of the senses and the other
world revealed when one penetrates the accidental phenomena
crowding in upon the senses. Here again Novalis is paraphrasing
the aim of the Romantic poet, namely to pass beyond the real to
the transcendental. While this chapter has introduced the poet
Heinrich by story and song to the spirit of militant Christianity
in the Crusades and the lure of the exotic East through the captive
Zulima, the aim for Heinrich, as for Novalis in the novel, is
ultimate harmony, the reconciliation of Christian and Muslim.

If Zulima the Muslim maiden can be taken as an example of
Romantic love of the exotic, the treatment of the next person
Heinrich meets in the novel is a perfect example of how Novalis
the Romantic gives the normal a magical aura, the familiar the
dignity of the unfamiliar. This man comes from strange lands,
wears strange clothes, and his stories and songs bear the imprint
of strangeness. He is a seeker after buried treasure, and he describes
the work that leads him into the hidden bowels of the earth as a
rare and secret art, characterized by secret signs and an un-
intelligible private language which only heightens the fascination
of it. The practice of his art is something which offers complete
satisfaction :

It is impossible to explain and describe this complete fulfilment of an inherent wish, this wonderful delight in things which might have a closer connection with our secret being, that is with occupations for which one is fated and equipped from the cradle (242).

All this sounds more like the absolute dedication of the artist to his art than a description of a miner's calling, for this is what he is! Like the poet's, the miner's art makes him happy and noble of spirit, it awakens in him faith in God's wisdom and the divine order and keeps him innocent and childlike at heart. Far removed from the claims of day-to-day existence he works underground in darkness and alone, free from the degrading lust for property and inspired only by the longing for greater insight into the mysteries of the natural world and a love of harmony :

In his loneliness he thinks in his inmost heart of his comrades and of his family with constantly renewed awareness of the mutual and indispensable ties of blood that bind all men together (245).

The art of mining as treated here is in effect "a serious symbol of all human existence". Like the Welsh miners, German miners are famous for their songs and Novalis' character is no exception, though his second song in particular seems somewhat Romantic, being "almost as obscure and incomprehensible as the music itself, which is exactly what made it so strangely attractive and entertaining, like a waking dream" (248).

If Romanticism is the poetry of night and moonlight then the power of the moon for the Romantic poet is particularly apparent in the description of evening which now follows :

The moon hung in gentle radiance over the hills giving rise to wonderful dreams in all creatures. Itself looking like something dreamt by the sun, it lay turned in upon itself over the dream world and led a nature divided into countless parts back to that mythical age when every seed slumbered by itself and, lonely and intact, longed in vain to unfold the dark abundance of its incommensurable being. Heinrich's mind mirrored the fairy tale of the evening. He felt as if the world were lying opened up within him showing all its treasures and concealed delights as if to a welcome guest. The great simple spectacle struck him as so comprehensible. Nature seemed to him to be incomprehensible only because it heaped such a mass of close and familiar things with such an extravagance of multifarious forms round people (252).

Here, as with Zulima's Romantic landscape, the significant thing is the sudden ability to see through the mass of natural phenomena which normally cloud the senses. This it is in the power of the moonlight to accomplish, leading divided nature back to a primeval state of unity and harmony. This the miner's words have also accomplished for Heinrich. They have opened a secret door within him :

He saw his little room built on to a lofty cathedral, while from the cathedral's stone floor rose up the stern world of the past to be greeted by the clear happy future . . . Suddenly now he sees all his relationships to the great world about him in proper perspective . . . (252)

From such reflections and inner musings which are such a feature of the novel, the narrative takes our hero into the strange underground realm of the miner, a world of its own beneath one's feet, teeming with traces of life dating back to the beginning of time. Here a distant voice rises out of the depths in song announcing the presence of a hermit, Friedrich von Hohenzollern. Like the miner's, his is a life of loneliness, dedication to piety and contemplation of the natural world. Though youthful fantasy had drawn him early in life to the contemplative life of a hermit, he had lacked the inner resources and it is only after a hectic period as a soldier that he has returned to it. In other words, he has travelled both paths described by Heinrich, namely the path of contemplation and the path of experience. Now living in the world of memories, what this recluse has developed, looking back over his own rich store of them, is a sense of their real inter-connection, the deeper significance in their sequence and the meaning of what they reveal. What follows is a statement of the Romantic view, not only of memory but of history. A true sense of history :

develops late, and more with the quiet exercise of memory than under the pressure of present experience. Most recent events seem only loosely connected, but they sympathize all the more wonderfully with remoter events; and it is only when one is in a position to survey a long sequence, neither taking everything literally nor jumbling the real order with capricious dreams, that one can discern the secret concatenation of past and future and learn how to piece together history out of hope and memory (257).

Like the Romantic landscape in which the poet can see the message of the past and the hieroglyphs of God, so too history must be like a beam of light from the dome of a church setting everything off in the most appropriate and attractive light and illuminating the ultimate meaning as with a divine spirit. The writer of history must also be something of a poet, for only the poet knows the art of revealing the proper relationship between events, hence there is more essential truth in the tales of the poets than in the learned compendia of disparate facts the chroniclers produce. In history, as in everything else, the goal is to break through the multiplicity of confusing trivia to the spirit of the age. If this is achieved then incidental details do not matter. Once again the scale of the novel opens up with reflections like these to embrace the infinites of geological time and the difference between the chaos that was the rule during the phases of creation and the peace and harmony that are the rule in nature at the present time is once again stressed.

But however fruitful the hermit's linking of history and poetry are, for Heinrich the most fateful and mysterious event is still to come, for in one of the hermit's books he sees himself as he is at present, in the cave with the hermit and the miner; he sees his own past and he sees himself in situations of which he has as yet no knowledge. This is more than a mere Romantic awareness of fate, it means not only that his life is already pre-determined, but also that he is living a life that has been lived before. He is more than a mere historical personality, he is the archetypal figure of the poet as such, who can appear in any age :

Novalis' hero is the poet of all generations. In portraying his fate Novalis is seeking to depict what is universal in the fate of all poets. When we recall that Novalis described *Heinrich von Ofterdingen* itself as an "apotheosis of poetry" Hohenzollern's description of this book—"a novel . . . in which poetry is praised and depicted in its various aspects"—assumes further significance. Novalis would seem to suggest that his own novel is a restatement of the one true theme of poetry, the praise of the spirit of poetry in all its manifestations. In view of the fact that Novalis' novel remained a fragment at his death, Hohenzollern's closing words—"The end of the manuscript is missing"—have a poignantly *ironic* quality.[22]

From a technical point of view this "window technique"[23] is characteristic of Novalis' Romantic aim always to press beyond the real to the transcendental, to reveal the truth behind the surface reality. Not only are veils constantly being lifted, curtains being drawn back, secret doors opened, tunnels and shafts explored, not only does one moment of *insight* succeed another when all becomes clear and connections are established, the novel is also characterized by a kind of "romantic irony" whereby it reflects upon itself. There is the dream within a dream, the story within a story, the *Märchen* within a *Märchen,* or, as here, the novel within a novel. The real is thereby revealed as the point of departure for the ideal and perspectives are opened up into all infinity. The process is endless.

Chapter Six starts with a general discussion of the difference between men of action and those quiet anonymous individuals whose world is their mind, whose activity is contemplation, whose life is a quiet developing of their inner powers. Once again it is stressed that this does not mean an escape from real life, but rather an attempt by contemplation to arrive at its essence or spirit. Hence the importance of the rôle of the mind. It quickly becomes obvious that the poet, for this is who is meant, will not expose himself personally to the wealth of experience and the "countless phenomena" of the real world. He does not need great and remote events in his personal life :

> Instead their fine senses will be occupied enough with the unimportant phenomena near at hand, which reveal that other great world in miniature, and they will never take a step without making the most surprising discoveries inside themselves on the nature and meaning of these discoveries (267).

The true source of poetry is what the poet knows best. Poets are like birds of passage wandering through the habitations of man breathing new life into man's ancient cults and objects of worship, the stars, spring, love, happiness, fertility, health and happiness. Poets are like kings, sages, heroes. Heinrich is born to be a poet and a multitude of apparently unconnected events seem to be combining to complete his education towards this goal. But so far his vision is still of a world of vast and ever-changing relationships, its soul has not yet spoken to him. Now at journey's end the culminating encounter awaits him in a poet and a young girl. The revelation of his own mother-tongue combined with the touch of her lips will suffice to unseal his lips and develop the simple chord into infinite melodies. Heinrich has now passed from the narrow confines of his unpoetic home in the north to the artistically more congenial south, the land of the great poet Klingsohr. The arrival in his grandfather's home is auspicious, for here Heinrich meets Klingsohr and Mathilde his daughter, "the visible spirit of song". Schwaning's house is like a paradise on earth filled with the enjoyment of life, "a sounding tree laden with golden fruit", and in this house he has another great moment of insight when he too "understands" what enjoyment of life means. He meets the master poet and falls in love with his daughter. Everything falls into place as he grasps the connection between Mathilde, the dream of the blue flower, the fateful book, etc. "She will be my inmost soul, the keeper of my sacred fire". This is immediately followed by a mysterious dream in which Mathilde is drowned in a deep blue river, and a dream within a dream, marked off by the transition from the initial terrors and sorrows of parting to the joys of homecoming and eternal union with Mathilde. For the time being the Romantic dichotomy between the extremes of gladness and sadness remains unresolved, for though Mathilde whispers a wonderful magic word that "resounded to the core of his being" he cannot recall it on waking. One is reminded of the power of the magic word in the poem which, according to Tieck, was also to take its place in the novel : [24]

> Wenn nicht mehr Zahlen und Figuren
> Sind Schlüssel aller Kreaturen,
> Wenn die, so singen oder küssen
> Mehr als die Tiefgelehrten wissen
> Wenn sich die Welt ins freie Leben,
> Und in die (freie) Welt wird zurückbegeben,
> Wenn dann sich wieder Licht und Schatten
> Zu echter Klarheit wieder gatten
> Und man in Märchen und Gedichten
> Erkennt die (alten) wahren Weltgeschichten,
> Dann fliegt vor einem geheimen Wort
> Das ganze verkehrte Wesen fort (344).

The action of the novel has now virtually ceased and all that remains in the chapters preceding the great *Märchen* are the conversations between Heinrich and Klingsohr and his declaration of love for Mathilde. His conversation with Klingsohr, which develops into a fundamental exchange over the nature of poetry, must be read particularly carefully. First of all it needs to be decided whether Klingsohr's definition of poetry is also Novalis' own :

> I cannot commend to you strongly enough the reinforcing with diligence and effort of your understanding, of your natural impulse to know how everything happens and how all things are interconnected through laws of causality. What is absolutely essential for the poet is insight into the nature of every type of activity, knowledge of the means required to achieve every effect, and presence of mind to choose those most appropriate according to the particular fashions and circumstances of the time. Inspiration without understanding is useless and dangerous, and the poet will be able to perform few miracles if he is himself astonished at miracles (281).

At this point Heinrich introduces the problem of *Fate* (a key concept for the Romantics) but still Klingsohr continues:

> The young poet cannot be cool or detached enough . . . if there is a torrent raging in the poet's own breast then all that comes out is confused nonsense. Poetry must be practised as a strict art (281).

None of this sounds like the doctrine of art one would expect for Romantic poetry and here one must follow the conclusions arrived at by Heywood: [25]

> There would seem to be every good reason, judging from Klingsohr's words here quoted, for the belief held by many critics that in Klingsohr Novalis has given us his portrait of Goethe. They fail to draw the inference that Novalis here subtly suggests that Romantic poetry will transcend the poetry represented in his eyes by Goethe. The portrait is, of course, by no means intended to be entirely disparaging, but to show what Novalis regarded as definite failings in Goethe's art.

Heinrich gladly accepts the offer of apprenticeship to the great master and is no doubt as eager and willing to learn from him and his work as Novalis was to learn from Goethe's *Wilhelm Meister* for this novel. But equally it is certain that Novalis intended to surpass Goethe just as Romantic art was to accept all that was good in classical art, only to pass beyond this to a higher synthesis. For Novalis, as has been seen, the true path is *not* to allow the light to fall evenly over the objects of the real world in all their delightful multiplicity but to penetrate through this multiplicity to the transcendental.

Now Heinrich's journey is at an end, the period of expectation is over and the fulfilment about to come. The spirit of poetry has surrounded him everywhere and his companions on the way have been its voices. "In close proximity to the poet, poetry breaks out everywhere". He has encountered the Romantic East with all its melancholy, War with all its wild splendour has stirred his soul, Nature and History have been revealed to him in the miner and the recluse—to these is now added the divine revelation of Love. Chapter Eight concludes with a fantastic love duet between Heinrich and Mathilde in which almost every aspect of Romantic love is touched upon. Love is like a dream. Love is like the experience of pre-existence. Lovers must have known each other before. Love makes one fully aware of Life and Death: only now does she feel she is really living, but at the same time she is prepared to die for him. Love conquers Time. Now through love he knows what it is to feel *immortal*. There can be no parting, even death cannot separate them, they will always be together, in all *eternity*. Love is an awareness of Religion. Heaven has singled her out for his worship. He *adores* her. She is like the Virgin Mary and is the intermediary between him and God, the one through whom he knows God's inexhaustible love. "For what is religion if not infinite understanding, an eternal union of loving hearts". True love does not alter with the changing appearance of the loved one with age, for the eyes of love can see through the transience of surface charms to the wondrous image of the loved one beneath and this image is an eternal image, a part of the sacred world that surrounds us unseen. Hence love is a revelation of the higher world, it will endow the poet with the gift of prophecy, revealing to him the most sacred mysteries of life and the most arcane realms of the mind. Love can overcome the normal limitations of life and death and carry the lovers off to their home in paradise. Love is the *unio mystica* :

> Only the most boundless surrender can satisfy my love. This is what it means. Why, it is a mysterious confluence of our most intimate and essential beings (289).

In the discussion over the nature of poetry Heinrich had raised the question : Can any subject be too remote for poetry ? According to Klingsohr it can and he warns his young apprentice about the general rule applying to the "limits of the presentable". Young poets with their lively imaginations are only too prone to go for the outer limits and to express the unreal and the excessive. But according to him the best poetry stems from what we are most familiar with and an everyday subject is often the best. On the whole, as he sees it, poetry relies on experience of the known world, and that is why the *Märchen* which draws on the unknown and remote is so difficult. This difficult task is exactly the one which Novalis tackles in Chapter Nine, though he places the *Märchen* in the mouth of Klingsohr as one of that poet's youthful works. At first sight it does appear to contain all the dangers Klingsohr warns of; more "multiplicity" than simplicity of subject matter; more chaos than order, forcing the narrative well beyond the bounds of the presentable. Just as by this novel Novalis was competing with *Wilhelm Meister,* so with this final inclusion in the narrative he seems to be deliberately trying to surpass Goethe's famous *Märchen,* with the resultant difficulty and obscurity. But it is probably only when read in isolation as a separate entity that Novalis' *Märchen* seems difficult and wilfully obscure. When looked at together with the tale of Arion and Atlantis much of the mystery disappears. Heinz Ritter has even shown the parallels existing between the novel, the *Märchen,* and Novalis' private life in diagrammatic form as follows : [26]

Novel	*Märchen*	*Life*
Heinrich	Eros	Novalis
Mathilde	Freya	Julie von Charpentier
Klingsohr	Arctur	F. W. F. von Charpentier
Gottesmutter?	Sophie	Sophie von Kühn

While such parallels certainly exist it is perhaps misleading to rely too much on Novalis' private life as a "key" to the obscurities of the *Märchen*. There is no single key which will explain the mysteries, there is no moral to the story. On the contrary it has to be accepted for what it is : an allegorical, symbolical work of art, the appropriate climax to the first part of a novel which is itself *märchenhaft*. In all three of the novel's inserted stories the central theme is the nature of the poet and of his art, and the ultimate victory of poetry over all opposing forces. An equally constant theme is the collapse of an old and the rise of a new and higher order. The march of time is seen as a threefold movement from the golden age of the beginning through an intervening stage of disharmony to a return of the Golden Age at the end. The mystery of death and resurrection appears in each of the three tales, in the story of Arion with the poet's leap into the sea and his rescue by the dolphin, in the Atlantis story with the concealment of the princess underground and her reappearance as a mother, and in the Klingsohr *Märchen* with the death of the heart, which by this sacrifice becomes the potion of eternal life. This unified cycle of stories follows a rising pattern until by the final *Märchen* the original theme of the power of poetry over the natural world becomes a complex narrative of many strands which all have to be brought together to indicate the striving for cosmic harmony. With the progress through the three tales the area of conflict has become ever more extensive and the defeat of the forces of disruption makes greater and greater demands on the power of poetry. Nevertheless the three tales still show the progress of the threefold dialectic from harmony through disruption to a new harmony. Novalis uses not an historical sequence but his own vision of time to mark the progress of the world from its mythical beginnings through the time of the floods which buried Atlantis to the Ice Age at the beginning of the Klingsohr *Märchen,* a form which for Novalis marked the absolute poetic pinnacle known to Romantic art.[27]

The *Märchen* told by Klingsohr is the end of the first part of the novel, the end of the expectation and an indication of the fulfilment to come. Clearly its position in the work was strategic, marking this transition from the old to the new, from the real to the possible world, culminating in the vision of the Golden Age reborn through the power of poetry. Clearly too it is no naive retelling of a simple folk tale, but a highly complex and sophisticated work of the highest artistry. The *Märchen* for Novalis becomes a vehicle to express his philosophical beliefs, his religious longings and his faith in the power of poetry. Within the allegorical symbolism of the *Märchen* all the disparate worlds of Greek mythology, Germanic saga, Eastern mysticism can be combined with the modern world of astronomy, geology and electrical forces to form one great harmony. The *Märchen* itself gives a key to this harmony concealed behind its multiplicity of warring strands, for

> however marvellous and abrupt the transitions often were, there still seemed to be one simple theme joining the whole thing together (293).

Part Two of the novel starts with the poem of Astralis, the sidereal being, born of the embrace of Heinrich and Mathilde. This being was to speak between every two chapters. From the poem it is clear that the novel was to move into the new world of Klingsohr's *Märchen*, "a realm of poetry, where past and future are united, where the familiar is strange and wonderful and where the sympathy between all things is apparent".[28] Be this as it may, the action of the novel as it continues after the poem is still in the real and discernible world, though a great deal seems to have happened in the interval. Heinrich appears in the guise of a pilgrim wandering in the mountains and wrestling with "deep thoughts". What has driven him into the wild terrors of the mountains? As in Part One of the novel, we again see Heinrich as exposed to "voices", only now he is hearing voices borne on the wind, voices which still strike an echo within him though he is apparently unaware of them. Do they come from the regions of his childhood? Why is he torn by such Romantic extremes of emotion extending from fear and horror to the chill of despairing indifference? Why does he now need the comfort of nature to heal the destructive forces within him? Why does his soul explode in floods of tears? All these questions are raised by the strange "madness" that has come over him, paralleling his Romantic "madness" at the beginning of the novel. Gradually it becomes clear that his life has taken a tragic plunge from the pinnacle of happiness to the depths of despair. Mathilde, his beloved, has died as foretold in his fateful dream and now in his bereaved and bemused state he mistakes a rock with a tree over it for his old friend the Court Chaplain and as he prays by the foot of it he seems to hear more voices, this time a chorus raised in song, and after the song he seems to hear Mathilde's voice and then a beam of light falls and he is vouchsafed a vision which removes all his sorrows and gives him back his peace of mind :

> The wild torments of loneliness, the bitter pain of an unspeakable loss, the dark ghastly vacuum, the mortal apathy, had all departed and the pilgrim saw himself once again in a full and meaningful universe. Voice and speech had come to life within him again, and he now had the feeling that everything was much more familiar and prophetic than before, so that death appeared to him like a higher revelation of life (320).

All this is still capable of "normal" explanation in terms of the psychological state of a deeply bereaved person; the key phrase always singled out, however, is the truly Romantic idea of "death as a higher revelation of life". What this deepened insight means for Heinrich the poet is clear, for now at last he is capable of song and in consecration of the place of his vision he sings of heaven and of gratitude to Mathilde, who, as the Virgin Mary, has interceded on his behalf, so that now the distressed man can go on his way, illuminated by an inner light. As his song finishes he becomes aware of Cyane who has come to guide him. In the cryptic conversation which he has with her it becomes apparent that now even the barriers of individuation have fallen and all the characters begin to flow together just as Heinrich and Mathilde have flown together into one in their mystic union. Cyane, who has already experienced death and rebirth, seems to be the spirit of Mathilde. Hohenzollern is both her father and Heinrich's. The old man Sylvester, whom Heinrich now meets, resembles the miner and also seems to be the antiquary who told Heinrich's father of the blue flower.

The action of the novel in the second part follows the discursive pattern already evolved in the first, for Heinrich is quickly engaged with Sylvester in discussing some of the key problems which exercized the Romantic mind : *education, nature, fate, conscience.* Education, being concerned with growth from childhood, is particularly important for the Romantic and the ideal education which Heinrich has enjoyed at his father's hands is given an extended gloss :

> There is a spirit at work here which comes fresh from the inexhaustible fountainhead, and this feeling of the superiority of the child in ultimate things, the irresistible thought of a closer guidance of this innocent being on the threshold of such a momentous career, the imprint of a wonderful world as yet not defaced by any of this earth's torrents, and finally the sympathy of the self-memory of that fabled time when the world

struck us as brighter, friendlier and stranger and the spirit of
prophecy almost visibly accompanied us (327).

Nature and childhood are closely related, for "flowers are like
children's doubles".

We can see here the full wealth of unending life, the mighty
powers of later times, the glory of the Judgment Day and the
Golden Age of all things still joined in intimate embrace, and
yet at the same time at such a tender early age. The mighty
power of love is already active, but it does not burst into flame.
It is still not a devouring flame, only a fleeting fragrance. And
however intimate the union of tender souls is, there are still no
concomitant violent emotions or devouring rage as in animals.
So childhood is closest in depth to the earth, while clouds are
perhaps the visible forms of that second, higher childhood,
paradise regained, and that is why they drop their rain on the
flowers (329).

Fate is linked with mind, moral philosophy with religion, poetry
with science, but the aim remains the same :

What previously struck our innermost nature as incomprehensible necessity, a general law without body, is now seen
to be a wonderful, homely, infinitely inexhaustible and completely satisfactory universe; it becomes an incomprehensibly
intimate community of all the blessed in the Lord, and the
perceptible, immortalizing presence of the supreme being or of
His will, His love in our deepest self (333).

At this point the novel breaks off. It would be pointless to
engage here in debates over whether Novalis, or indeed any poet,
was capable of completing the work; in particular whether Novalis,
who was such a master at revealing the inward path of the poet,
would also have been so successful in the *Faust II*-like passage of
the poet outwards into the world, to the Imperial Court, to Rome,
Greece, the Orient, etc. Some critics have seen it as a characteristic of the Romantic author that he should be incapable of
raising to further heights the mood of aspiration raised in the
first part and hence the spell of Romantic yearning is left lingering
on without any hope of the fulfilment. Other critics more favourably disposed to Novalis have claimed that he was indeed capable
of triumphantly solving the problems implicit in the continuation.
But the debate is fruitless, for the work remains a fragment. What
can be said, however, is that, as with other famous German literary
fragments (e.g. Kafka's novels), the very incompleteness of the
work, with its unresolved problems and mysterious hints, almost

adds an element of fascination to it. At the same time it can be argued that there is a sense in which the fragment is complete as it stands, since the essential message has been successfully conveyed. Certainly Novalis cannot be dismissed as an amiable enthusiast, poetic dreamer, simple-minded German mystic or crack-brained rhapsodist. Tieck likened him to Dante, while Carlyle inclined rather to call him the German Pascal:

Both are of the purest, most affectionate moral nature; both of a high, fine discursive intellect; both are mathematicians and naturalists, yet occupy themselves chiefly with Religion; nay, the best writings of both are left in the shape of "thoughts", materials of a grand scheme, which each of them, with the views peculiar to his age, had planned, we may say, for the furtherance of Religion, and which neither of them lived to execute.[29]

NOTES

1. *Monatshefte* 39 (1947), p. 523.
2. Korff, H. A., op. cit., p. 605.
3. Schlegel, F., "Athenäumsfragment 216". cf. *Kritische Friedrich-Schlegel-Ausgabe,* Vol. 2, ed. Hans Eichner (München, 1967), p. 198.
4. Rose, W., op. cit., p. 182.
5. Müller, Andreas, "Die Auseinandersetzung der Romantik mit den Ideen der Revolution", *D.V.J.*–Buchreihe, Bd. 16, p. 280.
6. Samuel, R., *Der deutsche Roman,* p. 265.
7. Ryan, L., *Periods in German Literature,* Vol. I, p. 138.
8. Lovejoy, A. O., op. cit., p. 73.
9. Samuel, R., *Der deutsche Roman,* p. 257.
10. Kahn, Robert L., op. cit., p. 49 ff.
11. Schulz, G., "Die Poetik des Romans bei Novalis", *Jahrbuch des freien deutschen Hochstifts,* 1964, p. 123.
12. Samuel, R., *Der deutsche Roman,* pp. 253–5.
13. Quoted bv G. Schulz, op. cit., p. 142, from Kluckhohn, Bd. 3., p. 298 (Hs. K., Bl. 19. Juni 1800).
14. Mähl, H. J., op. cit., p. 420.
15. Kahn, R. L., op. cit., p. 51.
16. Willson, A. L., "The Blaue Blume: A New Dimension", *Germanic Review,* XXXIV (1959), p. 51 ff. See also J. Christopher Middleton: "Two Mountain Scenes in Novalis and the Question of Symbolic Style", in *Literary Symbolism. A Symposium,* ed. and intro. H. Rehder, University of Texas (Austin & London, 1965).
17. Willson, A. L., op. cit., p. 51.
18. If the times would only stop being so mutually unfriendly
Past, present and future would be one,
Spring would unite with autumn and summer with winter,
Playful sobriety would couple youth with age;

Then, sweet spouse, all torments would expire at source
And every heart's desire be granted.

19. Ryan, L., op. cit., p. 129.
20. Salmon, P. B., *Literature in Medieval Germany* (London, 1967), pp. 244–5, for literature on *The Wartburgkrieg* and Heinrich von Ofterdingen and attempts to identify him.
21. Samuel, R., *Der deutsche Roman*, p. 276.
22. Haywood, B., op. cit., p. 107.
23. Korff, H. A., op. cit., p. 595.
24. When numbers and figures stop
    Being the key to all creatures,
    When singers and lovers
    Know more than the vastly learned
    When the world turns back to the free life
    And the free world,
    When light and shade
    Unite in true clarity
    And the world's true and ancient histories
    Are grasped in tales and poems
    Then one magic word will put
    The whole topsy-turvy state of things to flight.
25. Haywood, B., op. cit., p. 111.
26. Ritter, H., op. cit., p. 222.
27. Voerster, E., op. cit., p. 120 ff.
28. Haywood, B., op. cit., p. 137.
29. Carlyle, T., op. cit., p. 53.

BIBLIOGRAPHY

All references in the text are to Novalis, *Schriften*, Bd. 1 hrsg. Paul Kluckhohn und Richard Samuel unter Mitarbeit von Heinz Ritter und Gerhard Schulz (Stuttgart 1960).

Borcherdt, H. H., *Der Roman der Goethezeit* (Urach-Stuttgart, 1949), pp. 363–82.

Carlyle, Thomas, *Critical and Miscellaneous Essays*, Vol. II (London, 1899), pp. 1–55.

Ehrensperger, O. S., *Die epische Struktur in Novalis Heinrich von Ofterdingen* (Winterthur, 1965).

Häring, Theodor, *Novalis als Philosoph* (Stuttgart, 1954).

Haywood, Bruce, *Novalis: The Veil of Imagery* ('s-Gravenhage, 1959).

Heilborn, Ernst, *Novalis der Romantiker* (Berlin, 1901).

Hiebel, Friedrich, *Novalis. Der Dichter der blauen Blume* (Bern, 1951).

Hiebel, Friedrich, Novalis and the Problem of Romanticism, *Monatshefte* 39 (1947), pp. 515–23.

Kahn, Robert L., "Tieck's Franz Sternbalds Wanderungen and Novalis' Heinrich von Ofterdingen", *Studies in Romanticism*, VII (1967), pp. 40–64.

Korff, H. A., *Geist der Goethezeit*, Bd. 3, 2. Aufl. (Leipzig, 1949), pp. 588–627.

Lovejoy, A. O., "On the meaning of romantic in early German Romanticism", *M.L.N.*, XXXI (1916), pp. 385–96; XXXII (1917), pp. 65–77.

Mähl, H. J., *Die Idee des Goldenen Zeitalters im Werk des Novalis* (Heidelberg, 1965).

May, K., "Weltbild und innere Form der Klassik und Romantik im Wilhelm Meister und Heinrich von Ofterdingen", in: *Romantik-Forschungen, D.V.J.–Buchreihe*, Bd. 16 (Halle, 1929), pp. 185–203.

Müller, A., "Die Auseinandersetzung der Romantik mit den Ideen der Revolution", in: *Romantik-Forschungen, D.V.J.–Buchreihe*, Bd. 16 (Halle, 1929), pp. 245–333.

Nivelle, A., "Der symbolische Gehalt des Heinrich von Ofterdingen", *Tijdschrift voor de levende talen*, XVI (1950), pp. 404-27.

Ritter, Heinz. *Der unbekannte Novalis* (Göttingen, 1967).

Rose, W., *Men, Myths and Movements in German Literature* (London, 1931).

Ryan, L., "Romanticism" in: *Periods in German Literature*, Vol. 1, ed. J. M. Ritchie (London, 1966).

Samuel, Richard, *Die poetische Staats- und Geschichtsauffassung F.v. Hardenbergs* (Frankfurt/M., 1925).

Samuel, Richard, "Heinrich von Ofterdingen" in: *Der deutsche Roman* ed. Benno von Wiese (Düsseldorf, 1963) pp. 252–300.

Schulz, G., "Die Poetik des Romans bei Novalis", *Jahrbuch des Freien deutschen Hochstifts*, 1964, pp. 120–57.

Thalmann, M., *Das Märchen und die Moderne* (Stuttgart, 1961).

Tymms, R., *German Romantic Literature* (London, 1955), pp. 190–206.

Voerster, E., *Märchen und Novelle im klassisch-romantischen Roman* (Bonn, 1966).

Walzel, Oskar, "Die Formkunst von Hardenbergs Heinrich von Ofterdingen", *Germanisch-Romanische Monatsschrift*, VII, 1919, pp. 403–79.

Willson, A. L., "The 'Blaue Blume'—A New Dimension", *Germanic Review*, XXXIV (1959), pp. 50–8.

Willson, A. L., *A Mythical Image: The ideal of India in German Romanticism* (Durham, N. C., 1964).

Stifter's *Nachsommer* and Biedermeier

VII

Stifter's *Nachsommer* and Biedermeier

M. J. NORST

ADALBERT STIFTER has been called the most representative writer of the *Biedermeier* period and *Der Nachsommer,* the first of his two long novels, has been described as the most typically *Biedermeier* of his works.[1] The following discussion considers what relevance such a description has for the *Nachsommer;* what contribution it can make to our better understanding of this work in the full knowledge that discussing a work as representative of a particular period or movement is an undertaking fraught with difficulties. In what sense does any writer represent a period? What is involved in saying that he does so? Do we demand from him a picture of the time? Do we expect to find in his writings the essence of commonly-held attitudes of the time; or some typical literary rejection of these? Do we look to him to illustrate the accepted literary style of the period or the acceptable stylistic innovation? A literary work is not as a rule a literary manifesto, and if the writer himself does not lay claim to representing a particular literary movement, by what criteria is the critic to confirm him in this office? Stifter himself made only the most general statements about his literary affiliations.[2] The situation is further complicated if, as in the case of *Biedermeier,* the use of the term itself is problematic.[3] For some literary historians it defines a socio-political unit extending from about 1815 to 1848 and including everything written in this *Biedermeierzeit;* others use the term *biedermeierlich* to label certain attitudes to life held by some individuals in all periods (perhaps by most at given moments in their lives) but felt to be particularly pronounced in this period; still another group applies it to a particularly *Biedermeier* literary style which it considers to predominate at that time. Viewing Stifter's *Nachsommer* as a *Biedermeier* work seems thus to be a matter of defining the unknown in terms of the unknown. It would of course be simplest to restrict oneself to *Biedermeier* as the label of a purely literary category, were it not that the history of the term *Biedermeier,* as applied to literature, clearly shows that the stylistic features said to characterize it, have been derived from four or five important writers and a very limited number of works, one of them certainly Stifter's *Nachsommer.* If a label is specifically devised to fit a

147

book, it would necessarily be a rather unrewarding exercise to reveal that the book fits the label.

Yet it is difficult to quarrel with literary taxonomy as such, since there is an obvious need to associate single items meaningfully with each other, to establish connections, reveal differences, evaluate within a context. Categorization can be demonstrated to be successful if it leads to more adequate interpretation of the whole (i.e. the period or movement), the parts (i.e. the individual works) and their interrelation. And categorization demands labels to provide a short-hand method of recognition.

It may be best to begin with a consideration of the term *Biedermeier* in its application to the *Nachsommer* by summarizing those aspects of the period about which there is general agreement. Socio-politically, it coincides with the *Restaurationszeit,* that is, its beginning can be traced to 1815 and the Congress of Vienna. It is the literary period which follows on Romanticism showing a clear reaction to many of its ideals while never rejecting it violently as, for instance, Storm and Stress writers rejected the Enlightenment. No longer is the hero asocial, the passionate, self-conscious creative individual, who glories in his subjectivity and yet yearns to lose himself in the cosmos. He is now the harmonious, rational, well-adjusted *Bürger,* mistrustful of the irrational, striving to achieve limited, realizable goals and very conscious of and concerned about his place in the community. There is no yearning for the infinite but a correspondingly greater concentration on the finite for its own sake. Seen from the point of view of the Romantics, a book like Stifter's *Nachsommer* is strangely sober and lacking in emotional impact, concerned not with conjuring up irrational forces and illustrating their potent intervention through chance happenings, inexplicable occurrences, but bent on explaining away the mysterious by revealing causal connections. For the Romantics it is a novel abounding in detailed factual descriptions of the object world and its management by man. Stifter was very strongly influenced by the Romantics, particularly Jean Paul, in the days of his literary apprenticeship, and he took this new line very consciously and deliberately though never aggressively as the Young Germans did. A comparison of the early and later versions of many of his stories shows a careful excision of colourful emotive adjectives; the pruning of expected Romantic literary effects. The *Nachsommer* makes a conscious literary device of causal connections. Frequently the reader is presented first with the effect and then in subsequent pages made to trace the path to the cause. This process, the consequent recognition of such a connection by the reader (with the attendant satisfaction), is designed, consciously or unconsciously, to demonstrate a rational world order. Only once does Stifter in the *Nachsommer* seem to make some reference to a conscious rejection of the Romantic approach, and to suggest that this involves not merely gain but also loss. It is in a small scene at the beginning of the *Nachsommer* where Heinrich has been sitting alone in his room in the Rose House on the occasion of his first visit. He has a strange, inexplicable sensation (seltsame Empfindung) : "I felt as though I were sitting not in a room but in the open air, indeed in a silent forest". This feeling one might find described in any Romantic work, but instead of indulging the feeling as the Romantic hero would, Heinrich immediately seeks an explanation—and finds it. The sensation is due to the open windows and the sound of birds normally found only in the forest. The discovery does not fill him with the usual satisfaction, however, and he goes on to remark : "But now that I had discovered the reason for my sensation or thought I had discovered it, a great deal of its mystery and therefore of its agreeableness had disappeared".[4] This comment is unique within the context of the book and seems to make sense only in terms of Stifter's still ambivalent attitude to the Romantics.

How long *Biedermeier* can be said to continue is a matter of dispute. It would seem to be most useful to see it as a part of the German form of Realism, lasting until the 1870s and the unification of Germany after the Franco-Prussian War. Perhaps one should call the whole of German Realism *Biedermeier,* if only to stop once and for all the invidious comparisons with Realism as the rest of Europe understood and practised it. During this time, there were writers who might have led a literary revolution, but they died early, like Büchner, became exiles, like Heine, or, like the group termed the Young Germans, made a considerable impact on the political situation but were not strong enough as artists to effect a real change in literary fashion.

The significant reaction to German Realism (of which *Biedermeier* is then seen as the beginning) did not come until the 1880s and Naturalism. Only then is there a will to change the direction forcibly, to produce something violently different, called "modern" with "faithful presentation of life to the strict exclusion of the romantic element";[5] only then is there a strong new line which challenges and provokes vigorous opposition. Naturalism, unlike German Realism, is European rather than provincial, indeed it is in these years that German writing re-enters the mainstream of European literature. It is not merely rationally orientated like Biedermeier-Realism, but often fiercely anti-metaphysical. For this generation moreover, as for earlier ones in England and France, industrialization is a fact of life, not a monster against which farm gates can still be locked. Immediate social problems predominate, the favoured genre is the social drama, and the writer sees himself as Fighter rather than as Philosopher-Teacher or aesthetic High Priest. Stifter's realism, recognizable as such to the Romantics, would not have been realism as the Naturalists understood it. For them the idyllicism of a Stifter is false and dangerous, preventing an honest assessment of society and fostering those social ills which they felt called upon to expose. As the critic Lunding remarks :

> How little Stifter, despite all his realism depicts the reality of life as lived, emerges from the reception by and the reaction of this materialistic and realistically inclined epoch.[6]

If, then, one wants to consider Stifter's *Nachsommer* within a literary historical context, one can establish that context as lying between a recognizable Romanticism and Naturalism, differing from both in ideas, style and of course the socio-political situation.

In what sense can Stifter's *Nachsommer* be said to represent German literature between 1815 and 1880? The novel, in three volumes, appeared on 12 September 1857, and was not well received. Stifter's reputation had been made on his *Novellen,* the genre then favoured as Feuchtersleben has testified : "Novellen, nothing but Novellen! That is the 'bread and circuses' of the modern public".[7] Weigel quotes a contemporary critic as saying : "Adalbert Stifter had the great good fortune to be promoted by the correspondent of a widely read periodical. The result? Stifter's *Novellen* have become high fashion and a source of envy among rival publishers".[8] Blackall confirms this : "By 1848 his reputation as a writer was firmly established, each new story was read by a wide public with eager interest".[9] But the *Nachsommer* found no such acclaim and Blackall comments : "I have not been able to trace any contemporary notice which could be called favourable".[10] This was due partly, no doubt, to the length—with shorter genres in favour, the thousand-page novel would have strained the loyalty of the most faithful readers of Stifter's popular *Novellen.* Stifter himself, realizing that in some significant way he was not in tune with the time, offers stylistic reasons for the alienation of his public :

> And the form of the book, tracing as it does the inner develop- ment of a character, is contrary to the fashion of today's books, thus those who are caught up in the fashion will be bewildered by the book.[11]

The term "irre werden", which Stifter uses, is interesting because the readers were in fact not antagonized but confused by the novel.

If plot is "what happens" then in nineteenth-century terms the *Nachsommer* appeared to have no plot. A young man, Heinrich, tells his own story. He grows up as the only son in a well-to-do middle-class family where he is given freedom to develop by wise and watchful parents. One day on a tour through the mountains, he meets Risach, a retired gentleman who owns a property. They argue about the likelihood of rain and Heinrich is invited in to await the outcome; there are more visits and Heinrich meets Risach's foster-daughter, Natalie, and eventually marries her. If this outline suggests a plot, it falsifies the impression Stifter creates. For in the thousand pages the "happening" is consistently avoided. It is difficult to isolate incidents in the story because it is not built up on incidents. No tensions develop, no conflicts arise. Within the novel there is only one segment which is more traditional. This is the chapter *Der Rückblick* (Reminiscence), which is like a *Novelle*. Here Risach tells the story of his life. As a young man he was tutor in a family with a son and daughter. He falls in love with the daughter, Mathilde (later Natalie's mother), and they decide to marry. Her parents, when they learn of this for the first time, ask them to wait. Risach agrees with them, and Mathilde is so angry and humiliated at his acquiescence that she breaks off the relationship altogether. Each of them marries, and in both cases the marriage partner dies. Eventually they meet again, there is a reconciliation and they establish a harmonious, platonic friendship, mutually caring for Mathilde's children, Natalie and Gustav. The function of this section within the whole is as an "abschreckendes Beispiel", as an awful warning of the consequences of sudden passion, of ill-considered, hasty action.

If in some ways then, the *Nachsommer* did not meet the expectations of his public, in others, of course, it did. The values which Stifter espouses here are precisely those which had made his *Novellen* so acceptable to the contemporary public; his ideals are without exception "gut biedermeierlich", generally speaking eminently Victorian. Staiger refers to the *Nachsommer* as "rules for the beautiful life",[12] and while one may well quarrel with the absolute flavour of the description, in a relative sense it is certainly true that the novel codifies the values of its own generation, presenting them in the guise of fiction.

A synopsis of these ideas is contained in the preface to the collection of stories entitled *Bunte Steine* which appeared in 1853. This, as Thurnher has pointed out, is in a very real sense the preface to the *Nachsommer*, the fable of which was begun in 1847 and called first *Der alte Hofmeister*, later *Der alte Vogelfreund*. Stifter extracted it from the collection for which it had

originally been intended in order to develop it into a novel.[13] He
refers to this obliquely in the preface itself :

> I have selected a number of these experiences and attempted to
> give them poetic form, but the views which I have here
> developed, and the experience of recent years, have taught me
> to doubt my power; let these attempts, therefore, be laid aside
> until they have been worked out more thoroughly, or being of
> no importance have been destroyed.[14]

According to this preface and the novel, Stifter sees art as the
handmaiden of religion; literature as the noblest of the arts, and
the writer as the High Priest of Beauty, and Benefactor of Mankind.[15] As such the writer has, according to Stifter, one clear
obligation : to enunciate clearly and promote enthusiastically that
law which he deems to be the fundamental moral law governing
earthly existence—the gentle law (das sanfte Gesetz) :

> Let us strive to recognize the gentle law, which guides the
> human race. There are forces . . . which work for the continued
> existence of all mankind, which may not be limited by individual
> forces, but on the contrary must act as a restraint on them . . .
> It is the law of these forces.[16]

Stifter, strongly influenced by Wolff's version of Leibnitz,[17]
assumes a pre-established harmony, not one established after
painful struggle with forces held in precarious balance. This
guarantees that the individual's interests and the community's
interests will always be identical.[18] This Christian-rational view
is fairly typical of conservative attitudes in the first half of the
nineteenth century.

Typical also is Stifter's faith in and fervent espousal of the
natural sciences as the hope of mankind. Like Goethe, he rejects
speculative philosophy in favour of scientific observation. The
study of natural phenomena is for Stifter the best way in which
man can use his reason to discover the rationality of the world
order, and thus provide himself with the key to reasonable human
existence. The natural scientist, according to Stifter, while he is
concerned with minute observations, with the conscientious collection of data, directs all his activity to establishing the meaningful
pattern of the whole; there is a tacit understanding that the
individual pieces derive their significance from their place in it.

The natural sciences, while pursued for their own sake, thus
have always a religious function providing guidelines for human
behaviour.

In the *Nachsommer,* as well as in the educational programmes
which he introduced as Inspector of Schools in Upper Austria,

the natural sciences are the fundamental study upon which all others rest. In the novel, this is shown in the education of Heinrich, who sets out to be a scientist "in general", and of Gustav, Natalie, Klothilde, Mathilde and her brother Alfred. The highly significant first meeting between Heinrich and Risach is occasioned by a problem in the field of natural science. Will it or will it not rain? Heinrich, not very experienced, draws his conclusions from a limited field of observation and on the basis of these maintains doggedly that it will; Risach, with greater experience, knows which observations are likely to yield more significant results. He does not restrict himself to the cloud-formation and the degree of electricity in the air, but notes the reaction of animals and insects, and deduces from these observations that it will not rain. And the events prove him right.

For Stifter, as for the nineteenth century in general, there is no essential difference between natural laws and those governing human behaviour. He coins the word *Menschenforscher* (behavioural scientist?)[19] by analogy with *Naturforscher* (natural scientist), and Risach says in the *Nachsommer*: "I have often thought that research concerned with human beings and their activities, yes, even their history is only another branch of the natural sciences".[20] The natural scientist has to proclaim the fundamental gentle law as "welterhaltend" (world preserving); the writer, as behavioural scientist, has to proclaim the same law, under the aspect of moral law, as that law which preserves mankind "menschenerhaltend". Both have a duty to stress the glory of slow, organic growth, the eternal cycle, the whole; both must avoid creating the impression that the singular, spectacular event, particularly if it is destructive, is more interesting or worthy of particular attention.[21]

The assumption that the fundamental Law is gentle, rational, together with the implication that it demands individual integration in a very fixed hierarchial order, are ideas Stifter absorbed while at the Monastery of Kremsmünster. They were fostered by his natural conservatism and confirmed by the turmoil of the 1848 Revolution. Coupled with a quasi-philosophical interest in the natural sciences and marked educational optimism, these ideas provide us with a reasonably firm time signature for the mid-century. The attitudes developed in the novel confirm this. The inviolable basic unit of the social structure is the family. "My son", says Risach to Heinrich "your first duty is to establish family life which is noble, pure and well-ordered . . . It is the family that our age needs . . . On the family rests art, science, human progress, the state".[22] The family unit—father, mother, and two children—pictured in their "Häuslichkeit"—opens the novel; the larger family unit, formed when the two families merge and a third emerges, is the final picture :

Thereupon my friend took my mother's arm, my father took Mathilde's, I took Natalie's, Gustav Klothilde's, and thus we went through the wrought iron gate into the garden and into the house.[23]

In a very real sense, the whole novel has shown the development from one pattern to the other. This final image of family relationships (Stifter's term is "Familienzusammengehörigkeit"), so reminiscent of the final scene in Lessing's *Nathan der Weise,* where everyone is so related that they *cannot* marry, is very instructive in its difference. For the eighteenth century writer, the family relationships are a symbol of human brotherhood, extending beyond any family group, triumphant in the face of religious intolerance; for Stifter, in the nineteenth century, the emphasis is on the family group itself as an organism, and the image necessarily includes the marriage of Natalie and Heinrich to indicate its growth and development. Within the family, the values which the *Nachsommer* stresses are domestic tranquillity, safety, the love of simplicity and moderation, the sense of tradition and conversattion, the reverent maintaining of social customs. These values are in every way representative of the period between Romanticism and Naturalism, and as clearly illustrated in a work like Ludwig's *Zwischen Himmel und Erde;* the effect is different in the *Nachsommer* because we are shown only the positive, never the negative. Characteristic also is the fact that the resignation which results from the withdrawal from passion, violence and all disruptive forces, is presented not as a compromise but as a positive value.

The values enunciated in the preface and demonstrated in the *Nachsommer* are unequivocally *biedermeierlich,* and critics have tended to accept or reject Stifter entirely on the basis of these views.[24] Patterns of thought rather than patterns of expression have provided most of the material of Stifter criticism. He is extolled, especially in immediate post-war periods, because he preaches non-violence, order, love of nature, harmonious family life. Some, while praising his idyllic *Nachsommer* world, also tacitly assume that it is a realistic picture of the world of the 1830s before railways. These are the critics whom Lunding has called the Apollonian School, who praise Stifter for the values he upholds. There is another school which projects the demonic Stifter image. These, realizing the unacceptability of many of Stifter's ideas in the twentieth century, but responding to some quality in his writing, value Stifter for the ideas which he in fact suppresses and thus expresses only indirectly through the resulting tension. Certainly one can agree with Pascal about "that gnawing uncertainty which always lowers on the horizon of this apparently soothing book",[25] but the real issue is whether the true value of the *Nachsommer* lies in its ideas, whether the best approach to this work is from a consideration of patterns of thought.

Those who, like Arno Schmidt, demand from an author "a picture of the times",[26] castigate Stifter for writing idylls in a revolutionary period. He is accused of a lack of awareness or of callous indifference, and the argument again is based entirely on a consideration of the issues which Stifter did not raise in the *Nachsommer* though they were demonstrably vital ones at the time. These critics are supported by that fierce army of biographers who devote their lives to discovering discrepancies between biographical fact and literary utterance. This kind of evidence, introduced as a corrective to Stifter's moral views as enunciated by a Risach or Heinrich or Mathilde, cannot be trusted. It may be poignant and revealing for biographer and reader to know that Stifter's literary world is very different from his actual one, but to use this discrepancy as a measure of his inadequacy or insincerity as a writer is the most basic confusion of life and art. The attack of those who, like Arno Schmidt, declare it to be an author's duty to reflect the socio-political situation of his time, does, however, raise the question of Stifter's representativeness as a *Biedermeierzeit* writer. Schmidt and others demand not only that issues of the day be brought up but also that a particular stand should be assumed. Were writers really to conform in this way, one would in fact know less about the times—not more; fortunately, they do not. Even when a writer makes no overt reference to the political events or the social climate of his time, the tension between literary reality and literal (socio-political) reality is of course present. If one understands the relationship between the writer and his society as a compulsive dialogue, then the evasions are as significant as the clear thrust and riposte. It is significant that Stifter writing during the time of social and political upheaval during and after 1848, reacts to this situation by pointedly ignoring it in his works. The revolution of 1848, the war of 1859 and the battles of 1866 find no direct mention in his work. Nor do the problems attendant on industrialization, the rise of nationalism, the class and religious conflicts of the day. Stifter's attitude to the use of contemporary material in literature is unequivocal and is justified by him on literary grounds. In a letter to Heckenast in 1845, he writes :

Most of all I feared the Young Germans, since I do not at all approve of one aspect of the movement, namely the introduction of contemporary problems and contemporary feelings into literature, but quite on the contrary maintain that the beautiful has no other purpose but to be beautiful and that political policies are not implemented in verses and declamations but by first acquiring training in the political sciences and following this up by appropriate action whether in writing, word or deed. I have interested myself in political science for many years, am for ever reading political journals, and it would indeed be strange if a man of feeling (which I would claim to be) could then avoid taking sides. One is strong enough, however, to refrain from introducing one's views on the Custom's Union where one is intent on depicting the beauties of God and the world.[27]

Five years later when defending his *Studien*, he writes again on this subject to Heckenast :

These (the *Studien*) will continue to exist in all their simplicity and naturalness when all the revolutionary poetry, tendentious novels, political party writing, clique views, etc. have disappeared or at best are regarded as items of curiosity by a succeeding generation, which cannot comprehend the feelings of former times; for there is no poetry in these things, while in the *Studien* there are . . . warm feelings, morality, enduring human behaviour, which ensure that the reader will return to the books.[28]

Stifter here reveals very clearly his attitude to literature—one very typical of nineteenth-century Germany and Austria (an attitude persisting among many readers, if a lesser number of writers, to the present day) in marked contrast to the rest of Europe. "Schöne Literatur" has to be "schön" (beautiful and elevating); the everyday world is not, therefore it must be banished from its pages. Confronted by the beginnings of professional journalism in Germany, promoted by writers like Heine, Stifter saw a threat to literature as he understood it. He therefore felt called upon to defend the art which he saw as something apart from and superior to the work-a-day world, by demarcating it very clearly from journalism. In this attitude to literature as well as in his political views, Stifter demonstrates a consistent conservatism. In this he voices the opinion of the majority, particularly after 1848, when the realities of revolution, the fear of disorder, drove many to extreme conservatism.[29]

The existence of these attitudes can be traced through biographical data or alternatively established by reading the *Nachsommer*, which, as Stifter explained, was consciously conceived as a model :

I wanted to set up a great, simple moral force in opposition to this wretched depravity . . . I wanted to depict a deeper, richer life in this work than that which normally occurs . . . The whole situation as well as the characters of the people, should be, as I see it, more elevated, lift the reader above his ordinary life and set an atmosphere for him in which he can, as a human being, come to a purer and greater self-realization.[30]

Stifter avoids the issues of the day in the *Nachsommer* because he believes that it is possible for literature to exist outside time, and because he feels that it ought to concern itself with absolutes. The view is summed up in the praise accorded a minor character in the *Nachsommer* : "He does not pay homage to the taste of the time but only to the essential nature of things".[31] Writing in a revolutionary period he sees it as his duty as a writer and *Menschenforscher* not to reflect the turmoil of the day and so give it emphasis, but to create a climate so inimical to disorder of any kind as to make wars and revolutions seem inconceivable. Stifter's attitudes to contemporary life are not in any way remarkable for the time, and represent a strong trend which marked the Restoration era, the *Biedermeierzeit*. Seen from the literary sociologist's point of view, this represents a significant response to a social situation which when it has been interpreted, can be used together with the interpreted responses of writers like Gutzkow, Keller, Spielhagen, Heine, Freiligrath, von Fallersleben, Büchner, Grillparzer, etc. and a series of minor writers to reconstruct the period.

We have seen that the *Nachsommer* is *biedermeierlich* in its values and in the attitudes it assumes towards its own *Biedermeierzeit*. What, then, is paradoxical is the fact that a work which embodied all the most acceptable ideas of an established author should have been unpopular in its own day and yet survive in an age when the ideas are largely unacceptable, the attitudes irrelevant. Clearly, what makes the *Nachsommer* interesting is precisely what made it atypical and not acceptable to the reader of 1857—not its ideas, but the literary presentation of them. If the *Nachsommer* still has interest as a literary work and not merely as an historical document or philosophical compendium, then this is due to Stifter's experimentation with expression which extended the possibilities of the medium. This is the context in which it is best judged, the one most relevant to it, the one which it has helped to fashion. What is typically *Biedermeier* about the *Nachsommer* is least interesting, what is most interesting has not been adequately categorized and is not covered by the term. Stifter has always been a writer's writer and his literary advocates—such

as Nietzsche, Thomas Mann and Hofmannsthal—did not feel drawn
to him because of his moral attitudes or social commitment; they
responded to him as an experimental artist.

It is possible to gain some insight into the essential quality
of the *Nachsommer,* if one considers the peculiar literary problem
with which Stifter wrestled. He took *Biedermeier* thinking to its
logical conclusion and wrote a plotless, conflictless novel in which
the theme of organic growth was presented not polyphonically,
with counter-melodies providing arresting dissonances, but as a
single melody line with every literary device from story, motif,
image to the word itself, contributing to the density of the pattern.
The *Nachsommer* is a highly structured work in which theme and
form are indissoluble, the form being in a very real sense the subject
matter of the book. The problem for Stifter is how to represent
organic growth entirely positively and, as such, persuasively. How
to depict only the easy steady flow of the stream in its inconspicuous
and constant movement, not the sudden violent collision which
forces change. It was on this literary issue that he was so
diametrically opposed to Hebbel. And Stifter has achieved what
he set out to do. Those who attack the *Nachsommer* today because
they are sceptical of the virtues of Brave New World conditions
in which storms do not occur, and doubt the possibility of growth
which is free of conflict and pain, do not deny, though they do
not discuss it, that as a writer Stifter has succeeded in creating
such a world. How Stifter achieved this, technically, is very
interesting and far in advance of his own time. In the *Nachsommer,*
we find the development towards a style which is essentially
abstract, using the term in the sense in which it has been applied
to art. It demands from the reader an emotional reaction to formal
elements; to dynamic relationships of words emptied of association, to patterns of repetition. Blackall comments on this,
though he does not stress how far Stifter has gone in this direction :

> Stifter in this novel (i.e. the *Nachsommer*) penetrates to the heart
> of experience and presents it as a series of shapes and patterns,
> which recur in the separate happenings and feelings of individual
> lives. He presents the permanent content of experience made
> transient in our lives by the incidentals of time and space, and
> hence his presentation is devoid of these incidentals—but not of
> reality. Indeed it has a deeper reality. This applies to everything
> in the book—the characters, the setting, the situations and the
> conversations. We must beware of mistaking extreme love of
> pattern for artificiality and unreality.[32]

The effect on character portrayal has also been noted by
Blackall. Stifter makes no attempt to write a psychological novel;

in the *Nachsommer* we do not find the workings of the individual mind exposed and explained. As in the old epics "the characters appear only through the medium of their appearance, their observations on matters of common interest, their behaviour".[33]

All the characters are in a sense *one* character illustrating growth. Each character is shown in movement, but viewed in relation to the others, each also illustrates a fixed stage, a constant interval in the line of development as a whole. Thus Heinrich's own growth is traced minutely, but at the same time earlier and later stages of his development are represented by Gustav and Alfred, by Risach and his father. Similarly, Natalie's development is shown dynamically, but if one views the line of development, she represents one stage, while Klothilde, Mathilde and Heinrich's mother represent others.[34]

Essentially, Stifter's problem is how to create the awareness of time passing slowly; he departs from the usual method of marking a time scale by dispensing with vivid incidents. Superficially, the normal narrative technique seems to have been inverted. The apparently trivial is related with a wealth of circumstantial detail; the apparently significant fact is often slipped into a subordinate clause. But the incidents do not function directly as time markers at all. The novel is structured by Heinrich's round of visits : home, the mountains, the Asperhof and Sternenhof, home. These follow the seasons and we sense the significance when there is the slightest break in the sequence—when Heinrich climbs the mountain in winter, when he visits his friends twice in one autumn. These regular visits are the most natural vehicle to reveal and effect steady change, since absence heightens awareness of change and promotes a mutual exchange on the subject. Everything is shown as part of a process. Getting into the Rose House which presents a great problem for Heinrich at first, gradually becomes easier, and eventually is automatic; Risach shows him the house in very slow stages, needing to be prompted before showing yet another room; names of characters are revealed so gradually that Heinrich is sure of his bride's surname only on the day he marries her. Clothes and customs which seem strange gradually become familiar and eventually are adopted. Retardation is not *one* element but *the* element in the novel. Early in the story (p. 141) a rare cactus—cereus peruvianus—is mentioned as belonging to the Inghof. It is a plant whose potential beauty will not be realized unless it is carefully nurtured in the right atmosphere. It is taken to Risach's Asperhof, seen in various stages (pp. 313, 348, 664), until it finally blooms gloriously on Heinrich and Natalie's wedding day (p. 966). This in itself would not be a very remarkable use of a flower symbol, but one becomes aware that *every* image used is, in fact, part of a developmental pattern. Seen in this light, the irrelevancies of which Stifter is so often accused, assume total relevance.

The *Nachsommer* has been called a *Bildungsroman*, and frequently compared with *Wilhelm Meister, Der grüne Heinrich,* and *Heinrich von Ofterdingen,* and in some sense it is of course just that, but it is a *Bildungsroman* with a difference. The traditional form is that in which the hero is acted upon by the environment. In being forced to adapt in order to cope with its demands in a series of instances, he is brought to self-realization and maturity. In the *Nachsommer,* the development consists in a gradual process, no abrupt changes of direction take place, expectations are realized in the fulness of time. The emphasis is not on the collision of individual and environment which produces change, which can be termed growth; but on the growth itself which takes place almost imperceptibly given favourable conditions. A process in which every stage is essential, a prerequisite for the next, leading eventually to the activating of all potential in the human being. The educational process is shown as resulting from the fusion of external preparation and internal maturation. Since for some stages a variety of interacting preparatory ones must have taken place, the pattern is revealed as being very complex. Heinrich's educational development, which leads him from nature to human nature and art, is shown in associative patterns. Heinrich involved in nature study sees a dead stag and thinks of beauty and human tragedy; he sees a play and thinks of human tragedy; he sees a girl and is reminded of Greek art, he loves the girl and is aware of the beauty of Greek art. All of this is shown without commentary. The gradual development of consciousness, the progress from unconscious to conscious feeling and full awareness, is conveyed with consummate skill, best of all perhaps in Heinrich's relationship with Natalie. He goes to a performance of *King Lear* at the moment when he is emotionally ready to appreciate human feelings; though his response to the play as a play is as yet very naïve and but a stage removed from his earlier definition of plays as lies ("erlogene Geschichten"), he is deeply moved. He sees Natalie for the first time at the play but is not truly conscious of her as a person and has later to be reminded that it was she. He then sees her on innumerable occasions, but usually they do not speak. He is conscious of her as he is conscious of the marble statue of the muse without being fully aware. When he eventually becomes aware of Natalie, his inner eye is ready to perceive the beauties of the statue, too. "Now, indeed, that has been fulfilled which was prepared".[35]

Repetition, sometimes with minute variations in word or phrase, is part of Stifter's technique. Repetition of images, of syntactical structures, of words.[36] The favourite syntactical pattern is the logical series (if, if, if . . . then) which creates the impression of a closed world order, an unbroken causality which excludes the possibility of chance happening.

The web of repeated words, the meshing of developmental images produces so tightly woven a fabric that to isolate one strand is to unravel the whole pattern.

Stifter produces a strange, windless world of uncanny silences and subtle movement, which carries its own conviction provided the reader, as Vanesa suggests, learns to read again,[37] for nothing in the nineteenth century, not even the late Goethe, as is often suggested, prepares one adequately for this novel.

Is Stifter's *Nachsommer* a *Biedermeier* novel? It mirrors faithfully many of the beliefs and values of the time even in its refusal to deal with contemporary problems. As a literary work however, it is not representative, because stylistically Stifter attempted something for which his own age had no understanding. Stifter himself seemed to be aware of the pitfalls of classification. In the *Nachsommer* he has Heinrich say: "experience showed me that according to my description the plants which belonged in a group were different from those which the experts recorded as belonging together". The experts classified them according to one or several characteristics which they shared, but this often meant that very different plants were grouped together. Heinrich continues: "I retained the usual classification but added my descriptions. In these descriptions the plans were grouped according to characteristic lines and, if I may express it in this way, according to their structure".[38] This problem and its solution seem very relevant to the *Nachsommer*.

NOTES

References are to the following editions:

Nachsommer: *ed.* Hümmler (Düsseldorf, 1953). 3. Aufl.
Vorrede: *ed.* Stefl (Leipzig, 1942).
Briefe: *ed.* Schumacher (Zürich, 1947).

1. cf. Bollnow, O., "Der Nachsommer und der Bildungsgedanke des Biedermeier" in: *Beiträge zur Einheit von Bildung und Sprache im geistigen Sein* (Berlin, 1957): p. 15, "Biedermeier has found its purest expression in Adalbert Stifter . . . Hence this work (*Nachsommer*) is, as it were, Biedermeier showing its own ideal of 'Bildung' . . ."; p. 30, "Only when the two works *Wilhelm Meister* and *Nachsommer* are contrasted is Stifter's true quality revealed and then Stifter can be taken as standing for Biedermeier as a whole".
Bietak, W., "Probleme der Biedermeierdichtung" in: *Neue Beiträge*

zum Grillparzer- und Stifter-Bild (Graz, 1965): p. 15, "Stifters *Nachsommer* can be taken as the ultimate development of Biedermeier, despite its lonely eminence".

2. e.g. "While I am admittedly no Goethe, I am one of his family and the seeds of all that is pure, high-minded and natural reach the heart of the readers of all my writings" (letter to Heckenast 13 September 1854, p. 207), and about the *Nachsommer*: "It is written with all Goethe's love of art" (letter to Heckenast, 11 February 1858, p. 281).

3. cf. Norst, M., "Biedermeier" in: *Periods in German Literature* (Lond., Wolff, 1966) for an account of the problem. For the sake of clarity, the terms *biedermeierlich* (attitudes, values); *Biedermeier* (literary style); *Biedermeierzeit* (political period suggested there, will also be used in the following discussion).

4. *Nachsommer*, p. 56–7.

5. Ruprecht, E.: *Literarische Manifeste des Naturalismus 1880–92* (Stuttgart, 1962), p. 59 quoted by Schulz, G.: *Periods in German Literature* (Naturalism), ibid., p. 205.

6. Lunding, E.: "Probleme und Ergebnisse der Stifterforschung 1945–54", *Euphorion,* Bd. 49, Heft 2, Heidelberg, Winter 1955, p. 206.

7. Feuchtersleben, quoted Kluckhohn, P., "Biedermeier als literarische Epochenbezeichnung", *DVjs.*, Vol. 13, 1935, p. 28.

8. Weigel, H., *Flucht vor der Große* (Wien, 1960), p. 157.

9. Blackall, E., *Adalbert Stifter* (C.U.P., 1948), p. 226.

10. Ibid., p. 33, footnote.

11. Stifter in a letter to Heckenast, 11 February 1858 (*Briefe,* Manesse, p. 282) Cf. also 22 March 1857, p. 264.

12. Staiger, E., *Meisterwerke deutscher Sprache* (Zürich, Atlantis, 1961), p. 188.

13. Thurnher, E., p. 396. Also letter to Heckenast, 3 February 1852, p. 170.

14. *Vorrede* to Bunte Steine, p. 10.

15. *Vorrede* to Bunte Steine, p. 3: cf. *Nachsommer*, p. 370 and p. 484. Cf. also letter to Louise von Eichendorff, 23 March 1852, p. 171.

16. *Vorrede*, p. 6.

17. See Enzinger, M., *Adalbert Stifters Studienjahre* (Augsburg, Kraft, 1950).

18. *Nachsommer*, p. 15: "Man is not primarily there for the sake of human society but for his own sake. And if every man were to follow this precept in the best way possible, then this would also be for the best as far as society is concerned"; p. 772: "man ought to chose that life's path which is the best for the complete realization of all his potential. This is the best way he can serve the whole."

19. *Vorrede*, p. 7; *Nachsommer*, p. 771.

20. *Nachsommer*, p. 131: "We find the natural sciences much more comprehensible than the behavioural sciences . . . because we can stand back from natural objects and observe them, while human objects of study are obscured by our own values."

21. *Vorrede*, p. 9.

22. *Nachsommer*, p. 897.
23. *Nachsommer*, p. 873.
24. The details are, of course, often *biedermeierlich*, too. Absolute obedience is expected of children (e.g. p. 16, p. 829, p. 835); physical exertion is bad for girls (p. 807); a woman's place is in the home (p. 386); great respect is accorded to displays of excessive modesty in both men and women (p. 205); and a scene such as that where the family is shown painting, reading, making music (p. 812) could have been painted by Ludwig Richter.
25. Pascal, R., *The German Novel* (Manchester, *M.U.P.* 1956), p. 70.
26. Schmidt, A., "Der sanfte Unmensch, Einhundert Jahre Nachsommer", in: *Dya Na Sore*, Ullstein, p. 75: "Every writer should be obliged to do one thing sometime: to leave behind a picture of the times in which he lived!"
27. Letter to Heckenast, 9 January 1845, pp. 94–5.
28. Letter to Heckenast, 22 April 1850, p. 159.
29. Amongst the writers Grillparzer, whom Stifter much admired, and Hebbel, to whom he was bitterly opposed, showed the same development.
30. Letter to Heckenast, 11 February 1858, p. 281. Cf. letter to Hoefer, 15 October 1861, p. 348.
31. *Nachsommer*, p. 903
32. Blackall, E., *Adalbert Stifter* (C.U.P., 1948), pp. 326–8.
33. Pascal, R., *The German Novel* (M.U.P., 1956), p. 68.
34. Cf. Stifter's letter to Heckenast, 11 February 1858, p. 281 ff.
35. *Nachsommer*, p. 614. Cf. also letter to Heckenast, 29 February 1856, p. 246.
36. Typical for Stifter is repetition of a word or movement to convey movement; e.g. *Nachsommer*, p. 546 (cf. also p. 538 and 544): "Ich weiß nicht, wie lange ich *gegangen bin*", antwortete sie, "ich *ging* zwischen den Feldern hin, auf denen die ungeheure Menge des Getreides steht, ich *ging* an manchem Strauche hin, den der Rain enthält, ich *ging* an manchem Baume vorbei, der in dem Getreide steht, und kam zu dem roten Kreuze, das aus den Saaten empor ragt".
37. Vancsa, K., "Ist Stifters dichterische Welt eine Utopie?", *A–S–I–* Jhrg., 5, H.4, 1956, p. 162.
38. *Nachsommer*, p. 31 ff.

BIBLIOGRAPHY

Blackall, E., *Adalbert Stifter*, A critical Study (C.U.P., 1948).
David, C., *Zwischen Romantik und Symbolismus 1820–85* (Gütersloh, 1966).
Hallmore, G. J., "The Symbolism of the Marble Muse in Stifter's Nachsommer", *P.M.L.A.*, Vol. LXXIV, No. 4, 1959.
Hohoff, C., *Adalbert Stifter, seine dichterischen Mittel und die Prosa des 19. Jahrhunderts* (Düsseldorf, 1949).
Lunding, E., "Probleme und Ergebnisse der Stifterforschung, 1945–54", *Euphorion* 49, Heft 2, 1955.

Pascal, R., *The German Novel*: Studies (M.U.P., 1956).

Paulsen, W., "Adalbert Stifter und der Nachsommer", in: *Corona Studies in celebration of the 80th birthday of Samuel Singer* (Duke University Press, 1941).

Rehm, W., *Nachsommer. Zur Deutung von Stifters Dichtung* (München, 1951).

For full bibliographical information on Stifter see: Eisenmeier, E.: *Adalbert Stifter Bibliographie* (Linz, Oberösterreichische Landesverlag, 1964).

Fontane's *Irrungen, Wirrungen* and the
novel of Realism

VIII

Fontane's *Irrungen, Wirrungen* and the novel of Realism

M. A. McHAFFIE

FONTANE is a late-comer among the German Realists. Keller, Raabe and Storm, for instance, all began producing their fiction around the middle of the nineteenth century, yet although Fontane is Keller's exact contemporary—both men were born in 1819—he did not publish his first novel *Before the Storm* until 1878. *Irrungen, Wirrungen* (*Errors, Entanglements*), his ninth work of fiction, first appeared in serial form in the *Vossische Zeitung* in 1887 and was then published in book form in the following year.

It has often been suggested that Fontane differs from the other Realists, not only in the lateness of his début as a novelist, but in other more radical ways. Demetz has recently made a brilliant, if sometimes overstated, case for seeing Fontane as a late inheritor of the novel of society practised by Jane Austen and Thackeray, as a writer whose affinities are with the English novelists of the earlier part of the nineteenth century rather than with the German Realists of the second half :

> Seen from Germany in the epoch of Raabe and Stifter, Fontane appears as an odd exception, from the European standpoint as the rule.[1]

Brinkmann expresses a similar, if rather more cautiously formulated view :

> In the German Realism of the nineteenth-century Fontane is in significant aspects an exception.[2]

It is entirely in the spirit of Fontane to point out that both of these statements can also be reversed. From a European standpoint, in the age of Zola and Turgenev, Fontane appears as an exception, in a German context as the rule, and for all the individual differences which spring from his temperament and from the point in time at which he writes he remains in significant aspects representative of the German Realism of the nineteenth century. Fontane as a novelist works within well-established literary traditions, some European, some German. While it is true, as Demetz has demon-

167

strated, that there are resemblances between Fontane's novels and those of Jane Austen and Thackeray, there are also differences which mark Fontane's novels as the product of a later and more problematic age. He retains marked affinities with the kind of Realism that existed in Germany in the latter half of the century. Though he works in an individual way, he thinks of himself as a Realist and works within the Realist mode. *Irrungen, Wirrungen* is an example of Fontane's personal modification of a recognizable period style.

In theory at least, as Brinkmann concedes, Fontane is a convinced apologist of the Realism which began to dominate German literature after 1848. Fontane in an essay written in 1853[3] expresses his warm approval of the new tone of Realism apparent in both life and art, and goes on to formulate a concept of Realism drawn from a survey of the fiction and lyrical poetry produced in Germany since 1848 :

> Realism in art is as old as art itself, indeed it is more : *it is art.* Our modern tendency is merely a return to the only right road, the recovery of an invalid, which could not fail to take place as long as the organism was still capable of living at all. Lessing's beautiful, still unrivalled Realism, in accordance with an eternal law, had to follow Gottsched's unnatural affectation, and the extravagant nonsense which had developed out of untruthful sentimentality and the confusion of empty imagery in the Thirties of this century was bound to be succeeded as necessary reaction by a period of honest feeling and healthy commonsense, a period which we boldly assert is here . . . Realism is the sworn enemy of all pretentiousness and extravagance . . . Above all, we do *not* understand by it the naked reproduction of everyday life, least of all of its misery and sombre aspects. Sad enough that it is necessary to have to insist still on such self-evident things. But it is not all that long ago since people (particularly in painting) confused wretchedness with Realism and imagined that in depicting a dying proletarian surrounded by starving children or in producing those so-called "Tendenzbilder" (Silesian weavers, the game laws and other things of the kind) they had indicated a brilliant tendency for art to adopt. That tendency has the same relationship to genuine Realism as raw ore has to metal : the refining process is missing . . . It [Realism] is the reflection of all real life, all true forces in the element of art.

In his allusion to the antiquity of Realism, Fontane touches here on one of the main difficulties which has bedevilled attempts to define the nature of German Realist writing. If Realism is as old as art itself, what are the distinguishing features of German Realism in the second half of the nineteenth century? Fontane supplies at least part of the answer when he declares Realism's hostility to immoderation and excess and rejects "naked prosaic Realism" in favour of the "genuine Realism" which aims at the fusion of reality and poetry. Keller, Raabe and Storm, as well as Fontane, believe that real life is always only the raw material which has to be shaped and transformed by art and that the direct depiction of squalor and social misery is outside their province. In their individual ways, all of the Realists demand and practise the "poetization", or, to use Fontane's term, the "transfiguration" (*Verklärung*) of reality.

There is, as the Realists themselves are aware, nothing particularly new about this. The literature of many periods and many countries has shaped the raw material of real life into works of art. What distinguishes the work of the German Realists from the literature of earlier periods is the nature of their reality and their manner of transfiguring it. The reality which they set out to make poetic is for the most part the complexity of life in the second half of the nineteenth century, or rather those segments of the complexity which fall within their individual experience. Their manner of expressing this reality is characterized by selectiveness, restraint and discretion.

To assume that Realist writing is, for this reason, always positive, harmonious and optimistic is a fallacy which has now been finally discredited. Realism is frequently melancholy and elegiac. Indeed, Otto Brahm saw "a negating and pessimistic impulse"[4] as one of the decisive characteristics which distinguished the literature of the Realist period from that of earlier times, and recent reappraisals of Realism have all found confirmation of this impression. As Martini[5] and Ritchie[6] have recently pointed out, the Realist writer is well aware of the tensions and contradictions of his age and of the radical changes taking place as the century advances. But German Realism is more reticent than the contemporary literature of other European countries. Where Dickens and Zola deal directly with social and political issues in a spirit of militancy, the German Realist expresses the problematic aspects of his age in a veiled and oblique way in a spirit of melancholy or humorous resignation. Measured against the literature of the Age of Goethe and of European Realism, German Realism represents a process of withdrawal from the world of metaphysical, universal or public issues to the world of the private individual in his day-to-day existence. The reduction in range and scope is accompanied by a preference for obliquity of expression, a predilection for the suggestion and the hint rather than the direct or explicit statement.

The avoidance of the explicit does not, however, mean vagueness or imprecision. On the contrary, Realism is characterized by the attention which it pays to precise detail and nuance, to the minutiæ of everyday life, to concrete reality and to the psychological processes of the human mind. External reality is linked with subjective reaction to it, and the details of concrete reality are frequently introduced, not for their own sake, but as elucidating comment on the character or situation of the human beings who live among them.

German Realism's divergence from the path taken by European Realism does not always spring from ineptitude or timidity. In Fontane's case it springs from aesthetic conviction. He is aware of the novels of European Realism, but he has no wish to emulate them. His attitude to Zola and Turgenev is characteristic and revealing. Although he concedes Zola's talent and admires aspects of Turgenev's work, he repeatedly expresses grave reservations about both the French and the Russian novelist :

> Life is not like that, and if it were, then the transfiguring veil of poetry would have to be created for it. But this "creating" is not at all necessary; the beauty is there, one must only have eyes for it or at least not close them on purpose. Genuine Realism will always be full of beauty; for beauty . . . belongs to life just as much as ugliness.[7]

He objects to the work of Zola and Turgenev on two counts. Firstly, that in concentrating on ugliness and squalor they are presenting only a partial view of real life, and secondly, that their presentation of their material is prosaic. Turgenev's *Novellen,* he claims, show "the Muse in sackcloth and ashes, Apollo with toothache".[8] Much as he admires the sharpness of the Russian's observation and the lack of cant and posturing in his work, he confesses his basic dissatisfaction with Turgenev's literary method :

> I cannot enjoy this way of writing . . . it bores me, because it reproduces things in such a boundlessly prosaic way, so completely *untransfigured.* But without this transfiguration there is no real art . . . A man with talents of this kind must write *essays* about Russia, but not *Novellen.*[9]

Comments of this sort are scattered liberally through letters written in the 1880s. They indicate how little Fontane's concept of Realism has changed since he first formulated it some thirty years earlier. In 1878 he began to translate this concept into the practical realities of his novels.

In the essay of 1853, Fontane argues that Realism embraces the whole richness of life, in both its highest and its most unassuming forms. It is interested in everything that is real : Columbus, who presented the old world with the gift of a new one, as well as the minute creature whose universe is a drop of water, the loftiest thought as well as the deepest feeling, the meditations of a Goethe as well as the joy and pain of a Gretchen. But, however persuasively he urges the claim for the all-inclusiveness of Realism in theory, he is, like the other Realists, highly selective in fact. There are no discoverers of new worlds, no great artists or intellectuals among the characters who people Fontane's novels, and the only form of heroism which he allows them is the bleak and limited heroism of insight into their own inadequacies and the realities of their situation. Great men, whether of action or of intellect, are exceptional beings, they represent a form of the extreme. Fontane, like the other Realists, is interested, not in the exception, but in the norm, not in the extreme, but in the average. In practice, he avoids the world of great events and epoch-making figures and confines himself to the modest sphere of unremarkable people in their daily lives.

This does not, however, mean that he confines himself to the sphere of middle class characters. He does on occasion deal with such characters, sometimes, as in *Frau Jenny Treibel* (1892), in a spirit of humorous irony, sometimes, as in the portrayal of the Gundermanns in *Der Stechlin* (1898), in a tone of icy distaste. But he also extends the social range upwards. His characters are often chosen from a higher social stratum than those of the other Realists. They are often members of the aristocracy, landowners, officers and high-ranking civil servants rather than the *Bürger* and *Bauer* favoured by other Realist writers. Nevertheless, this does not mean a break with Realist practice, only a modification of it. In his choice of characters, whatever their social position, Fontane adheres in essentials to the Realist preference for ordinary, average people. The great figures who make history and shape politics, if they are present at all, are present only peripherally and obliquely, in the consciousness of Fontane's characters. Bismarck, for instance, plays a marginal part in *Effi Briest* (1895), but only as the distant, invisible employer who makes Innstetten's frequent absences from his young wife necessary. In *Irrungen, Wirrungen*, he is the target for the choleric Baron Osten's vituperations in Chapter 7, the powerful, unseen, hated eroder of the privileges of the old Prussian aristocracy, the parvenu reserve officer, the scribbler of telegrams who has dared to engineer the downfall of a Harry von Arnim; and in Chapter 8, in the conversation of the officers in the club, he is alluded to mockingly by Pitt and Wedell, who is a distant cousin of Bismarck's wife. In neither novel does the great man play any direct or important part. In both novels, Fontane mentions him primarily to illuminate aspects of the society which he dominates and the characters and attitudes of the men who hate or serve him. In *Irrungen, Wirrungen,* the allusions to Bismarck help to establish the historical and social background against which Fontane sets the story of the aristocratic officer Botho von Rienäcker and the laundress Lene Nimptsch. Fontane's fictional world reverses the values of the real world to ensure that the reader, like the gossiping officers, will find the problems of Botho more engrossing than the policies of Bismarck.

If Fontane's characters never scale the pinnacles of greatness, they never sink to the lowest depths either. Although his letters reveal that he is clearly aware of the existence of poverty, social wretchedness and the problems of the industrial worker, as a novelist he remains faithful to the conviction expressed in the early essay and ignores those topics. Like the great man, the proletarian, if he is seen at all, remains on the periphery of Fontane's work. *Irrungen, Wirrungen* provides one of Fontane's rare glimpses of the industrial worker, when in Chapter 14 Botho rides past a factory and sees the workers with their wives and babies as they sit in front of the factory eating their midday meal. The nature of the glimpse is, as Demetz demonstrates, calculated to reassure the reader rather than stir him into awareness of the problems which industrialization means for the worker:[10]

> One of the finest artistic devices which Fontane likes to use on the boundaries of his narrative world aims at making socially problematic phenomena innocuous as works of plastic art, or better, as genre-painting. The most significant example of this pictorial or tableau method is to be found in *Irrungen, Wirrungen.* Botho approaches a big establishment—Fontane here does not even dare to use the word "factory". The aristocratic hero is not permitted to see the people at work. Midday repose. The world of the proletarian workers has been transformed back into a rustic idyll. The sun filters through the grass; shade, men, women, babies, gaiety; robust country life, which almost recalls a Dutch genre-painting . . . The count (*sic*), and with him the reader, is "enchanted" by the picture, and the foreign element, thus isolated and assimilated, is not allowed to endanger the aesthetically unified world of the novel.

The characters of humble origin who do appear in Fontane's novels are often merely adjuncts to the aristocratic or affluent way of life, nursemaids, parlourmaids and cooks, coachmen and family retainers, innkeepers and waiters who work in the restaurants, clubs and hotels which the aristocratic customers frequent. *Irrungen,*

Wirrungen has its complement of such figures, but it also contains others from the same social sphere who have no such direct link with the aristocracy. Where such people appear as important characters, as they do in *Irrungen, Wirrungen,* Fontane tends to stress the positive rather than the negative aspects of the way in which they live. They are self-employed, like the market-gardener Dörr and his wife, or they work at home, like Lene. They appear more often in their leisure hours than at work. The inadequacies of the houses in which they live are compensated for by the poetic nature of their situation. Poverty is not an acute problem : Lene can afford to have a new fireplace built for her foster-mother when they move to the Luisenufer (Chapter 17), Frau Nimptsch has been able to save money to pay for the kind of funeral that she wants (Chapter 19), the grasping Dörr can, when he has a mind to, present his wife with the ridiculously expensive hat which she wears on the walk towards Wilmersdorf (Chapter 9). They are clearly aware of the stratification of society and of their place in it. They are people who can be linked with the aristocracy only as Fontane links them in *Irrungen, Wirrungen* : by means of an accidental meeting which leads to a love affair.

The plot of the novel is a simple one, though, as we shall see later, it is treated in a highly sophisticated way. Botho and Lene, who have met on Easter Monday 1875, have a brief love affair which ends at the beginning of July in the same year. Botho leaves Lene, whom he loves, and marries his rich cousin Käthe von Sellenthin. The lovers part in Chapter 16 and Fontane devotes the remaining ten chapters to an account of their lives after the parting, Botho's in his marriage to Käthe, Lene's in the three years that elapse until her marriage with Gideon Franke in the summer of 1878.

Precise details about time are given at the beginning of the novel, and the precision is maintained throughout. When Frau Nimptsch and Frau Dörr have their conversation in the opening chapter, it is a fine evening in the week after Whitsun 1875. The letter from Botho's mother, which makes Botho realize (in Chapter 14) that he must acquiesce in the marriage arranged for him, is dated 29 June 1875, and the lovers meet for the last time on the day after he has read the letter. His marriage takes place in the middle of September, and Lene catches her painful glimpse of Botho and Käthe together in the third week of October. Even when the dates are not given, Fontane constantly reminds the reader of the time sequence of the events taking place : this or that meeting or conversation happens "on the next day" or "the same evening" or "two and a half years later" in relation to exactly specified points in time. The same attention to the calendar is apparent in the latter part of the novel. It is the 24 June 1878 when Käthe leaves on her journey to Schlangenbad, when Frau Nimptsch dies. Gideon Franke pays his visit to Botho three weeks after Frau Nimptsch's funeral, Käthe returns from the spa four days after the visit, and the novel ends three weeks after Käthe's return, on the day after Lene's wedding.

The precise dating of the story is matched by a similar precision in establishing the locality in which it happens. Berlin is evoked in exact topographical detail. The cottage in the Dörrs' nursery garden which Lene occupies with her foster-mother is situated opposite the "Zoo" at the point where the Kurfürstendamm and the Kurfürstenstraße intersect. Botho leaves his bachelor flat in the Bellevuestraße to live with Käthe in a flat in the Landgrafenstraße. On the rare occasions when they venture out of the seclusion of the Dörr garden, the lovers make their expeditions to precisely named places, in the direction of Wilmersdorf, to Hankels Ablage.

The use of real place names in fiction is not, of course, peculiar to Fontane or even to Realism. As Demetz has pointed out,[11] it is a traditional element of the European novel. Smollett, Jane Austen and Thackeray, Tolstoy and Henry James are among the many novelists who also name the towns and streets where their characters live and send them off on excursions and journeys to Bath and Brighton, Florence, Moscow, Paris and London. Precision of locality is also a feature of German Realist writing. Even if they sometimes have assumed names, the landscapes and townscapes in the fiction of Raabe and Keller are usually individualized and recognizable. In Realist novels, precision of locality is one of the devices used to strengthen the impression of verisimilitude. But it is not always combined, as Fontane combines it, with such exactness of date. The care which Fontane expends in establishing that the events of *Irrungen, Wirrungen* take place in Berlin between 1875 and 1878 suggests that he is interested in more than mere verisimilitude.

If it is true to say, as we did earlier, that the mention of Bismarck is one of the means of establishing the historical and social background for the story of the aristocratic officer and the humble laundress, the converse is also true. The individual story of Botho and Lene illuminates the general nature of society in the Germany of the 1870s. *Irrungen, Wirrungen* is not only a love story, it is also a social novel. It is an illustration of the belief about the function of the novel which Fontane had formulated in 1875, in a review of Freytag's *Our Forefathers*.[12] "What should a novel do?" he asks, and goes on to give the answer:

It should, while avoiding everything exaggerated and ugly, relate a story in which we believe. It should speak to our imagination and our hearts, it should stimulate, without exciting us; it should make a world of fiction appear to us for moments as a world of reality . . . The modern novel should be a picture of the age, of *its* age. Everything epoch-making, certainly everything lasting produced by the narrative literature of the past 150 years corresponds in essentials to this requirement.

In *Irrungen, Wirrungen,* with the familiar rejection of exaggerations and ugliness, the distrust of extremes which characterize German Realism generally, Fontane sets out to present a picture of German society in the decade after unification. It is, as Martini comments, a picture of "qualitative" rather than "quantitative" totality".[13] Fontane's method of suggesting social reality is to use a comparatively small number of characters, and by showing characteristic episodes from their lives to indicate the nature of the society to which they belong. The characters of *Irrungen, Wirrungen* are human beings who are also social beings, individuals whose behaviour and actions are determined, not by immutable moral laws, but by the social conventions and taboos which prevail in this place at this historical moment. Like Fontane's other novels, *Irrungen, Wirrungen* is concerned with the way in which individual lives are influenced by the time and place in which they are lived. What happens to Botho and Lene is only a particular instance of a general rule.

Fontane makes this clear by peopling the novel with subsidiary characters who provide both a parallel and a contrast with Botho and Lene. Frau Dörr has had an illicit affair with an elderly count before settling down to the respectability of married life in the nursery garden. The mistresses whom Botho's fellow officers bring with them to Hankels Ablage are from the same social milieu as Lene, and the oldest of them, the corpulent Isabeau, has plans for marriage with a widower of her own class when her affair with Balafré is over. In the eyes of society, the relationship between Botho and Lene is a replica of the others. The fact that this particular relationship is characterized by the mutual love and respect which the others lack cannot save it from sharing their fate. While it will tolerate an ephemeral affair as a manly peccadillo, the social code of the time will not sanction a permanent or legitimized union between an aristocrat and a girl from a lower social stratum. Rexin, the officer who asks for Botho's advice in Chapter 23, finds himself in a position similar to Botho's earlier one. He, too, loves his mistress and would like to marry her. But he, too, is aware that the society that exists in Germany in 1878 will not permit such a marriage :

> If instead of riding by this boring canal, as boring and unbending as the forms and formalities of our society, if, I say, we were riding by the Sacramento River instead of here by this miserable ditch, and if instead of the Tegel shooting ranges we had the gold diggings in front of us, then I would marry Jette right away. I can't live without her, I love her, and her naturalness, simplicity and real love are worth ten countesses to me. But it can't be. I can't do it to my parents, nor do I want to leave the army at the age of twenty-seven, to become a cowboy in Texas or a waiter on a Mississippi steamer.[14]

In a different kind of society, Botho and Rexin might have the freedom to marry the girls whom they love. In this one, however much Rexin may rail against the rigidity of the social code, they cannot. However relative to time and place the social conventions may be, they are binding and inescapable for the human beings who live then and there. Rexin's allusion to the possibilities open to him if he marries beneath him is anticipated in the bitter self-interrogation to which Botho submits himself in Chapter 14 :

> Who am I? An average human being from the so-called higher reaches of society. And what can I do? I can put a horse through its paces, carve a capon and play cards. That's all, and so I have the choice then between circus rider, head waiter and croupier. At the most I can add cavalry trooper, if I'm prepared to join a foreign legion. And then Lene with me as daughter of the regiment. I can see her already in the short skirt and the high-heeled boots and a little pack on her back.[15]

A permanent relationship with Lene is possible only if he is prepared to make himself an outcast in the world of the barracks and the club and exile himself from the company of his social equals. If he is cast out for offending the conventions of his class, his talents as an officer and a gentleman fit him only for professions on the seedy periphery of his own world. The fact that he cannot pay this price does not mean that he is especially weak. Fontane depicts him as an average man of his position, caught in a web of social and family obligations from which he cannot escape. His real choice is, in fact, not between happiness with Lene and unhappiness without her, but only between two forms of unhappiness. He cannot in the long term hope to be happy with Lene, since he is clear-sighted enough to see that the consequent estrangement from society would sap his self-respect and, as he later puts it to Rexin, make him "an abomination and a burden" to himself.[16]

He cannot be happy without Lene, to whom he is bound by one of those "mysterious forces", one of those "affinities from heaven or hell" to which he alludes in Chapter 22.[17] It is a choice of evils, and he is in a position where he cannot help but make the choice of which society approves. When he renounces Lene, he is making the only decision possible for a man of his circumstances living in a society organized as this one is.

Fontane devotes considerable care to illustrating that the renunciation is inevitable. From the first moment that it is mentioned, the affair between Lene and Botho is depicted as something necessarily transient. Lene is not introduced directly until Chapter 3, Botho does not appear until Chaper 4, but before we have seen either of them, the conversation of Frau Dörr and Frau Nimptsch in the opening chapter suggests that the affair is unlikely to last. Frau Dörr sees Lene's present experience as an interesting and more aesthetic variant of her past liaison with the count, and it does not occur to her for a moment that Lene's affair can be anything more than the episode which hers was. What both she and Frau Nimptsch fear is that Lene may be taking everything too seriously, that she is so emotionally involved that she will be badly hurt when the affair comes to its inevitable end, that she has perhaps begun to imagine that there is a possibility of permanent happiness with her Baron. They are both right and wrong. They are right in supposing that Lene's affections are deeply engaged, and that she will be hurt when she and Botho have to part. They are wrong in suspecting that she has an optimistic view of the future. Lene imagines nothing. She is, in every sense of the term, "realistic". She and her intimate circle know that she loves Botho and that the feeling is reciprocated, but they also assume correctly that the relationship will be broken off sooner or later, and that this will happen because of the social differences between the laundress and the Baron. No reassuring contradiction is possible, when, in Chapter 5, Lene tells Botho how she assesses their situation and its prospects :

"One day you'll have flown away ... Don't shake your head, it's as I'm saying. You love me and are faithful to me, at least I'm childish and vain enough in my love to imagine so. But fly away you will, I see that clearly and surely. You will have to. They always say love makes you blind, but it also makes you clear and far-sighted".

"Oh, Lene, you don't know how much I love you at all".

"Yes, I do know. And I know too that you regard your Lene as something special and that you think every day : if only she were a countess. But it's too late for that, that I can't manage any more. You love me and you're weak. That can't be changed. All handsome men are weak, and are dominated by what is stronger . . . And the stronger thing . . . yes, what is this stronger thing? Well, either it's your mother or what people will say or circumstances. Or perhaps all three . . ."[18]

Both of them know, although Botho is still reluctant to admit it, that she is right. Even without the complicating family circumstances revealed in Chapter 7, Botho will have to leave Lene. Their affair cannot be anything but an interlude which the claims of society are bound to terminate. Lene and Botho belong to two quite different worlds, and the gulf between them cannot be permanently bridged.

Even temporarily, the bridge leads in only one direction. It is possible for Botho to appear in the privacy of the Dörr garden, to sit in front of Frau Nimptsch's fire with Lene and the Dörr family, enchanted by the simplicity and naturalness which he finds in Lene's way of life. She has no access to his social world, as it is exemplified in his elegant flat, Hiller's restaurant and the officers' club. Botho and Lene can be happy together only when they are alone or in the company of her social circle. The sour ending to the excursion to Hankels Ablage demonstrates what happens to their relationship in the presence of representatives of his. When Botho's friends arrive with their "ladies", the happiness which Botho and Lene have experienced in the solitude of Hankels Ablage is destroyed. Not only are their plans for the day frustrated. The relationship between the three officers and their companions provides a kind of distorting mirror, in which Lene is made to see how she and her relationship with Botho appear in the eyes of Botho's world. It is a reflection which threatens to rob them of their individuality and depersonalize them to fit the frivolous social cliché which the others represent. The essentially frivolous tone of the officers' affairs is finely suggested by the pseudo-discretion of the nicknames and of the way in which their companions are introduced. The "password" for the day is Schiller's *Maid of Orleans*. The girls are presented as "the daughters of Thibaut d'Arc", the older woman as Queen Isabeau, and in the presence of his intimates, Botho becomes the "Gaston" of the club, and Lene loses her own identity for the counterfeit one of "Agnes Sorel", the King's mistress. With the intrusion of figures from Botho's real world, simple enjoyment and natural feeling are superseded by the rather cynical mechanism of social ritual. The idyll is degraded into the conventional excursion. Routine replaces inclination, and the experienced Isabeau dictates the shape of the day. Botho cannot evade the claims of social convention. He has to join his friends in the card game suggested by Isabeau, and Lene is banished to the bored company of the other women, with whom she has nothing in common except the fact that she, too, is the mistress of an aristocratic officer. The excursion which was initially the occasion of the lovers' greatest happiness goes on to underline the extent of the social gap between them and concludes with the bleak realization that their happiness cannot survive for much longer.

The affair ends two days later. The timing of the inevitable renunciation is determined by the existence of specific family duties. Botho is not only in a position where social considerations make marriage with Lene impossible, he is also in a position where financial considerations make it imperative for him to marry his rich cousin Käthe. As his uncle Osten has reminded him over lunch at Hiller's in Chapter 7, a previously contracted family arrangement already half binds him to Käthe. Marriage with her is the obvious solution to the family's acute financial problems. Botho knows that his family wish him to marry Käthe and that he must do so soon or not at all. By making it clear to the reader that Botho is subject to this family pressure before the episodes of the Wilmersdorf walk and the excursion to Hankels Ablage, Fontane achieves in them a curiously elegiac atmosphere. The episodes which show us the lovers at their happiest are also full of awareness of the precariousness and impermanence of their happiness. They take place with the reader sharing Botho's consciousness of the forces of financial crisis and family duty which are working to end the affair. They are permeated, as indeed the whole novel is, by the melancholy awareness of transience which pervades so much of German Realism.

His mother's letter, which reaches Botho on the day after the return from Hankels Ablage, is an ultimatum which makes any further postponement of the inevitable impossible. The break with Lene must be made at once, the marriage with Käthe undertaken as soon as possible. It is a decision which Lene accepts without rancour or recrimination when Botho comes to take leave of her:

"I've seen this coming from the beginning, and what is happening is only what has to happen. When people have had a beautiful dream, then they must thank God for it and not complain that the dream is ending and reality beginning again; It's hard now, but we'll forget it all or it will all look brighter again. And one day you'll be happy again and perhaps I shall as well".

"Do you think so? And if not, what then?"

"Then we'll live without happiness".[19]

The treatment of the lovers' last meeting is an illustration of the Realist way of dealing with painful or unpleasant material. The whole episode is handled with characteristic moderation. There are no outbursts of despair, no flamboyant manifestations of grief, no melodramatic gestures. The pain is there, but its expression is muted and restrained, and the emotional stress of the occasion is made bearable by Lene's attitude of understanding, acceptance and resignation.

It is an admirable attitude, as Lene is an admirable character. In her integrity and honesty, she seems very much the moral superior of any of the other figures in the novel. But Fontane avoids the dangers of idealizing her or making her seem too good to be true. She is, as Frau Dörr remarks in the opening chapter, not an angel. She has had a much earlier affair with a man called Kuhlwein, which she and Frau Nimptsch allude to in Chapter 17 and 18. Her comments on Frau Dörr's person and marriage have the spice of occasional malice (Chapter 5). There is sometimes a hint of bitterness about the fact that she and Botho cannot appear together in public (Chapters 5 and 9). Even at Hankels Ablage, when Botho asks her to choose between the boats "The Trout" and "Hope", she cannot resist the pinprick of allusion to their affair: "The trout naturally. What should we do with hope".[20] Fontane draws her with just enough imperfections to make her virtues seem entirely credible. In his characterization, Fontane treads the Realist path of moderation and avoidance of extremes.

Similar restraint is evident in the later part of the novel. Botho's bitter picture of himself as an outcast (Chapter 14) expresses what would have happened to him if he had defied social taboos and tried to make his relationship with Lene permanent. The second part of the novel shows us what becomes of him when he conforms to the social code by abandoning Lene and marrying Käthe. On the surface, his lot seems an enviable one. But Fontane looks beneath the surface to reveal the essential hollowness of Botho's existence with Käthe and his painful perception of loss.

In an illuminating comparison of *Irrungen, Wirrungen* with Goethe's *Kindred by Choice*, Killy has pointed out both the resemblances and the significant differences between the two novels:

> *Irrungen, Wirrungen* is in many respects related to the older work in its form, indeed it even shares with it the same basic theme: "there are such mysterious forces, such affinities from heaven or hell and now I am bound and can't get away again".[21]

Lene and Botho, like Eduard and Ottilie, are caught in a conflict between the force which draws them to each other and the claims of a moral order. But where Goethe represents the moral order as an absolute one, Fontane, as we have seen, shows it as something historical and relative, a conventional moral code rather than a timeless moral law. It is, however, in the treatment of the common theme of renunciation that the essential difference between the two novels becomes clearest. The comparison emphasizes the Realist nature of *Irrungen, Wirrungen*. Compared with Goethe's novel, Fontane's represents the limitation in scope and the reduction in intensity which characterize the period :

The end in both cases is tragic, even if this may escape many readers of the later novel. For where there fate emerges in a demonic way and uses dreadful portents and destructive accidents, everything here is tuned down to the reasonable tone of an age which regards itself as enlightened and is moved into the light of a story which replaces heroic annihilation with destruction by everyday triviality.

The tragic process has been flattened, but it has not disappeared. It has changed its character, not its result.[22]

The tragedy in *Irrungen, Wirrungen* has been muted to the threshold of audibility. The tragic situation is presented with characteristic moderation, and the bleakness of Botho's life after he leaves Lene is revealed gradually and discreetly.

Where a lesser novelist might have been tempted into the oversimplification of making the rich cousin a disagreeable character and the marriage with her overtly distasteful, the Realist Fontane rejects any trace of sensationalism. The only outward hint that the relationship with Käthe is basically empty and sterile is the continuing childlessness of the marriage. Otherwise everything about the life which the couple leads together appears outwardly to be in exemplary order. Käthe is not only rich, beautiful and socially suitable, she is also amiable, gay and charming, and Botho, far from being desperately unhappy in his marriage, is initially entirely captivated by her charm. It is Lene's realization of this which makes her involuntary glimpse of the couple so hurtful. The pain which she feels when she sees them together springs mainly from the sight of their apparent happiness with each other, not because she resents Botho's seeming happy, but because the sight intensifies her own sense of loss and desolation. She is alone, her life goes on monotonously, there is as yet nothing to fill the vacuum left by the severance of her relationship with Botho. Initially Botho seems more fortunate. He has an attractive and vivacious wife and numerous agreeable distractions to help him over the misery of separation. And yet, when Lene sees the laughing couple, Botho has already begun to discover the flaw in his marriage, the basic incompatibility of temperament between himself and Käthe which will lead him in time to the realization that his marriage is no more than existence with an endearing doll. Käthe's shallowness and incorrigible frivolity, her predilection for comical trivialities, first become entirely clear to him as they return from their honeymoon. Fontane avoids any hint of flamboyance in Botho's reaction. The discovery of Käthe's superficiality produces nothing more intense than uneasiness. As time passes, her lack of seriousness occasionally provokes him to a moment of irritation and leads him involuntarily to think of Lene, who has the depth and complexity of character which Käthe lacks. But the moments of irritation, the memories of Lene are, until Franke's visit in Chapter 20, only occasional. There is no hint of desperation or despair. The marriage is presented as an affectionate, good-humoured, moderately successful relationship with a wife whom Botho sometimes finds a little silly and frivolous, who sometimes causes him to remember Lene with nostalgia and regret.

It is not until Franke's visit that he becomes fully and sharply conscious of the inadequacies of his marriage. Franke's question forces him to recall Lene and his relationship with her with painful clarity, and, in thinking of the past, to realize, both how much is lacking in his present existence and to what extent he is still emotionally bound to Lene. She does not appear directly in the novel after Chapter 19, except for the brief description of her arrival for her wedding in the final chapter, where she is seen from the perspective of the curious spectators, titillated by the absence of the bride's virginal wreath. But through the medium of Botho's memory she remains an important character to the last. In Botho's pilgrimage to Frau Nimptsch's grave (Chapters 21–22) with the wreath of everlasting flowers which he had promised her in Chapter 10, in the burning of Lene's letters and the faded flowers from Hankels Ablage in Chapter 22, in the conversation with Rexin in Chapter 23, Botho is made to relive the past and the pain of leaving Lene and to realize that his present life is devoid of real happiness. The realization changes nothing, is in no way disruptive, produces no great upheaval. Botho's unhappiness is tempered with resignation. When Käthe returns, he is pleased to have her back—"She chatters in a silly way, well yes, but a silly young wife is still better than none"[23]—and after her return, his feelings are suggested on only two occasions and in the most unobtrusive of ways. After Käthe's discovery of the ashes, his failure to attend to her gossip about fellow-guests at the spa allows the reader to discern that he is preoccupied with memories of Lene and of the relics which he has burnt. His thoughts are indicated not by words, but by his silence. His reaction to the newspaper notice of Lene's wedding is expressed in a similarly subdued way in the *double entendre* of the remark with which the novel ends : " 'Just what have you against Gideon, Käthe? Gideon is better than Botho' ".[24] The words convey with the utmost brevity and discretion the essence of his resigned acceptance of a life without happiness. In Fontane's version of "the conflict between the poetry of the heart and the opposing prose of circumstances",[25] the victory of circumstances is registered quietly and without fuss.

The choice of unremarkable characters and commonplace situations entails for Fontane, as for the other Realists, the problem of making them interesting. In a discussion of Ibsen's *Wild Duck*, Fontane remarks that it is the hardest (and perhaps the highest) thing in the world :

> to illuminate everyday life in such a way that what was just now indifferent and prosaic suddenly moves us with the most entrancing magic of poetry.[26]

Irrungen, Wirrungen illustrates the Realist method of achieving this illumination : by careful composition, attention to balance and symmetry, skilful deployment of symbols and leitmotifs, the unobtrusive use of allusions and cross references and of the telling detail of human behaviour or of external reality, which suggests far more than it says explicitly.

Irrungen, Wirrungen is highly symmetrical in structure. The novel begins on an evening in the Dörr nursery garden, it ends on a morning in the flat in the Landgrafenstraße. The intervening chapters are arranged in blocks which alternate between Lene's and Botho's worlds, with the confrontation of the two worlds at Hankels Ablage occupying a central position. Fontane uses a technique of alternation and contrast which serves two purposes. By providing insight into two different social spheres, it contributes to the impression of social totality. At the same time, it helps to emphasize the nature of the social differences which make the lovers' parting inevitable.

The double function of the structure is only one example of the admirable economy with which Fontane contrives the maximum effect with the minimum of means. He is a master in "the abbreviation of complex reality".[27] With unobtrusive brilliance he manipulates the simple events in the foreground to open social vistas for the reader and to suggest both the individual and the typical aspects of Botho's and Lene's experience. Even the fact that we are not shown the lovers' meeting, but only the final stages of the affair, is calculated to indicate something significant about the nature of the age. It is, as Chapter 7 makes clear, an age of transition. Baron Osten's tirade against Bismarck suggests that the standards and assumptions of an old way of life still exist, but that they are no longer unchallenged. The transience of the lovers' affair hints that the old way of life is also coming to an end.

Fontane was a prolific writer of ballads long before he became a novelist, and his technique as a novelist remains consciously balladesque :

I was a writer of ballads from the age of sixteen . . . and for that reason, by nature and habit, I cannot get away from the ballad. The ballad loves leaps; indeed those leaps are its law, the condition essential to its life . . . This balladesque feeling guides me in everything that I write.[28]

It is this feeling which determines the narrative shape of *Irrungen, Wirrungen*. For all the meticulous attention to the passage of time in the novel, it makes no attempt to give an uninterrupted picture of chronological progression, but springs from one place and one point in time to another. Fontane's manner of narrating is episodic. Moments of an outwardly trivial nature are made to assume representative quality. The essence of the lovers' relationship is conveyed in the depiction of an evening in front of Frau Nimptsch's fire, a stroll in the garden, a country walk, the first part of the excursion to Hankels Ablage; while a lunch at Hiller's restaurant, an afternoon in the club, a dinner party in Botho's flat capture the essential nature of his way of life. Each episode, taken by itself, provides a wealth of information about the characters' situation and the social reality of the time and is simultaneously bound by an intricate web of detail and allusion to all the others.

In a review of *Debit and Credit* which he wrote in 1855 Fontane praises the exemplary form of Freytag's novel :

There is not a nail hammered in throughout the first volume, on 'which there is not something or other hung in the third volume, be it a coat or a human being".[29]

With the twofold reservation that Fontane is briefer and subtler than Freytag, the comment applies equally well to *Irrungen, Wirrungen*. The novel is remarkable for the skill with which Fontane uses the devices of anticipation, echo and parallel motifs to connect its various parts. Botho's imitation of the sort of conversation heard at fashionable dinner parties, with which he entertains Lene's circle in Chapter 4, is, for instance, an anticipation of Käthe's prattle, an early example of the art of chattering pleasing trivialities which she practises with such mastery over her dinner table and in her letters, and Botho's reaction to her letters is an echo of Lene's comment on his imitation. This is only one of many instances of the way in which Fontane repeats and varies motifs, points forward and harks back. The moment when Käthe waltzes with Botho to the sound of music from the concert in the Zoo (Chapter 17) must remind Botho, as it does the reader, of the occasion in the past when he and Lene danced to similar music (Chapter 4). When, after their presence has wrecked the lovers' idyll, Isabeau looks for strawberries for Balafré (Chapter 13), the reader can share Lene's memory of the evening in the Dörr garden when she picked a strawberry for Botho, and be aware with her of the painful contrast between then and now. Botho's capitulation to social ritual at Hankels Ablage foreshadows his necessary surrender on a larger scale. On his way to the cemetery, he hears again the song which they sang on the way back from Wilmersdorf in Chapter 9. On occasion, the fairly obvious link between past and present is accompanied by a further muted hint of what is going on beneath the surface. When, for instance, Botho buys the wreath of everlasting flowers in Chapter 21, it is clear that the evening when he made his promise to Frau Nimptsch must be in his mind. When he chooses the yellow, rather than the red or white wreath, there is the almost imperceptible suggestion that his choice is determined by memories of Hankels Ablage and of the yellow immortelle which Lene included among the flowers.

The unobtrusiveness of such details is matched by Fontane's unobtrusiveness as author. While he is not as rigid as Spielhagen, who demanded the total withdrawal of the author and strict adherence to an objective or "dramatic" method of narrating,[30] Fontane is prepared to concede that the intervention of the author should be kept to a minimum :

> The intervention of the author is almost always harmful, or at least superfluous. And what is superfluous is wrong. It is true enough that it is often difficult to ascertain where intervention begins. The writer must inevitably do and say a great deal. Otherwise it just doesn't work or artifice results. But he must refrain from judging, preaching, from being clever and wise.[31]

Irrungen, Wirrungen displays the same kind of sensible compromise. For much of the novel, Fontane retires behind his characters and allows them to reveal themselves and their own situation, or the situation of other characters, in conversation, in letters or, occasionally, in an interior monologue. It is Frau Nimptsch and Frau Dörr, not Fontane, who acquaint us with the existence of the affair, and Baron Osten who reveals to Wedell, and to us, the special circumstances which determine when the affair must end. The advantages of the conversational method

are obvious. It enormously strengthens the impression of naturalness and verisimilitude for which the Realist writer strives :
Fontane is a virtuoso in the art of "making human beings speak
as they really speak".[82] It enriches the fabric of the novel by
introducing a number of different perspectives : we hear how the
lovers' affair appears to Frau Dörr and to Botho's friends as well
as to Botho and Lene themselves. It is also economical. By his
skill in catching the differences in tone between Lene's circle and
the aristocratic characters, Fontane briefly but effectively reinforces
once more the sense of social difference which plays such an
important part in determining the lovers' fate. The conversational
passages of the novel have, on occasion, yet another purpose. It
is in the conversations that Fontane most frequently introduces
the humorous note with which the Realist writer so often tries
to reconcile the tensions and problematic aspects of reality. Much
of the humour in *Irrungen, Wirrungen* centres round the persons
of the robust and earthy Frau Dörr and the charming but scatter-
brained Käthe. Each woman, in her individual way, is an
uninhibited and enthusiastic talker. In both cases, their own words
humorously reveal both their likeable qualities and their weaknesses and foibles. Through them, Fontane creates the humorous
aura round the tragic story of frustrated love, which helps to
give the novel its characteristically unsensational tone.

Fontane does not make only his human characters speak. As
Martini remarks, he makes things speak as well.[33] The details of
the external world are made to elucidate and comment on the
situation and feelings of the protagonists. The fireworks which
flare and fade in Chapter 4 add their confirmation to Lene's
realization of the intensity and the transience of her relationship
with Botho. The fly which buzzes round Botho's head in Chapter
14 is not only the "herald of disaster"[34] which anticipates the
arrival of the ultimatum from his mother, it is also the external
equivalent of the uneasy thoughts which are tormenting Botho
in the aftermath of Hankels Ablage. On occasion, the characters
themselves are aware of the relevance of concrete reality to their
own experience. This is so in Chapter 21, when Botho rides out
to the cemetery. His way takes him through a street lined with
the tawdry booths of a fairground and the yards of the stone-
masons who make gravestones for the many cemeteries in the
neighbourhood. The bizarre juxtaposition of the fairground
placards and the advertisements for gravestones has both an
individual and a universal relevance. Signs of the human quest
for happiness, or at least in pleasure, are linked with the *memento
mori* which emphasizes how short-lived and fragile happiness is.
The point is reinforced by the sight of the cart piled with broken

glass, which Botho immediately relates to his own experience of loss :

"Happiness and glass" . . . He looked at it with reluctance, with the sensation in all his fingertips that the fragments were cutting him.[35]

Details such as these demonstrate Fontane's ability to endow the most mundane of objects with poetry and human significance.

Irrungen, Wirrungen exemplifies the Realist method of transfiguring reality. Simple subject matter, average characters and everyday situations are handled with a subtlety and sophistication which give them "that intensity, clarity, transparency and roundedness and consequently that intensity of feeling, which is the transfiguring power of art".[36] It is a novel which displays how Realism at its best is capable of transcending its self-imposed limitations to achieve a credible and convincing picture of the life lived in Germany in the second half of the nineteenth century. *Irrungen, Wirrungen* does more. The shrewdness of Fontane's psychological insight, his humorous and melancholy grasp of the potentialities and limitations of human nature ensure that the story of Botho and Lene has more than merely local or historical validity. The characters of *Irrungen, Wirrungen* wear the costumes of the 1870s and their behaviour is conditioned by the customs of the age in which they live. But Fontane's poetic imagination has achieved the fusion of the specific with the universal which distinguishes all writing of high literary rank. In his depiction of the characters and customs of a now vanished age, he captures the authentic note of recurring human experience.

NOTES

1. Peter Demetz, *Formen des Realismus: Theodor Fontane* (München, 1964), p. 223.
2. Richard Brinkmann, *Theodor Fontane. Über die Verbindlichkeit des Unverbindlichen* (München, 1967), p. 180.
3. *"Unsere lyrische und epische Poesie seit 1848"*, *Sämtliche Werke*. Hrsg. von Edgar Groß, Kurt Schreinert u.a. (Nymphenburger Ausgabe, München, 1959 ff.) Vol. XXI, p. 9.
4 Otto Brahm. "Gottfried Keller", in: *Meisterwerke deutscher Literaturkritik* herausgegeben und eingeleitet von Hans Mayer (Berlin, 1956), Vol. 2, p. 747.
5. Fritz Martini, *Deutsche Literatur im bürgerlichen Realismus* (Stuttgart, 1962).
6. J. M. Ritchie, "Realism", in: *Periods in German Literature* (London, 1966).

7. 14 June 1883, *Gesammelte Werke* (Berlin 1905-11), 2nd series, Vol. 7, p. 35.
8. 9 July 1881, *Familienbriefe*, hrsg. von Friedrich Fontane (Berlin, 1937), p. 183.
9. 24 June 1881, *Ges. Werke*, II, Vol. 6, p. 314.
10. Demetz, op. cit., p. 150.
11. Ibid., p. 116.
12. *Sämtliche Werke*, Vol. XXI, p. 239.
13. Martini, op. cit., p. 851.
14. *Sämtliche Werke*, Vol. 3, p. 220.
15. Ibid., p. 169.
16. Ibid., p. 221.
17. Ibid., p. 214.
18. Ibid., p. 117.
19. Ibid., p. 174.
20. Ibid., p. 145.
21. Walther Killy, *Romane des* EF, *Jahrhunderts. Wirklichkeit und Kunstcharakter* (Göttingen, 1967), p. 206.
22. Ibid., p. 206.
23. *Sämtliche Werke*, Vol 3, p. 217.
24. Ibid., p. 232.
25. Friedrich Hegel, *Sämtliche Werke*, hrsg. von Hermann Glockner, 1928, Vol. 14, p. 395.
26. *Causerien über Theater, Sämtliche Werke*, Vol. XXII/2, p. 696.
27. Killy, op. cit., p. 195.
28. *"Ein Stück Autokritik"*, in *Sämtliche Werke*, Vol. XXI, p. 496.
29. *Sämtliche Werke*, Vol. XXI, p. 219.
30. Friedrich Spielhagen, *Beiträge zur Theorie und Technik des Romans*, 1883.
31. 15 February 1896, *Ges. Werke*, II, Vol. XI, p. 373.
32. 24 August 1882, *Theodor Fontanes Briefe. Erste Sammlung*, 1911, Vol. 2, p. 22.
34. Martini, op. cit., p. 749.
34. *Sämtliche Werke*, Vol. 3, p. 166.
35. Ibid., p. 211.
36. *Aus dem Nachlaß. Ges. Werke*, II, Vol. IX, p. 270.

BIBLIOGRAPHY

Brinkmann, R., *Theodor Fontane, Über die Verbindlichkeit des Unverbindlichen* (München, 1967).
Brinkmann, R., ed., *Zur Begriffsbestimmung des Realismus* (Wisbu, 1969).
Demetz, P., *Formen des Realismus: Theodor Fontane* (München, 1964).
Friedrich, G. "Die Frage nach dem Glück in Fontanes Irrungen, Wirrungen", *Deutschunterricht*, 1959, Jg. 11 April.
Gansberg, M. L., *Der Prosa-Wortschatz des deutschen Realismus. Unter besonderer Berücksichtigung des vorausgehenden Sprachwandels 1835–1855* (Bonn, 1964).

Killy, W., *Romane des 19. Jahrhunderts. Wirklichkeit und Kunstcharakter* (Göttingen, 1967).

Lukács, G., *Essays über Realismus* (Berlin, 1948); *Deutsche Realisten des neunzehnten Jahrhunderts* (Berlin, 1951).

Martini, F., *Deutsche Literatur im bürgerlichen Realismus 1848-1898* (Stuttgart, 1962).

Preisendanz, W., *"Voraussetzungen des poetischen Realismus in der deutschen Erzählkunst des 19. Jahrhunderts"*, in: *Formkräfte der deutschen Dichtung vom Barock bis zur Gegenwart* (Göttingen, 1963).

Preisendanz, W., *Humor als dichterische Einbildungskraft. Studien zur Erzählkunst des poetischen Realismus* (München, 1963).

Ritchie, J. M., *"Realism"*, in: *Periods in German Literature* (London, 1966).

Sasse, H. C., *Theodor Fontane. An Introduction to the Novels and Novellen* (Oxford, 1968).

Thanner, J., *Die Stilistik Theodor Fontanes* (The Hague, 1967).

Die Familie Selicke and the Drama of Naturalism

IX

Die Familie Selicke and the Drama of Naturalism

DAVID TURNER

I

IN his essay *Die Kunst—Ihr Wesen und ihre Gesetze* (1891) Arno Holz set up a hierarchy of the arts, in which literature held pride of place, because its artistic means, words, were more comprehensive, better able to reproduce the totality of nature[1]—and thereby of course to fulfil the requirements of his famous law that art has the tendency to become nature. Taking the premise a step further, Wolfgang Kayser has shown how within the sphere of literature it was drama, with its additional advantages of a room filled with real objects and of real men and women to speak the words and provide appropriate gestures, that was the most suitable medium for realizing the artistic revolution envisaged by Holz.[2] Historically, too, drama occupied a central position in German Naturalism, whose heyday can justifiably be said to have coincided with the activity of the *Freie Bühne* of Berlin,[3] the theatre club founded by Otto Brahm in 1889 to promote the production of what were mostly controversial works by modern playwrights.

Die Familie Selicke, the fruit of collaboration between Holz and his slightly older colleague, Johannes Schlaf, was first performed on 7 April 1890, after considerable backstage manœuvring and lobbying,[3a] under the auspices of the *Freie Bühne*, as part of the international programme of plays—French, Russian, Norwegian and German—produced between 1889 and 1891. In terms of public scandal its impact was relatively small, although one newspaper, on learning that the play was to be presented, suggested that no woman concerned for her reputation would dare to show her face there and that gentlemen would have to sneak into the performances as if visiting some house of ill fame.[4] And in terms of artistic merit it can scarcely claim to have been the greatest work seen by the *Freie Bühne* audiences, even among those from the pen of German authors. Nevertheless in its very shortcomings *Die Familie Selicke* points to some of the major theoretical and practical concerns of German Naturalism. And in certain technical features it genuinely breaks new ground, much more so, for example, than Hauptmann's *Vor Sonnenaufgang* and Tolstoy's *The Power of Darkness* with their more sensational subject-matter.

II

As in so much of Naturalism, the keynote of *Die Familie Selicke* is suffering, coupled with pity for the victims. Of Hauptmann's *Die Weber*, a play also compounded of suffering and pity, it has been said that there is no hero in the traditional sense, but that the weavers as a whole are the hero, even that misery itself is the hero. Although *Die Familie Selicke* has a much smaller list of characters and therefore provides more opportunity for our interest to be focused on one particular character, the same basic impression prevails. The suffering depicted is not that of any one character, but rather, as the title of the play makes plain, of a whole family. This is not to say that either the causes of distress or the ways in which it affects the characters are the same for each of them. Indeed, much of the skill shown by the authors is precisely in the subtle gradations and variations of suffering. Nevertheless the ultimate impact of the play is that of a tormented family, whose agony is only increased because its members are so closely involved with each other. Like ungreased ball-bearings they are gradually worn away by constantly rubbing against each other. And like ball-bearings they seem completely encased. The fact that the scene never changes from the living room of the Selicke's is no act of deference to the classical unities. That is why Wolfgang Kayser speaks of "Einheit des Raumes" as opposed to "Einheit des Ortes".[5]

There is little communication with their surroundings and the world outside. It is an enclosed space, a cage almost, in which two married people make their lives a hell and their children suffer.

In seeking to assess the causes of suffering in *Die Familie Selicke* it is important to keep the whole background of the period— scientific and philosophical as well as literary—in mind. In this connection determinism is the key-word. At this time man was no longer seen as a free agent, capable of making significant decisions which directed the course of his life. He appeared rather as a product of heredity and environment, physical, social, intellectual and spiritual; and ultimately he could not escape from this self which had been moulded by so many forces outside him. The French novelist Zola, for example, had spoken of man as a thinking animal, subject to the many various influences of the soil on which he grew.[6] The German, Wilhelm Bölsche, relying partly on his scientific background and partly on his acquaintance with Zola's novels, stated quite confidently :

> For the writer, however, I can see only the highest gain in the fact that man has no free will. I boldly declare that, if he had, a truly realistic literature would be absolutely impossible. Only by stirring ourselves until we fathom out laws in human thought, only by realizing that a human action, of whatever kind, is bound to be nothing more than the product of certain factors, of an external cause and an inner disposition, and that this disposition also can be derived from given quantities—only then can we ever hope to arrive at a true, mathematical penetration of a man's entire mode of action and to conjure up before our mind's eye characters who are as logical as nature.[7]

And Julius Röhr, in an essay entitled *Das Milieu in Kunst und Wissenschaft* (1891), also took up some of Zola's ideas and developed them further for the German public. The strange thing was that Röhr, who seems to have considered only novels, accused the Germans of having so far failed to take the importance of milieu, understood in the widest sense, into account.[8] Even though his essay appeared in the organ of the *Freie Bühne*, he apparently ignored what had gone on there under his very nose, so to speak. There had already been Hauptmann's *Vor Sonnenaufgang* with its stress on the demoralizing consequences of newly acquired wealth and on hereditary dipsomania, *Das Friedensfest*, which in an attempted family reconciliation had shown the ultimate powerlessness of man's good intentions against the forces of heredity and upbringing, and *Einsame Menschen*, whose main character, Johannes Vockerat, finally proved too weak to break free from the stifling intellectual atmosphere of his tradition-bound family. And the next few years were to bring further clear examples of the powerful determining forces at work in modern society.

With this general picture of the period in mind it is tempting to see *Die Familie Selicke* simply as another case of suffering engendered by forces—particularly social forces—outside man's control. But that would indeed be to see things simply; in reality they are much too complex to allow a single, neat answer. Thus it is with perhaps the most obvious contender among the possible causes of suffering—poverty. The Selicke's are poor of course : they are deeply in debt; they cannot afford proper treatment for Linchen, having to make do with the quack, Kopelke; Linchen recalls the mockery she had to endure at school because of her shabby clothes; Toni has to drudge even over Christmas in order to scrape together a little extra. But the picture of poverty is nowhere as harrowing as it sometimes is with Hauptmann, who has labourers stealing scraps from cattle troughs (*Vor Sonnenaufgang*) or weavers slaughtering their pet dog to provide meat (*Die Weber*). Moreover, Selicke does have a job as a clerk and the eldest son, Albert, is also earning, if only as an apprentice. Frau Selicke speaks at one point of another family, originally no better off than they, who by good management have got on and now have a house (pp. 41–42).[9] And the point of this is clearly to show that more than finances is involved in their situation. Much more significant, one feels, is the behaviour of the two main breadwinners of the family. If the father spent less on drink and Albert less on smart clothes, the financial position would be at least tolerable. Altogether the poverty shown in *Die Familie Selicke* is as much "effect" as it is "cause".

Put the other way round, the burden of suffering which the various characters individually have to bear is for the most part unrelated to their lack of money. The source of Linchen's suffering, for example, is much less the physical fact of her illness and the lack of proper treatment than the atmosphere of discord in the home. This emerges from a most revealing daydream in which she indulges. In it she imagines herself being well enough again to go and stay with her uncle in the country. Not only will she be well-fed and have a fine dress to go to church in, but, more important for her, one senses :

> Uncle doesn't quarrel—with auntie—not even once! . . . No swear-words! . . . And Anna and Otto—are always—so good! (p. 40).

A few years later, in his *Hanneles Himmelfahrt*, Hauptmann was to expand this basic situation into an entire play, in which the young heroine's delirious dream of a fairy-tale heaven was to take on dramatic reality. But in both cases the idyllic fantasy can be regarded as a psychological means of compensation for the hardships of a deprived child.[10] Another clear indication of the true source of Linchen's suffering is the pathetic way in which she comes actually to enjoy her illness, because her mother no longer scolds her now :

> LINCHEN. Mum—my? . . .
> FRAU SELICKE. Hm?
> LINCHEN (*smiling*). It's nice being poorly!
> FRAU SELICKE. O my goodness! . . . My poor, silly little girl! . . . Whatever for? (*Leans tenderly over Linchen.*)
> LINCHEN. Because . . . because then . . . you're always . . . so kind . . . (pp. 37–38).

In Toni's case the suffering is much more difficult to assess, because, being uncomplaining by nature, she rarely communicates her sorrows. We can be certain, however, that they go at least as deep as those of the others. When she tells Wendt in Act III that she wishes she were dead—a sentiment also expressed by both her parents—the accompanying stage direction, "weary, tormented", tells us all we need to know about the effects of the life she has had to lead. But what of the causes? Physical drudgery is only part of the story. For the rest it is the nervous tension and gnawing anguish involved for a person who almost heroically assumes a burden of responsibility for the lives of others, not only in caring for her sick sister, but also—and ultimately more crippling—in acting as referee and seeking some sort of reconciliation or truce between her wrangling parents. When at one point in Act II Toni seeks to restrain her drunken father from disturbing Linchen, his reaction is merely one of mockery and anger which almost spills over into physical violence. And such is the thanks she can generally expect for all her efforts to help. Thus, although sympathy compels one to attribute Toni's suffering for the most part to causes outside her, it must be stressed that these forces are principally human rather than hereditary or social in the normal sense.

As to the continuation of her suffering after the end of the play, one of the most depressing aspects of the whole work, the question of determinism, which again arises, must be decided in the light of what proves to be the most important "event" of the play, Toni's renunciation of possible escape with Wendt. Whether the early plays of Hauptmann end with a definite catastrophe or with a situation basically the same as before, the impression given is of men and women so conditioned by the circumstances of their life hitherto that they do not possess the mental or physical strength to win through and gain their ends or better their lot. In *Das Friedensfest* the inner conflicts of the Scholz family have become so ingrained in the various members that the will to reconciliation is eventually overtaken by the uncontrollable nature of the characters themselves. In *Einsame Menschen* Johannes Vockerat, out of tune with the inferior intellect of his wife and in rebellion against the narrow moral and religious climate of his home, is nevertheless still under the grip of these forces to the extent that he finds himself unable to make a clean break with them. And in *Die Weber* the fact that the last word on the revolt of the weavers indicates success still cannot hide its ultimate subsidence and the return to the *status quo* attested by history. Is Toni Selicke's failure to break free therefore also to be interpreted as an example of milieu eroding man's power to change his circumstances? Certainly there is evidence that Toni is a character without hope. And this pessimism, attributed by Wendt—with Toni's assent—to the general misery of the life she has been forced to lead (p. 32), may naturally be expected to cripple any plans for a better future. In fact, however, the authors have laid by far the greater emphasis on emotional ties and moral principle, making the matter truly one of decision and not of involuntary compulsion. The emotional ties are evident first from two pieces of mime placed at significant points in the play; for just as Act II ends with that tableau of Toni embracing her grief-stricken father, while Wendt opens the door and enters, so Act III opens with the picture of Selicke sitting by Linchen's bed mourning, while Toni stands to one side, embracing this time her mother. At the same time, leaving aside the question of whether blood is really thicker than water, there is reason to suspect that Toni's response to her parents derives more from pity than from real love. Consider, for example, the following passage from the final act :

> TONI. And even if they were *bad!* . . . But they're so good! Both of them! I'm so fond of them! . . .
>
> WENDT (*quietly; simply noting the fact, not reproachfully*). Yes! More than you are of me! . . .
>
> TONI. Oh, but you're so much happier!
>
> WENDT. Happier? Me?!
>
> TONI. Yes, you! You! . . . You're still young; you still have a lot before you! . . . But they've nothing more at all in the world! Nothing at all! . . . (pp. 58–59)

As to moral principle, probably the most significant single factor, her sense of obligation emerges clearly from the frequency with which the verb "dürfen" appears in Toni's argument, and from the way in which she gradually comes to see a future life with Wendt as lacking complete happiness, because of the constant torment—of conscience, one assumes (p. 59). In a genuinely deterministic scheme of things there can be no heroes, only passive victims, since the characters have no real say in what happens to them. In *Die Familie Selicke,* on the other hand, Toni makes a conscious sacrifice of personal happiness to moral duty, thereby stealing much of the limelight and almost turning herself into the heroine of a piece which is essentially a family affair. Moreover in deliberately turning her back on the possibility of happiness with Wendt she is falling into the same trap as Mrs. Alving in Ibsen's *Ghosts,* of whom it has been said that "she, the most dutiful of persons, is guilty of dereliction of the most important duty of all : to herself".[16]

Selicke too shares in the suffering. It is all too easy to dismiss him simply as the villain of the piece, utterly worthless and deserving no sympathy. At bottom, however, he is shown to be a man with a heart. In his clumsy, noisy, befuddled way he has genuine affection for Linchen, and when he wakes up from his drunken sleep to learn that she is dead, he collapses in grief. But his suffering is more than just grief. Selicke is a man deeply disappointed with life, particularly his marriage. In his eyes it has simply brought him a wife with no intelligence, no enterprise and no understanding for him, a woman capable only of complaining and spoiling the children. Although it is not stated explicitly, one wonders whether all this may not have been the cause of his drinking. Drunkenness of course was by no means uncommon in plays of the Naturalist period. Audiences at the *Freie Bühne* had already witnessed outstanding examples in Tolstoy's *Power of Darkness* and Hauptmann's *Vor Sonnenaufgang*. In the former case, however, the causes were seen as social and moral—drunkenness was one form of corruption by money—and in the latter they were largely hereditary. Here, on the other hand, the reasons are personal and private. Again, Selicke's assertion that he loves all his family, even his wife, need not be rejected because of what we hear of the beatings he gives her, for it is corroborated by such a close witness as Toni herself (pp. 49 and 58). Certainly, Selicke's shortcomings should not be white-washed, but at the same time his bitter disillusionment must be weighed in the balance, since it drives him to worse than drink—to the point where he can say :

(*In a hollow voice, stares in front of him.*) I'll string you—all up! All of you! . . . An' then—I'll shoot myself—dead! . . . (pp. 45–46)

Of the whole family, however, it is Frau Selicke on whom the weight of suffering falls most heavily. And this is true even allowing for her more complaining nature. The first speech in the entire play is her untranslatable sigh, "Ach Gott, ja!" The very same words are virtually the last we hear her speak. And in between they recur many times.[12] They as much as anything express the depth of her weariness with life. Its causes, however, are various. On the most basic level there are, first, the material problem of poverty, which the housewife naturally experiences most directly, and then the physical fact of pain, for Frau Selicke has some unspecified complaint in her foot. More important and destructive, however, are the anxiety and nervous tension of which her day-to-day life is constituted. The anxiety concerns her husband, whom she can see gradually making a wreck of his life, as well as her sick daughter, Linchen, who is slowly dying before her eyes. As a mother she knows she can do nothing to help the child. Kopelke is no more

than a silly, useless quack, but he is all she can afford; and in a
pathetic attempt to compensate for her own fundamental helplessness she resorts to such futile substitute comforts for her daughter
as soft pillows and hypocoristic diminutives ("Linchen", "Herz-
chen", "Puttchen", "Schäfchen", "Mäuschen", etc.) This use of
pet forms is strongly reminiscent of Frau Vockerat in Hauptmann's
Einsame Menschen. Behind it one senses both the inability to
cope with the incomprehensible and grim realities of life and the
desire to protect others from an open, adult awareness of them.
From here it is only a short step to the suppression of truth and
the self-deception that go on in *A Doll's House*. But for Frau Selicke
there is also the nervous tension produced by the continual bickering of her two sons, Albert and Walter, who do indeed seem to be
spoilt children, the former full of supercilious *ennui*, the latter
whining selfishly, and by the conduct of her husband, whose lateness
she complains of, but whose actual arrival she fears so much that
her first instinct is to run away. The physical results of all this
are evident from the opening stage-direction, which describes her,
a woman presumably in her forties, as "rather elderly and care-
worn", but it is once again the psychological consequences that
prove the more cruel. For although she knows in her heart that it
would be best to control herself and adopt a more conciliatory tone
towards her husband, she no longer has the mental power to do
this (p. 22); and her responses to life have become so blunted
that apart from Linchen, on whom all her interest is now focused,
she has ceased to care about anything (p. 41). This is precisely the
stage reached by Amalie, the wife of the tragic actor passé in
Papa Hamlet; and it is a most unhappy stage, which necessarily
precludes an improvement in the situation; human will-power
has been eroded.

When one considers Selicke and his wife in relation to each
other, an immediate obstacle appears to the passing of any judgement; the lack of valid, objective terms of reference. Each partner
complains and accuses the other of being the cause of his or her
wretched plight. But who is right? Or is there truth on both sides?
These are questions to which the play gives no clear answer. What
it does show, however, is that the Selicke's are caught up in what
one might call a vicious circle if it were not part of a downward
spiral : the husband is disappointed with the woman he has married
and with what he regards as her mismanagement of the home;
consequently he spends time away from home, drinking; this,
together with the attendant reduction in housekeeping money, dis-
tresses the wife and causes her to complain; which in turn further
alienates the husband and makes him rely on alcohol even more;
and so on and so on. This is an oversimplification of the situation,

and the starting point may seem arbitrary, but taken as a whole, it is a reasonably accurate picture of the basic links in this inseverable chain of circumstances. Even when, after the death of Linchen, Frau Selicke makes the first conciliatory gesture towards her husband, the attempted "new beginning" fails, and for reasons not only of personal deficiency, but also of circumstance outside the characters' control. Selicke's sole response to his wife's suggestion is what the stage direction calls "a dead, expressionless gaze". And the probable cause is not so much a general blunting of his sympathetic responses after years of wrangling as quite simply that his grief at Linchen's death has so dazed him that he is not properly aware of the world around him and therefore incapable of responding to anything. His silence, however, is enough to turn his wife against him once more making her unduly suspicious of his attitude; and her words express that profound pessimism so common in German Naturalism, that despair over future improvement:

> FRAU SELICKE. No! No! He'll *never* change; In that stare . . . the way he looked at me . . . I could read quite clearly: if only it had been *you!* . . . Oh, and I'd *gladly* make way for him! God only knows! . . . *So gladly!* (p. 55).

The fundamental mistake of the Selicke's is a thing of the past: the fact that they got married in the first place. Although one hesitates to compare the situation with that of Hauptmann's *Einsame Menschen,* where the intellectual gulf between man and wife stands at the centre of the action and is therefore much more clearly delineated, there are indications of a discrepancy of outlook as well as intellect in *Die Familie Selicke*—the plaster busts of Goethe and Schiller are doubtless the husband's—and these are confirmed by the analogy of the prose sketch *Papa Hamlet,* which has so many other elements in common with the play and where there is also a world of difference between the main character, with his literary pretensions, and his slovenly wife, between the ideal and the real world. In both *Einsame Menschen* and *Die Familie Selicke* the authors do not imply a criticism of any social conventions which might have led to the mismatch—as, for example, Fontane does in his *Effi Briest* and Ibsen does in his *Ghosts.* Instead they take the fact for granted and then show how the marriage has become a prison.

So much for the most interesting members of the Selicke family. But the theme of suffering also involves the two "outsiders" in the play, the old quack Kopelke and the theology student Wendt. The former knows the struggle for existence from first-hand experience and regards his whole life as a failure. But the interesting thing is that, when he speaks of the causes, his words sound like a piece of uncultivated Naturalist propaganda :

> KOPELKE. Yes! If a feller's always got lots o' money, yer know, then things are all right! Yes, the old spondulics! . . . Take me, for example! I was no duffer as a lad! I was always first in school! Take my word for it! . . . But it was circumstances, yer know! circumstances! No good, it wasn't! The ole man 'ad me become a cobbler! . . . Mind you, cobblin's gone to the dogs these days as well! Them ole factories, yer know! The ole factories ruin the little man! . . . (p. 16).

In these words are crystallized some of the most important ideas of the age—the economic factors governing man's personal progress, the social problems of mass industrialization, the decline of the artisan, with even a hint of man's alienation from his labour. And in these words Kopelke is speaking for thousands of others, especially in the big new cities of Wilhelminian Germany, where the prevailing economic and social conditions pushed them to the disreputable fringes of society. For him it meant quack-medicine; for a woman, like some in Paul Ernst's *Im Chambre Séparée* (1896), it might well have been prostitution. Nevertheless, for all that he appears as a representative spokesman of German Naturalism as a whole, Kopelke is still a minor figure in the play, whose experiences are not really shared by the Selicke family.

Wendt's case is interesting for different reasons. His suffering is more of a mental or spiritual kind; he is a man whose ideals have been shattered and who has lost his faith in God and man—a grave situation indeed for a man about to enter the ministry. The cause appears to lie in the social and moral degeneracy of the times. At the beginning of his studies he was full of hope and vigour, but having come to the metropolis and seen its terrible misery and poverty, he has suffered spiritual atrophy. Here, even more than in Linchen's pathetic dream of an idyllic life at her uncle's, the authors touch on one of the favourite themes of German Naturalism : the contrast between town and country. For it is only in a village setting, surrounded by luxuriant nature, that he can imagine himself assuming his rôle as pastor to God's people.

> Round about us a big, high wall, and we shall live inside, the two of us, quite shut off from the world, but without hatred, and that's the main thing (p. 31).

These words, taken from the scene in which Wendt paints a picture of his idyll for Toni, not only contain an uncanny echo of part of Goethe's poem *An den Mond* (*circa* 1776),[13] as though Wendt had unconsciously resorted to a poetic model for his ideal, but also anticipate closely the ideal of the city-hater, Johannes Vockerat, in *Einsame Menschen* : an extensive park surrounded by a high wall.[14] In Wendt's idyllic picture, however, there is the human element too, in the shape of Toni herself. And like the picture as a whole it corresponds to some deficiency in his present world, to the other important source of his spiritual suffering disillusionment with human beings as he has experienced them in the capital city of Berlin. Like Kopelke his image of man—based not on his own self but on what he has observed in others—is thoroughly deterministic. On the other hand, he sees the forces that control man not so much outside as inside him; they are those ungovernable urges which brutalize him and thereby rob him of his true humanity :

> Men are no longer what I considered them to be! They are selfish! Brutally selfish! They are nothing more than animals, artful beasts, a walking collection of instincts, which fight each other, blindly assert themselves to the destruction of each other! All the beautiful ideas they've dreamed up, about God, love and . . . bah! it's all nonsense! Nonsense! You . . . you just grope your way along. You're just a machine! (p. 29)

If Wendt is not exactly speaking *for* thousands of others, he is at least speaking *of* them. This picture of man stripped of personality and dignity, a creature of flesh and blood though scarcely of spirit, showing signs of motion but not of advance—this picture is common to much of Naturalism and persists, with variations of degree and emphasis, even into Expressionism and beyond. That Wendt speaks of the dehumanizing forces within man should not be allowed to obscure the fact that his disillusionment has come only with his move to Berlin. In other words, one may assume that it is the evil social influences of the big city that have let loose within man those ungovernable, brutalizing forces which now complete his degradation. As was the case with Kopelke's lament, however, Wendt's depiction of man is not central to the play; it appears only marginally relevant to the plight of the Selicke family as a whole.

The only bright spot on his horizon has been Toni, who is a source of spiritual refreshment—just as Helene Hoffman is to the enervated reformer Alfred Loth in *Vor Sonnenaufgang*—and she is ultimately the basis of what belief he can muster in the goodness of life. For him, moreover, religious faith is inextricably bound up with this. For those like old Hilse in *Die Weber* religion is basically a hope that compensates for the deprivations of life, a force that grows stronger rather than weaker the more wretched life becomes. But it is the very opposite in the case of Wendt, who treads dan-

gerous theological ground in making the existence of God depend
on pleasant natural surroundings and the love of a good companion. In this he displays the same sort of immaturity as Schiller's
Don Carlos, whose interest in the cause of freedom is initially sustained only by the love of the queen.

> The poor folks!—The poor folks!—Gawd! Wot I always say
> is : why on earth does there 'ave to be so much misery in the
> world? (p. 64).

These words, spoken by Old Kopelke near the end of the play,
bring us back again to the problem of suffering and its causes;
the question they pose is not simply the concern of one character,
but of the whole play, indeed of Naturalism itself. And to assess
the rôle of determinism is of great importance, for it radically
affects the tragic possibilities of the play. George Steiner has argued
convincingly that where the dramatic conflict can be resolved
through technical or social means, real tragedy is impossible, since
it should be irreparable, and that where, following the tradition of
Rousseauist belief, man is regarded as not naturally evil, but rather
as corrupted by society or environment and therefore not wholly
responsible, real tragedy is again ruled out, since the tragic per-
sonage cannot evade responsibility.[15] The situation in *Die Familie
Selicke* expounded above is by no means so thoroughly deterministic as to rule out tragedy on either of those scores. The
material hardship which undoubtedly exists in the play is not the
main cause of the suffering we witness. Man himself rather—
either as an individual or in his relations to others—emerges as
the most significant contributor to his own and other people's misfortune. But this is not to say that he is free and therefore entirely
to blame. The parents, who are after all the two characters at the
heart of the trouble, are prisoners, first of a marriage that is now
merely a constant source of friction and then of their own selves,
blunted by years of disillusionment or anxiety, so that they no
longer have the power to better the situation. The other members
of the family are embroiled in this and are either influenced by
the general atmosphere in such a way that they simply add their
own share to the volume of argument and complaint (Albert and
Walter) or else seek in vain to combat it (Toni). It is to the credit
of Holz and Schlaf that they avoid the crudely deterministic
approach—the sort of approach that threatens, for example, Hauptmann's *Vor Sonnenaufgang,* where Loth's inflexible belief in the
laws of heredity almost reduces him to cardboard. In this respect
their presentation is much more subtle, showing characters who
are guilty and yet not guilty, responsible but not completely so.
Once the original mistake of marriage has been made, the rest

follows naturally, almost mechanically. Thus, with only a few minor adjustments, what Zola wrote of his *Thérèse Raquin* might well be applied to *Die Familie Selicke* :

> . . . there was no longer a logic of actions but a logic of feelings and sentiments, and the dénouement became an arithmetical solution to the problem set.[16]

In a sense, therefore, the play represents a marriage of old and new, sharing something of the inevitability common to ancient tragedy and the scientific objectivity characteristic of the modern age. If *Die Familie Selicke* nevertheless falls short of the authentic tragic effect, it is because the emotions aroused are pathetic rather than shattering and because, being basically concerned with a static situation, it cannot release its tensions in a catastrophe. For this reason the term "schleichende Tragik" has aptly been applied to the play.[17]

III

This concept of "lingering tragedy" brings us to a most important formal aspect of *Die Familie Selicke*. For here what we normally understand by "plot" is reduced to a minimum and what we get instead is the presentation of a more or less static situation or of characters in a static setting.

> The characters on the stage are not there because of the plot, but rather the plot is there because of the characters. The plot is not the end but the means. Not the primary but the secondary consideration. In other words : the law of the theatre is not plot but the presentation of characters.[18]

This statement, delivered in the manner of a prophet transmitting divine revelation to an amazed audience, occurs in an article by Holz entitled *Pro Domo* (1897). It does not exclude the possibility of plot, but merely assigns a subservient rôle to it. Since life itself, however, does not proceed in a series of "plots", each with a clearly definable beginning and end, then an artistic form that seeks to do full justice to life and reproduce it faithfully will inevitably eschew action in the conventional sense and endeavour to convey something of the arbitrariness of events, even the banality of life. In this respect *Die Familie Selicke* is much more "consistent" in its Realism than other plays of the period, German or otherwise. Even though the main concern of so many of Ibsen's mature plays, for example, is the exposing of an essentially past situation, of characters who have made a mess of their lives, his analytical technique concentrates the action on a time of present crisis and then rounds it off in some conclusive way—often death—so that the same crisis and hence the unmasking of the past can never occur again.[19] And although Hauptmann's *Vor Sonnenaufgang*, with its sub-title "a social drama", can be interpreted as fundamentally the portrayal of a representative situation—the evil social consequences of newly-acquired wealth—a love interest creeps in which eventually so dominates the play that Helene, when abandoned by the Socialist-reformer Loth, becomes almost a tragic heroine and her suicide marks a definite conclusion, after which things can never be the same again.[20] By comparison *Die Familie Selicke* does genuinely seem plotless. Only three significant "events" occur in the play : the arrival home of Selicke, drunk; the death of the younger daughter, Linchen (which is not an act, it will be noted, but a matter to be endured passively); and the decision of the elder daughter, Toni, to remain with her family and renounce the possibility of escape and happiness with Wendt. Nor is there much sense of dynamic progression from one event to the other, so that they can scarcely be regarded as stages in one plot. Moreover, not one of them brings about a really new state of affairs. Selicke regularly comes home drunk. Linchen's death may have put an end to her suffering, but for the rest of the family it means only the aggravation of an already depressing situation, for although there is now one cause less for anxiety, her illness did nevertheless provide a focus of attention and care; for both parents she seems to have been the only reason for living. Thus, during the lull that follows the death Toni remarks sadly :

That won't last long! At the next opportunity—it will be—just like before, and—and much—much—worse . . . (p. 58).

As to Toni's decision to stay, it is of course the very denial of new possibilities. By the end of the play then, nothing fundamentally has changed : the family has fewer members and there will have to be a new lodger, but the bickering will go on, Selicke will continue to come home drunk, and Toni will still try to keep the peace. Indeed it is this, the thought that the spectacle we have just witnessed will be protracted endlessly after the curtain has fallen, that makes *Die Familie Selicke* such a depressing work. The novelist Theodor Fontane, reviewing the first performance of the play for the *Vossische Zeitung*, spoke of its form in terms of "virgin soil" and "the parting of the ways".[21] Although he did not define the nature of its originality, one senses that what he had in mind was precisely this concentration on situation and this renunciation of plot in the normal sense.

But while situations continue, plays must come to an end. Total reproduction of reality is of course impossible; even the dramatist's artistic means are ultimately deficient. Nevertheless Holz and

Schlaf have not only made the inevitable concession to choice in setting a final limit to their play; they have further divided it into acts, ignoring, as it were, that part of total reality, however trivial, which occurs in the gaps. Although perhaps obvious, this point is worth making, because it underlines how far from realization the Naturalist's aim of reproducing the whole of Nature was bound to be in practice. More interesting, however, is the question of how the two authors determine their division into acts, at what point they choose to let the curtain fall. Act I serves primarily to set the scene in the Selicke household. But it also projects possibilities into the future, by raising certain expectations, dreaded or desired : whether Linchen will die; when the father will return; whether he will be drunk again; whether Toni will be able to marry Wendt. This last matter occupies quite a long section at theend of the act, and the curtain comes down on a note quiet optimism, as Toni allows herself to contemplate the possibility of future happiness as the wife of a country clergyman. Act II is for the most part a continuation of what the first act has led us to expect, but it does also bring the fulfilment of two of the expectations raised, the drunken return of Selicke and the death of Linchen. It is the immediate results of the latter that provide the occasion for bringing the act to a close. The father breaks down in grief, and as Toni puts a consoling arm round his neck, Wendt appears at the door. With that the act leaves us. Act III is centred on the important scene between the two young lovers, which contains Toni's difficult decision to remain with her family; and the final curtain comes as Wendt actually takes his leave of the Selicke's. It is hard to discern one governing principle at work in all three acts. One could say that each curtain marks the arrival of a new situation, but in fact the first is no more than a temporary illusion, while the others involve enduring conditions. The most noteworthy feature is one shared by the endings of the second and third acts : namely, the pictorial quality. Here, the moment is chosen not for its dramatic potential, but because it allows the authors to group the characters into *tableaux vivants*. Linchen's death could never be a moment of tension released, because at no time is there any real hope of recovery and the poor girl has shown little sign of life as it is. In any case, however, the act does not finish immediately with the announcement of the death, but, with increasing emphasis on mime, pursues the reaction of the other members of the family, until Wendt comes into the room and one pictures the characters becoming frozen into a decorative pose. Similarly at the end of Act III the emotional temperature of the scene between Toni and Wendt is allowed to cool off by means of intrusions by Kopelke and then Frau Selicke. When the physical

leave-taking comes therefore, the spiritual struggle involved for
the lovers is already past, the matter decided and accepted. What
is left is a scene which again dissolves largely into mime, until
the curtain falls on another tableau.

> WENDT (*seizing her hand*). Thank you, Frau Selicke! Thank
> you! For—everything! (*Pressing her hand.*) Farewell! (*To
> Toni, who still has one arm clasped round her mother, seizing
> her hand also.*) Farewell! I . . . (*Toni has sunk down on to
> her mother's breast and cannot answer him. Her whole body
> is trembling from her sobs.*)
> WENDT (*bending suddenly over her hand, which he has still
> not released, and kissing it*). I'll come back! . . .

Both endings recall those sentimental Victorian genre paintings
and photographs, with titles like "Waiting for a letter" or "The
Soldier's return", which sought to capture moments of pathos in
a visual form. And this is not really surprising when one remembers
that, by concentrating on an essentially static situation within the
confines of one single room, *Die Familie Selicke* has in many
respects invaded the province of painting. The ending of Act I
on the other hand has no special pictorial quality; the curtain
falls at what really seems to be a random moment during the
temporary happiness of the two lovers.

The point of all this is that it again illustrates how difficult
it was in practice to give even the illusion of not having selected
one's material, which is strictly speaking a form of artificial tam-
pering with reality. The same problem presents itself in the various
short prose sketches which Holz and Schlaf wrote a short time
before *Die Familie Selicke*. Of these only *Die Papierne Passion*,
the portrayal of various characters in rather squalid Berlin
surroundings, conveys a real sense of random presentation. Indeed,
the title of the piece is symptomatic of its casual, seemingly un-
contrived manner of presentation. It refers to a silhouette of
Christ's Passion cut out of paper, which appears only towards
the end of the narrative in a completely inessential way.

A second interesting question of choice arises in connection with
the timing of the material presented in *Die Familie Selicke*. For
the dramatist concerned not with a definable plot but with a static
situation one would expect the time chosen to be immaterial, since
his subject-matter applies whatever the day. Holz and Schlaf,
however, have set their play on one very special day of the
calendar, Christmas Eve. Although one can only guess at their
reasons, it is clear that there is no necessary and inevitable connection between the three "events" of the play and this particular
day. The sole purpose behind the choice—as no doubt in *Die*

Papierne Passion, which also takes place on Christmas Eve—is probably no more than to squeeze that extra bit of pathos out of what happens, to make the spectators say to themselves, "How awful of the father to come home drunk on Christmas Eve! How sad to lose a child at Christmas of all times!" The point becomes clearer when one sets *Die Familie Selicke* beside Hauptmann's *Das Friedensfest,* first performed at the *Freie Bühne* only a couple of months later. Once again the time is Christmas Eve, but here it is essential to what happens. Without the opportunity it provides of a family reunion, the abortive attempt at reconciliation, which leads to the death of the father of this torn family, would not be possible.

If a note of criticism can be detected in the above remarks, this is largely because of the theoretical background against which they are made. A manner of reproduction which is completely "involuntary"[22] is impossible; selection cannot ultimately be avoided. And what the authors have done is to replace one kind of selection—based on the presentation of a linear plot—by another, determined by pictorial or emotional ends.

IV

Behind all these questions of choice lies the Naturalists' basic concern for truth; and this in turn brings us down to one of their major preoccupations: the development of adequate techniques for the reproduction of truth or "nature". Hence the second part of Holz's famous dictum stresses the importance of the means available to the artist and his ability to make proper use of them:

Art has the tendency to become nature again. *It will do so in proportion to the limitations of the reproductive means and the way in which these are handled.*

For the dramatist of German Naturalism one important step was therefore to adopt the recent achievements of the famous Meininger theatre company in matters of realistic stage setting—hitherto employed largely in historical plays—for his plays about modern life.[23] Together with the general increase of interest in the material circumstances of human life, this resulted in a tendency to long and detailed stage-directions, which, however, characterized the native German productions much more than the foreign plays being presented side by side with them. This is not to say that all plays had previously been performed in a sort of vacuum, but only that what the playwright had formerly left to the imagination of the stage designer he now took largely into his own hands, becoming almost microscopically thorough in his new task. The detail into which Holz and Schlaf have gone in setting the scene at the beginning of *Die Familie Selicke* is as great as any we are likely to find. They specify among other things the colour of a lampshade, the pattern on the sofa and the material from which the curtains are made; they call for lithographs of the Kaiser and Bismarck in only a *finger's breadth* of gold frame, tiny plaster busts of Schiller and Goethe, and a *steel* engraving by a particular artist depicting a particular scene from one of Goethe's novels. Unlike the stage-direction at the beginning of Act III of Hauptmann's *Die Weber* this opening description does not have the power to represent the physical milieu which almost palpably shapes the lives of those trapped within it—the uncertain rôle allotted to determinism in the play necessarily precludes that— and unlike the incongruous mixture of biblical paintings and portraits of Darwin and Haeckel that decorates the living-room of Johannes Vockerat in *Einsame Menschen* the assorted bric-à-brac here cannot serve as a visible and pointed symbol of a definite problem. Nevertheless the stage-direction as a whole does provide a plausible material setting, which aids characterization—it conjures up a world of sentimentality, patriotism and popular culture as well as of modest financial means—and to some extent explains the characters and their behaviour. Perhaps some of the details are too small to be perceptible to members of an audience,[24] but they do make sense to a reader. Indeed, one sometimes suspects that the authors had a reading public at least at the back of their minds (as when they speak of the "*well-known* steel-engraving by Kaulbach entitled 'Lotte cutting bread' "), which is hardly surprising when one remembers how thin the border-line is between their prose sketches, notably *Die papierne Passion,* and their play.

This interest in details of setting also extends quite naturally to costume and general physical appearance. Here the concern is not so much for accuracy in local colour as for making external appearance express character or situation. Thus, the stage-direction which describes Toni on her first appearance as having, among other things, a simple, rather serious facial expression, a plain dark dress, a long, yellowish brown autumn coat, and black, knitted woollen gloves presents an immediate picture of her drab existence (p. 17; the description of Albert, with kid-gloves sticking out of his breast-pocket, a cigarette between his teeth, an eye-glass dangling round his neck, and hat and cane beside him on the chair, marks him off as something of a dandy and selfish at that, since his interest in outward show is set against a background of deprivation (p. 7); and the first picture we are given of Kandidat Wendt, with his delicate, pale features, his shortish black hair, simply combed back, and his dark but scrupulously clean clothes of a non-clerical cut—some of it reminiscent of the sectarian Gideon Franke in Fontane's *Irrungen, Wirrungen*—tells us much of what we need to know about him as a man (p. 12).

But, as Zola reiterates, setting and costume cannot be considered in isolation :

> Lifelike costumes look wrong if the sets, the diction, the plays themselves are not lifelike. They must all march in step along the naturalistic road . . . It follows that "theatre language", that language of booming sonority, is vanishing. We are moving towards simplicity, the exact word spoken without emphasis, quite naturally . . . to create living people you must give them to the public not merely in accurate dress and in the environments that have made them what they are, but with their individual ways of thinking and expressing themselves.[25]

To the spoken word Zola might also have added the language of gesture and facial expression. For in Naturalism this too was taken considerably more into the province of the dramatist, no longer a matter left to the discretion of the actor or producer. And it received as much detailed attention as setting and costume, being an additional means of revealing situation, character, feeling, and so on. Although in *Die Familie Selicke* it does not assume such a leading rôle as in Hauptmann's *Die Weber,* where it is often an inevitable consequence of the weavers' inarticulateness and where, as in his descriptions of physical appearance, the author sometimes seems to act as spokesman for the weavers in their plight, nevertheless Holz and Schlaf do devote great attention to appropriate and eloquent gesture. Adjectives and adverbs in particular lay down not only the visible manner of these gestures, but frequently also their mental or emotional content, so that again one suspects a reading of the play might be more likely to realize the authors' intentions than a performance in the theatre. There are times in the play when these carefully calculated gestures communicate more than the dialogue. Consider, for example, the following passage near the beginning of Act III, in which the stage directions convey vital information about the various attitudes of those involved :

> FRAU SELICKE. *They're* cheerful ! . . . (*She walks over to Selicke and lays her hand gently on his shoulder; in a pitying, trembling voice.*) Father ! . . . (*Selicke, his face in his hand, his elbows resting on his knees, brooding to himself, takes no notice of her.*) Father ! . . . Come along ! . . . Father ! . . . (*Her words turn to weeping.*)

SELICKE (*stirs himself; indistinctly, tenderly*). Linchen! . . .
My Linchen! . . . (*Suppresses a sob.*)

FRAU SELICKE (*leans her head against his shoulder and weeps*).
Father, come along! Come away from here! . . .

SELICKE. Linchen! . . . My Linchen! . . . Why *you?* (*Stares
in front of him.*)

FRAU SELICKE (*still in the same position*). Come on, father! . . .
From now on let's . . . make a real effort . . . Let's be sen-
sible . . . Things are going to be different with us now . . .
Eh, father?

SELICKE (*turns his face upwards and looks at her with a dead,
expressionless gaze. Frau Selicke stares at him anxiously for a
while and then straightens her back, putting the edge of her
apron to her eyes. Selicke, who has got ponderously to his
feet, leans over the bed and kisses the corpse. Softly, gently*).
Fare well! . . . Fare well, my sweet Linchen . . . You're
lucky! You're lucky! . . . (*Looks at the corpse a moment
longer, then stands upright and staggers, griefstricken, into
the closet, while Walter on the sofa begins to weep more
loudly and Albert, his face turned towards the window, blows
his nose loudly.*) (pp. 52–53)

As to the spoken dialogue, it is here that German Naturalism
made its most important technical innovation in the drama.
Foreign works performed at the *Freie Bühne,* such as Ibsen's *Ghosts*
or even Zola's *Thérèse Raquin,* for all their bold subject-matter,
sound polite by comparison. Linguistic crudities and, more
especially, dialect and colloquialism come to play an important
rôle, and some playwrights are able to create more or less subtle
distinctions between the various social classes or types, as for
example between "Vorderhaus" and "Hinterhaus" in Sudermann's
Die Ehre. Although the world of *Die Familie Selicke* is basically
restricted to one class, Holz and Schlaf still achieve a certain
gradation in the use of the Berlin dialect; from Frau Selicke, to
Albert, to Old Kopelke the dialect becomes progressively more
marked. But crudity and dialect are not all; nor are they entirely
new. Examples of the former could have been cited from plays
of the *Sturm und Drang* period, while the then newly rediscovered
Georg Büchner could have provided a model or at least a stimulus
for the latter. The more thorough-going linguistic innovation lies
rather in the attempt to record human speech in all its hesitations
and stutterings, its incompleteness and even its inarticulate noises.
Thus Holz could speak of

those little gestures of liberty and prudishness, which are beyond
the reach of all syntax, logic and grammar and in which the

growth and formation of an idea, the unconscious reaction to the opinions and gestures of one's interlocutor, the anticipation of objections, *captatio benevolentiæ* and all those slight stirrings of the spirit find their expression.[26]

But this attempt was by no means made by all. Indeed, in the theatrical world, it is to *Die Familie Selicke* and some of the earlier plays of Hauptmann, who after all dedicated the first edition of his *Vor Sonnenaufgang* to "the consistent Realist, Bjarne P. Holmsen" (alias Holz and Schlaf), that we must look for the clearest and most extensive application of this principle. Even here of course the realistic principle is not pushed to its logical conclusion; the authors are still selective, using hesitations, grunts, and so on to express feelings and thoughts, not merely as symptoms of mental or speech deficiencies.[27] Nevertheless they clearly go further, are more "consistent" in their realism, than even their contemporaries; and perhaps they go as far as is possible in practice.

"Sekundenstil" is the term often applied to this minute recording of human speech, but the word also covers more. It describes in fact the whole detailed implementation of the wider principle of presenting a "slice of life" and involves, besides the careful attention to gesture and speech mentioned above, a minute-by-minute record of the other sounds to be heard and of life's many changing visual impressions. In his story *Bahnwärter Thiel* Hauptmann gives a detailed aural and visual account of an approaching train, but this is hardly "Sekundenstil". It is altogether too much of a selected highlight, rendered imaginatively and with a keen awareness of the poetic possibilities of the steam locomotive. More faithful "Sekundenstil", by contrast, acknowledges that the sound effects of "real" life are much more haphazard and for the most part more trivial. Nobody can deny that in many of their prose sketches Holz and Schlaf have done justice to the implications of this. The only trouble is that in seeking to pay proper respect to the humdrum truth of life they have often fallen over backwards and exaggerated the trivia. At times one is made to feel that life consists in little more than cats miaowing, flies buzzing, people snoring, or furniture creaking—to say nothing of woodworms nibbling! The result is therefore still a distortion of life, only a less interesting one. In this respect *Die Familie Selicke* is again much more moderate. Perhaps because it is not a narrative, which can use a single consciousness, that of the narrator or of one of the characters, to receive the impressions of the world around, those seemingly arbitrary sound and visual effects are reduced to a minimum. At the beginning of Act I we are told that the clock is ticking, at the beginning of Act II we are told that moonlight is falling through the window, and once or twice Old Kopelke blows his nose for no very significant reason. But that is as far as it goes. Elsewhere the sounds that do occur have a definite dramatic point : a noise off-stage in the kitchen marks the return of the long-awaited Selicke; his snoring and panting as Linchen lies dying emphasize his clumsy thoughtlessness; and the shouting and carolling of children outside on Christmas morning form a telling contrast to the silent mourning in the Selicke household. This is not the work of an impersonal tape-recorder, but of two conscious artists, moulding reality in a meaningful way.

Implicit in much of our discussion about *Die Familie Selicke* has been a picture of the artist as a passive observer, almost a receptacle, who regurgitates indiscriminately the data observed. Two things, however, need to be stressed about this. The first is that, even as an ideal, this view was never subscribed to by all German Naturalists. There were always those who firmly upheld the individuality of the artist. In his foreword to the first issue of the periodical *Freie Bühne für modernes Leben,* for example, Otto Brahm advocated Truth, certainly, but

> not objective truth, which eludes the man involved in struggle, but individual truth, freely created from man's deepest conviction and freely expressed—the truth of the individual spirit who has nothing to gloss over and nothing to hush up.[28]

And the second thing is that for those who upheld this image of the artist it was still only a theoretical goal, unattainable in practice, so that when Holz set up his famous formula, "Art= nature—x", he might well have included in the factor x the element of selection too. Nevertheless for him and those of a like mind the tendency towards the submergence of the artistic personality—in appearance if not in fact—still remains. And it is no accident that in his tragedy *Sonnenfinsternis* (1908) the sculptor, Lipsius, succeeds in creating a perfect work of art only by burying himself in his object and extinguishing his own personality; Naturalist theory is here enacted in personal terms.[29] As to *Die Familie Selicke,* the very fact that there are two authors is some concession to the principle, for each must inevitably surrender something of his autonomy. Examples of this are rare in literature, although, significantly, in the world of the natural sciences, where the empirical approach counts for much, it is relatively common to see papers published under the name of two or three authors. It would be interesting to find substantiation of such an empirical, "scientific" approach in the collaboration of Holz and Schlaf too, but where they do talk about the subject, in the foreword to *Papa Hamlet,* they give it a mystical air or imply a kind of telepathy:

Our methods of perceiving and of reproducing what we perceive have gradually become completely identical. There are passages, even whole pages, in *Papa Hamlet* where we would find it absolutely impossible now to say whether the original idea belongs to one, the subsequent form to the other, or *vice versa.* Often the same words of the same sentence flowed into our pens simultaneously; often one would complete a sentence just begun by the other.[30]

And the matter is not at all clarified by the way in which the two collaborators later wrangled about the authorship, each claiming the credit for himself.[31] Yet it is interesting to note that when Holz once learned of a reported remark by Schlaf to the effect that their collaboration had nothing to do with the former's literary theories, he did not simply reject the idea; instead, while still maintaining that he was the moving force in technical matters, he interpreted Schlaf (charitably?) as meaning that their book was a purely scientific work and would perhaps have arisen even if their particular collaboration had never taken place.[32] Denial of the artist's individual genius could hardly go further than that!

As we have seen, then, the artist's activities of selecting and moulding could never be eliminated in practice. Even so those hackneyed terms, "photographic reproduction of reality" and "a slice of life", may still prove useful if it is remembered that focus, exposure and camera-angle have a great influence on the finished photograph and that a cake at least can always be cut so as to have a cherry on every slice.

V

Any movement, literary or otherwise, which takes its starting point in opposition to prevailing attitudes runs the risk of exaggeration. For in seeking to show the errors of what it opposes and both the difference and rightness of its own position, it may overstate its case and thus distort the truth. This certainly holds good for Naturalism, which quite rightly reacted against the prevailing literary habit of ignoring or glossing over the pressing social problems and ugly realities of contemporary life, but which then frequently went too far in exposing the sordid and sensational by turning a blind eye to what was still there of beauty and goodness.[33] Accordingly, the audiences of the *Freie Bühne* were not spared their full share of grinding poverty and violent argument, drunkenness, lechery, adultery, prostitution, incest, and murder. There could certainly be no complaint that their playwrights had sought to conceal the truth, however grim. On the other hand, there was every reason to suspect that this was only a partial or even distorted truth; in many cases the picture presented by Naturalism was anything but "natural". Against such a background *Die Familie Selicke* once more appears a moderate work : it has none of those more sensational vices except drunkenness, which even then emerges as a matter for pity almost as much as for reproach. Almost the first thing that Frau Selicke does is to blow her nose. This act, in itself insignificant, is nevertheless fairly indicative of the humdrum level of squalor to be found in the play—domestic squabbles, the stresses and anxieties of the poor but not destitute. It is hardly the material of which headlines are made, even in the most sterile of provincial newspapers; it is not lurid but a drab grey. If the result of this is at times dull, it at least approximates to a more widespread truth in a way which is barred to a play such as *Vor Sonnenaufgang*. So much so, indeed, that Theodor Fontane, a sympathetic reviewer of the first performance, doubted whether a play like *Die Familie Selicke* could ever be repeated, because the public was unlikely to pay the price of admission a second time to see on the stage what it could witness every day for nothing on its own back doorstep.[34]

At the same time Holz and Schlaf have had the insight to relieve the general gloom of their play with some of those brief touches of humour that undoubtedly belong to life. There is, for example, the character of Old Kopelke, a sponger and a quack, but a man without pretensions, who drops repeated hints that he would like some coffee, only to leave before Frau Selicke has finished preparing it. One remembers also the passage where Frau Selicke looks for her glasses and then has them discovered for her on the end of her nose; and the perhaps unintentional comedy of the scene in which she beats a hasty retreat from her drunken husband despite the painful foot she has been complaining of. This is of course far removed from uproarious comedy, but even in its unremarkableness it is admirably suited to the everyday tenor of the whole play, which after all seeks basically to depict a representative slice of the life of one ordinary family.

Although, as a movement, German Naturalism did not last long, its influence as pioneer or irritant remained. And of course elements of the phenomenon Naturalism are still with us—as in the plays of Tennessee Williams and Arthur Miller. Is there therefore a real case for reviving a play like *Die Familie Selicke?* Certainly, in its basic situation, which captures the tragic possibilities of human beings caught in the threefold web of their own personalities, their relationships with others, and their social environment, its relevance has scarcely diminished. If one nevertheless hesitates to advocate a revival, it is largely because it takes its Naturalism so seriously and becomes such a good illustration of the extent to which the theories could be realized in practice. In shunning meretricious sensationalism so honestly and in paying such respect to the humdrum truth of life, it fails to sustain dramatic interest. The province of *Die Familie Selicke* has now been taken over by the film and television documentary, and perhaps one does well to leave it there.

NOTES

1. Cf. A. Holz, *Das Werk*, ed. Hans W. Fischer (Berlin, 1925), Vol. X, p. 189.
2. Wolfgang Kayser, "Zur Dramaturgie des naturalistischen Dramas", in: *Die Vortragsreise* (Bern, 1958), pp. 217–218.
3. Cf. G. Schulz, "Naturalism", in: *Periods in German Literature,* ea. J. M. Ritchie (London, 1966), p. 207.
3a. Details are given in Lee Baxandall, "The Naturalist Innovation on the German Stage: The *Freie Bühne* and its Influence", *Modern Drama,* Vol. V (1962–1963), p. 466.
4. Quoted in the preface to *Die Familie Selicke* as it appeared in the volume *Neue Gleise* (Berlin, 1892), p. 223.
5. Kayser, op. cit., pp. 220–221.
6. Quoted by Julius Röhr in his essay "Das Milieu in Kunst und Wissenschaft", in: *Die Deutsche Literatur: Texte und Zeugnisse. 20. Jahrhundert,* ed. Walther Killy (Munich, 1967), p. 71.
7. From his book *Die naturwissenschaftlichen Grundlagen der Poesie: Prolegomena einer realistischen Aesthetik,* reproduced in extracts in: *Literarische Manifeste des Naturalismus: 1880–1892,* ed. Erich Ruprecht (Stuttgart, 1962), p. 91.
8. J. Röhr, loc. cit., p. 74.
9. Page references to the text of *Die Familie Selicke* apply to the Reclam edition, ed. Fritz Martini (Stuttgart, 1966).
10. One is also reminded of the consumptive Lieschen in Zuckmayer's *Der Hauptmann von Köpenick,* a more recent play, but set in and around the Berlin of only a few years later than *Die Familie Selicke.* As this pathetic figure lies dying, she too enjoys, together with the hero, a day-dream of eternal sunshine up on the *Riesengebirge,* the opposite of her dull, flat, impoverished life hitherto.
11. J. W. McFarlane, in his introduction to the Oxford Ibsen, Vol. V, p. 5. Wendt hints at this failing in Toni when he reminds her (p. 31): "And then, there's us too".
12. Frau Abendroth in *Die papierne Passion* is characterized by the self-same sigh.

13. Cf. especially the lines:

"Selig, wer sich vor der Welt
Ohne Haß verschließt".

14. Gerhart Hauptmann, *Sämtliche Werke* (Frankfurt/M.-Berlin, 1966). Vol. I, p. 189. It is worth noting in passing, however, that Holz at least could at other times describe himself without shame or disappointment as a "child of the metropolis" and find poetry and "life" there too. Cf. the poem "Frühling" from *Das Buch der Zeit,* quoted in *Deutsche Literatur in Entwicklungsreihen: Naturalismus,* ed. Walther Linden (Leipzig, 1936), pp. 85–90.

15. George Steiner, *The Death of Tragedy* (London, 1963), pp. 8 and 127–8.

16. Emile Zola, *Théâtre* (Paris, 1878), p. 10.

17. Humphrey Trevelyan in his introduction to the play, published in the series "Cambridge Plain Texts" (Cambridge, 1950), p. VI.

18. Holz, loc. cit., p. 224.

19. Cf. Peter Szondi, *Theorie des modernen Dramas,* "edition suhrkamp" (Frankfurt/M., 1959), pp. 22–31.

20. Cf. ibid., pp. 62–8.

21. Theodor Fontane, *Sämtliche Werke* (Munich, 1959), Vol. XXII/2, p. 732.

22. Cf. Kayser, op. cit., p. 216.

23. Cf. Brigitte Schatzky, "Stage Setting in Naturalist Drama", *German Life and Letters,* Vol. VIII (1954–1955), pp. 162–4.

24. Cf. ibid., p. 166.

25. From "Naturalism in the Theatre", translated by Albert Bermel, in: *The Theory of the Modern Stage: An Introduction to Modern Theatre and Drama,* ed. Eric Bentley, Penguin Books (1968), pp. 369–71.

26. Holz, loc. cit., p. 254.

27. Cf. Kayser, op. cit., pp. 218–19.

28. Quoted from *Die deutsche Literatur: Texte und Zeugnisse,* p. 65.

29. Cf. Wilhelm Emrich, "Arno Holz und die moderne Kunst", in: *Protest und Verheißung: Studien zur klassischen und modernen Dichtung* (Frankfurt, 1960), p. 159.

30. *Neue Gleise,* pp. 92–3.

31. Cf. Robert Reß, *Arno Holz und seine künstlerische, weltkulturelle Bedeutung* (Dresden, 1913), circa p. 146.

32. Letter to Reinhard Piper on 12 November 1897, in: Arno Holz, *Briefe* (Munich, 1948), p. 118.

33. The Hart brothers saw a similar danger in French Naturalism: "Historically the rise of French Naturalism is easy to comprehend; it has emerged from conscious resistance to Romanticism, to the falsity and bombast of Victor Hugo, Dumas, Sue, but the reaction is so strong that literature is in danger of being thrust directly into the opposite system and thereby in its turn producing new lies and, instead of bombast, insipidity". Quoted in *Literarische Manifeste des Naturalismus,* p. 31.

34. Fontane, loc. cit., p. 734.

BIBLIOGRAPHY

Lee Baxandall, "The Naturalist Innovation on the German Stage: The *Freie Bühne* and its Influence", *Modern Drama*, Vol. V (1962–1963), pp. 454–476.

Wilhelm Emrich, "Arno Holz und die moderne Kunst", in: *Protest und Verheißung: Studien zur klassischen und modernen Dichtung* (Frankfurt/M., 1960), pp. 155–168.

Siegfried Hoefert: *Das Drama des Naturalismus,* Sammlung Metzler (Stuttgart, 1968).

Wolfgang Kayser, "Zur Dramaturgie des naturalistishen Dramas", in: *Die Vortragsreise* (Bern, 1958), pp. 214–31.

Walther Killy (ed.), *Die deutsche Literatur; 20. Jahrhundert: Texte und Zeugnisse* 1880-1933 (Munich, 1967).

Walther Linden (ed.), *Deutsche Literatur in Entwicklungsreihen: Naturalismus* (Leipzig, 1936).

Ursula Münchow, *Deutscher Naturalismus* (Berlin: Akademie Verlag, 1968).

Erich Ruprecht (ed.), *Literarische Manifeste des Naturalismus*: 1880–1892 (Stuttgart, 1962).

Brigitte Schatzky, "Stage Setting in Naturalist Drama", *German Life and Letters,* Vol. VIII (1954–1955), pp. 161–170.

Gernot Schley, *Die Freie Bühne in Berlin. Der Vorläufer der Volksbühnenbewegung: Ein Beitrag zur Theatergeschichte in Deutschland* (Berlin, 1967).

Peter Szondi, *Theorie des modernen Dramas,* "edition suhrkamp" (Frankfurt/M., 1959).

Emile Zola, "Naturalism in the Theatre", translated by Albert Bermel, in *The Theory of the Modern Stage: An Introduction to Modern Theatre and Drama,* ed. Eric Bentley (Pelican Original, 1968).

Thomas Mann's *Buddenbrooks* and the Turn of the Century

X

Thomas Mann's *Buddenbrooks* and the Turn of the Century

M. A. L. BROWN

BUDDENBROOKS is the only work discussed in this volume which is likely, to be known to the English (or indeed the Albanian, Finnish, Japanese) reader who has no knowledge of German. It is that rarity in German literature— a work which has been not only translated into English but widely read and even sold in paperback in that language; in the country of its origin its phenomenal popularity still continues. The fact of its popularity in the English-speaking world might qualify it as in some ways untypical of German literature as a whole; its popularity in Germany almost disqualifies it as a suitable choice to illustrate German literature at the turn of the century. For this was a time when the gap between the poet or artist and the public was an apparently unbridgeable gulf with enormous mutual distrust on both sides : the public saw the artist as idle and dissolute, while the artist saw the mass of the public as materialistic, provincial and philistine and himself as absolute in his standards of artistic integrity, open to new ideas especially from other countries, and concerned with questions of ultimate significance. References to this fundamental antagonism between artist and public during the 1890s and immediately afterwards and analyses of its causes have been many. A notable article by Schwerte has documented the increasing alienation of the artist (for reasons first noted specifically by Nietzsche) in the new German Empire.[1] This empire gave its middle-class citizens growing prosperity and a sense of accelerating economic and social progress continuing into the new century and a heady belief in the advance of civilization as measured in terms of industrial production and the standard of living. It refused, however, to allow the artist to analyze or comment in his own terms on contemporary reality : literature was forced into the rôle of an "opposition", a rôle it would continue to play in Germany far more than in France, U.S.A., or England, well into the twentieth century.

That this antagonism could be a valuable stimulus to the poet is shown by Stefan George's well-known formulation of one of the main assumptions underlying his whole artistic enterprise :

223

"Today, in truth, Art is a breach with Society".[2] It is also demonstrated with varying degrees of involvement or irony in three personal statements by Carossa, Mann, and Rilke. In *Das Jahr der schönen Täuschungen*, at a distance of forty years, Carossa recounts his own starry-eyed arrival in 1897 in the big city of Munich, the city of Dehmel and *Die Gesellschaft*, the journal of the new poetry, where Mann too had been domiciled since 1893. In particular, Carossa remembers a poetry-reading from which he and his student friends had expected little less than a revelation of divine truth and which was brought to a standstill by the ridicule of the middle-class members of the audience who found the "Himalayan air" of Dehmel's verses too much for their composure. The particular sting is in the remark from one of the two middle-class women who had been chatting warmly about measles just before the reading that "after all they had paid two marks entrance money".[3] Also forty years after the event Mann recalls in *Lübeck als geistige Lebensform* how the ordinary citizens of Lübeck had regarded Emmanuel Geibel as a real poet and his neoclassicistic rhetoric as real poetry. So much so that after his death an old woman was supposed to have been heard in the street asking: "Who'll get his job? Who's to be poet now?"[4]—a simpleminded confusion of the position of the poet with that perhaps of an official in a regular salaried appointment. This is to be taken as a well-meaning and harmless enough instance of a widespread, fundamental and harmful misconception. Rilke's testimony to this misunderstanding dates back to 1898: in the course of a lecture delivered in Prague in the spring of that year to the Deutscher Dilettantenverein (poetic justice!) on the subject of "modern" poetry he refers to the "fashionable view which loves to think of artists as excluded from the mainstream of life" and which sees in them "children or cretins".[5] Speaking first and foremost as a lyric poet he particularly wishes "to express to the German public for its continuing and longstanding lack of interest—his warmest thanks"! They have done German poetry and poets a service by their neglect.[6] The tone this time is of courteous but none the less direct, face-to-face provocation of which other examples readily spring to mind—the more aggressively provocative title of a Stefan George maxim "Verdrehtheit (Perversität) des Bürgers"[7]; or Mann's ironic stylization of himself in the self-portrait composed for the readers of the *Litterarisches Echo of* 1906[8], where he lists as drastically as possible all his personal failings and failures, as seen through bourgeois eyes, and wonders if it can really be true that he has not finished up in the gutter; or his more disgruntled reference in a very early letter to "modern literature which may be observed all too frequently going to the dogs in compromises with the misera plebs".[9] If these examples typify a general situation, they would suggest that popular success would in all sincerity be scorned by any young writer who took himself and his ambitions as seriously as Mann must have done from a tender age, to judge by the way he signs off his first published letter, namely, Th. Mann, Lyric-Dramatic Poet.[10] The misgivings expressed by Samuel Fischer, the publisher, to whom Mann sent the voluminous manuscript of *Buddenbrooks,* were not on the grounds that the work might be too "modern" or advanced for the reading public, but more simply : "How many people in this industrial age we live in have the time and the concentration to take in a work of several hundred pages?"[11] In fact the novel was a great success. After this it is rather comic but not surprising in view of the general situation to find Mann in a letter to a friend insisting how much *Buddenbrooks* really was *loved* by its readers, but then asking if this meant artistic failure : "Am I so sentimental, so sweet, so mediocre, I have asked myself more than once, that they love me so much?"[12]

On the basis of material assembled in the Thomas Mann Archive in Zürich it has now been firmly established that the composition of *Buddenbrooks* did, quite literally, extend from the last few years of the nineteenth century into the first months of the twentieth. P. Scherrer gives the following time-table for the different stages of the work : begun in June 1897, the main preliminary studies lasted through the summer and autumn till about the end of October of the same year; the first three parts of the novel in its final form were completed between the end of October 1897 and mid-February 1898, the remainder being finished (subject to some minor alterations) between mid-February 1898 and the despatch of the manuscript to the publisher early in August 1900; it was published in the autumn of 1901.[13] Its young author was then only twenty-six and by no means the Establishment figure he later became. Before leaving school he had tried his hand at poetry and journalism and since leaving it the sole occupations he had taken seriously and passionately—to judge by the evidence of his correspondence and his many autobiographical writings—were reading (especially contemporary French, Russian and Scandinavian novels and dramas), writing (some short stories were already published, the first one, which appeared in *Die Gesellschaft,* bringing him some welcome encouragement from Dehmel), and possibly concert-going. After leaving Lübeck he had lived partly in Italy where he and his elder brother, Heinrich, spent approximately eighteen months from the autumn of 1886 till April 1898, and partly in Munich. There he was briefly employed in an insurance company, spent some agonizing weeks on military service before being released as unfit, and found a more congenial occupation as a publisher's reader, though he refers to this in a moment of irritation as "mindless editing" and complains: "What a waste of time the rubbish is".[14] The ambivalence of Mann's feelings towards Munich and the artistic life of the city are well illustrated by his comments in *Geist und Kunst*[15] (a collection of post-humously published notes towards an unfinished essay) which he repeated some ten years later in *Die Betrachtungen eines Unpolitischen*. He writes: "Frank Wedekind once remarked that every citizen of Munich was an artist, because he wanted to be left in peace to enjoy himself—a most Munich-like definition of the artist's state which will scarcely be understood elsewhere; it is a definition against which my life has been a silent protest for the last twenty years".[16] Mann was not drawn to the Bohemianism or the carnival atmosphere which was near enough to hand. In other ways, however, Munich was the right place for a serious, non-Bohemian, non-dilettante artist. It was a lively literary and artistic centre very much in touch with the latest literary developments in Germany and abroad. It had had close associations with Naturalism especially through the journal *Die Gesellschaft* and its editor, M.-G. Conrad, who ensured that it remained progressive and "weltoffen". It was from Munich that the poetry of Dehmel, the prophet of anti-Naturalism, inspired the hearts of the younger generation of Germans. In Munich two of the leading new literary journals of the mid-1890s were founded, namely *Pan* and *Simplicissimus,* and it was in and about Munich that some of the most daring German experiments in Art Nouveau decoration and "Kunst-gewerbe" were carried out at the turn of the century.[17] The latter and their rapid commercialization are satirized by Mann with precision and scorn in the opening section of *Gladius Dei* (first published in 1902), the section which reaches its climax in the words: "Munich was radiant . . ." Munich, it is clear, had got the art it deserved. Both in its faults and its virtues, this southern city was the antithesis of Lübeck.

Despite the important scholarly studies which have appeared in recent years[18] there is still no agreement that German literature at the turn of the century, i.e. probably from 1890 till 1910, may be viewed essentially as a whole with the same underlying assumptions about literature or the same types of theme or subject-matter, far less the same style. One of the main reasons why the concept of "German Literature at the Turn of the Century" is gaining currency is a negative one, the conviction that the old system of labelling in terms of a chronological sequence from Naturalism to Neo-Romanticism and *l'art pour l'art* and thence to Impressionism was so visibly wrong. The simultaneity of these varying tendencies may be confirmed from any history of literature. The distinction between them certainly escaped the notice of the authors concerned. Equally, many contemporary critics did not regard them as fundamental or final : in an article in a Viennese journal of the early 1890s we find this :

Unquestionably the outstanding distinguishing feature of "modernity" in literature is that it is not a single, one-sided tendency—the most diverse and contradictory views and aspirations all have their place in it . . . Everyone is a Naturalist. The man who sets out to reproduce external reality in every detail as carefully as possible is—a Naturalist, in so far as he refuses categorically to exclude everything that is random and accidental, insignificant or irrelevant; the man who is immersed in internal reality and follows up every tiniest nuance of his spiritual existence with conscientious persistence is—a Naturalist; every Romantic is a Naturalist in so far as he is a Romantic unawares and is only led into the paths of Romantic transformation of reality by his own individual temperament despite his firm intention of giving a faithful picture of reality.[19]

The difficulty is still, as B. Coghlan has pointed out,[20] to find a term to characterize what is distinctively "turn of the century" in the markedly individual writings of the 1890s generation. W. Rasch has identified some common features, including the already mentioned antagonism between Artist and Society and the deliberate provocativeness arising from it. He proposes further that a much more important unifying principle is a particular concept of life itself which he finds shared by a wide range of authors of this time :

The young generation, inspired by Nietzsche, saw more clearly that the truth of Christianity had lost the greater part of its sustaining power and they sought refuge from the isolation of the individual self in Life-mysticism i.e. within a purely "this-worldly" framework.[21]

Mann himself used the term "Naturalist" fairly frequently to refer to *Buddenbrooks*, but he does not make the meaning of the adjective very clear except by the addition of the phrase "and as such international in its artistic disposition, European in its attitudes".[22] In a book review which he wrote in 1912, however, Mann does make clearer what he considers Naturalism as a historical phenomenon to have been. Entitled by Mann "A work of Naturalism",[23] the review shows what qualities in the work in question (a novel by Georg Hirschfeld) Mann associated with Naturalism. Vastness of scale which makes the work seem a colossal frame filled with a huge number of subsidiary characters, walk-on

figures, silhouettes, is to be expected of a Naturalist novel ; so too
underlying altruism, an ethic of pity and sympathy, the author's
apparent preference for the amoral, indecently-fertile workings
of nature, and a particular variety of "objective" humour.
What Mann misses in this work and by implication in the
whole premisses of Naturalism is that it possesses, alas! no
style, no playfulness or spirit, no irony or elevation, no verbal
excitement or artistic magic.[24] He finds the writing so colourless
as to be totally conventional and the dialogue lacking in any
personal intonation. And the absence of these qualities is not out-
weighed by the presence of the others, although he has considerable
sympathy for all of them except the very limited form of humour.
In two quite different and widely separated contexts Mann refers
to his whole generation as a Naturalist one, on the grounds, in
both cases, that their over-riding concern, as he sees it, was with
the "pathological". The first is in note-form, probably written in
1909 and intended as part of the uncompleted *Geist und Kunst*.
He quotes a sentence from a new younger writer, "One must take
hold of Life with healthy hands", and continues :

> No young writer of novellas would have said that ten years ago.
> At the age of twenty I was rooting about in psychology . . . Au
> fond the dominating interest of the generation to which Hofmann-
> sthal, Hauptmann and I belong is the interest in the pathological.
> Today's twenty-year-olds have passed all that.[25]

And much later in a letter discussing *Death in Venice* he wrote
that "the Naturalist attitude to things which my generation had and
which is so foreign to you youngsters, forced me to consider the
pathological aspects of this "case" (amongst others)"[26] and some
paragraphs later we read, "George has stated that in *Death in
Venice* the highest things have been dragged down into the sphere
of decadence, and he's quite right; my Naturalist training has left
its mark on me".[27] The demarcation line between himself and
following generations is drawn here baldly and firmly and perhaps
one could go further and conclude that the juxtaposition of
"psychology" and "the pathological" in the first quotation also
has a significance for a whole generation to whom "abnormal
psychology" was almost the norm.

The source of much of the "modern" psychology, Nietzsche,
was another bond linking writers born about 1870—not that they
alone were influenced by him, but that his impact on them was
inescapable. The range and content of Nietzsche's influence on
succeeding literary generations till well into the twentieth century
has been the subject of many specialist studies which can draw
on the personal testimonies of innumerable writers, painters,

musicians and thinkers in Germany and elsewhere. The massively documented study *Impressionism*[28] by R. Hamann and J. Hermand contains twenty-nine references to Nietzsche and notes particularly, apart from the general vogue in the 1890s for Nietzsche-orgies, the inspiration his works provided to the composers of the 1894–1904 decade, e.g. R. Strauss, Mahler, Delius; the concluding and also by far the longest section of P. Pütz's survey of Nietzsche[29] is devoted to his influence and impact in its different phases from his life-time to the present day; Arnold's study of the literary sources of German Expressionism[30] includes Nietzsche's contribution to the thematic material of that movement; W. Rasch refers to him in the passage already cited as having made a radical "this-worldliness" not only desirable but indispensable for a generation whose starting-point was the death of God. A simple demonstration of the 1890s Nietzsche vogue amongst young intellectuals and aspiring poets is provided by the same Carossa reminiscence. He mentions that one of the non-bourgeois members of the audience at the literary reading was a girl nicknamed Zarathustrine because she drank her absinth in the Café Stephanie with Nietzsche's work on the table beside her glass; one of the poems recited by Dehmel was—inevitably—by Nietzsche, his *Nachtlied*.

Mann wrote eloquently of his admiration for Nietzsche on many occasions, and on one of them he states definitely that Nietzsche's influence both on the thought-content and the style of his earliest published prose-pieces is clearly recognizable, his own intellectual development having been largely determined by contact with Nietzsche's works.[31] Despite this statement which was made many years later there has been some doubt whether Mann's personal "Nietzsche-Erlebnis" in fact took place in time to colour the writing of *Buddenbrooks*. It has always seemed as though one could ascribe any internal evidence in the novel of acquaintance with Nietzschean ideas only to the general currency of Nietzsche's name and ideas in this decade. However, the notes to *Geist und Kunst*[32] which were not published till 1967 do contain a precise reference to Mann reading Nietzsche's critique of Wagner with burning interest for the first time at the age of nineteen, so the possibility of Nietzsche's psychological analysis of the decadent "modern" artist as an important source, e.g. for the characterization of Christian, both as an "ape" and a neurotic ("Nervenmensch") is plausible again. Schopenhauer's ideas, too, were in the air partly through the mediacy of Nietzsche, and Mann first read him in the course of his Italian visit when his work on *Buddenbrooks* was already begun. And Schopenhauer too had elaborated a "modern" psychology which exposed the extent to which men are commonly mistaken

as to the real motives for their actions and behaviour and are prepared to rationalize rather than face the truth about themselves.

Buddenbrooks is a long and closely-written work (in the former
respect untypical of a period which favoured "Kleinformen",
whether in lyric poetry, prose fiction, or drama). It relates in
detail the history of a wealthy family of Lübeck merchants over
the period 1835–77 against the background of the many social
and economic changes which the family experiences. Its popularity
may well be largely due to the interest of the subject-matter and
the fascination the average reader finds in facts. It is realistic in
the unsophisticated sense that it is a mine of detailed information
about upper-class social habits in a particular place at a particular
time—the sense which the nineteenth century German novel of
poetic or "bürgerlicher" Realism, unlike the French, English,
Russian or Scandinavian one, had neglected. The pattern of the
family chronicle—the genealogical novel was a favourite nineteenth
century form—allows the author every opportunity to describe
day-to-day details as well as producing climaxes usually in the
shape of births, deaths, and marriages, and Mann neglects none
of them. We read about furniture and dress, menus and medical
symptoms, divorce laws and procedures for election to senates,
bankruptcies and legacies, customs in mourning and in holidays,
in gay bachelor entertainment and in school-teaching methods and,
if at the end we have not mastered the intricacies of strawberry-
jam making into which *Anna Karenina* initiates its readers, we
could certainly have a try at a "Plettenpudding". All this factual
information is very skilfully and carefully interwoven with the
narration and even the dialogue so that, for example, it is prac-
tically impossible to "skip" the explanatory or descriptive passages
and concentrate on the forward movement of the action. Mann's
publisher asked if this "epic breadth", which he implied was
old-fashioned, could not be modified a little as a concession to
the probable tastes of his readers. He suggested courteously that
by dwelling on factual details the young author too often made
matters of secondary importance into essentials.[33] It is interesting
to compare this with Rilke's comment on the same aspect of the
work written in a review of *Buddenbrooks* in 1902.[34] He finds
Mann's technique as a chronicler "modern" in that he does not
"isolate a few outstanding moments, but conscientiously records
everything apparently slight and insignificant, including a
thousand individual details, since after all everything actual is of
value, forms a tiny piece of that life which he [Mann] had undertaken to depict. In this way", Rilke continues, "by immersing himself affectionately in individual processes, by dispensing the same
generous justice to everything which happens he achieves a par-

ticular liveliness of presentation".[35] The Realism of reported fact and authentic detail as well as the unhurried pace of the narration —though not the unrelieved bleakness of the ending—might well prompt the reader of *Buddenbrooks* to feel that Mann here more than anywhere else is a "child of the nineteenth century" as he called himself in *Die Betrachtungen eines Unpolitischen;* Rilke's response is to see in these very qualities evidence of what W. Rasch calls the most characteristic aspect of the literature of the turn of the century, namely, a particular conception of the totality of life.[36] Such a conception is not available to the novel's characters who are involved in the processes and events referred to. Their awareness is of the opposite—of an earlier totality of life which had included a meaningful religious dimension but is now in an ever-increasing state of disintegration. The one experience of totality, and it is only momentary, is Thomas Buddenbrook's at the height of his ecstatic nocturnal vision :

> The walls of his native town, in which he had wistfully and consciously shut himself up, opened out; they opened and disclosed to his view the entire world . . . The deceptive perceptions of space, time, and history . . . his spirit now put aside. He was no longer prevented from grasping eternity. Nothing began, nothing left off.[37]

This form of "Lebensmystik", however, which is also "Todesmystik" with roots in Novalis as much as in Schopenhauer, is only a fleeting vision for Thomas. Soon the intoxication wears off and the banality of his everyday problems reasserts itself. Rilke does not appear to have felt either that *Buddenbrooks* is at all nostalgic in the way that nineteenth-century German Realism frequently is, but it is not difficult to see something of the spirit of the earlier Realism in Mann's novel in this respect. J. M. Ritchie's statement that "always at the heart of the works of the Realists is the awareness of TIME, for essentially they were concerned not to record reality as they saw it, but to preserve the ideal image of the old world before it disappeared for ever",[38] could almost be applied to *Buddenbrooks,* strongly permeated as it is by a sense of a great age whose values the author admires and envies, and whose richness, serenity and strength he records in Part One of the novel. However, Mann is much more "modern" than this. His point is that the old world in question *has* disappeared for ever by the time the novel came to be written and that one should face the fact without sentimentality. But, making the work much more complex, his point is also that the destruction of one great age has produced new qualities and values—of artistry and self-awareness—which he also admires but which are not "lebensfähig".

This novel both records the new reality as Mann saw it *and* preserves the image of an old world.

The historical events on which the novel is based (the family chronicles of the Manns), are pushed back in time by Mann so that, for example, Thomas Buddenbrook dies in 1875, whereas the original, Mann's own father, had died in 1891, only ten years before the publication of the novel. The reader of the work may be surprised to discover on checking carefully in the course of the final chapters that events have moved only forty years forward since he first encountered Tony and her grandparents; the course of the social, economic, personal and spiritual transformations which he has witnessed taking place has been related so deliberately and its final outcome is so overwhelmingly complete that despite the carefully inserted dates it is easy to feel, perhaps naïvely, that not just an epoch but a whole century has passed. In fact the century *was* near its end when Mann's father died and it is tempting to speculate why he altered the dates so that, for example, the economic decline and its concomitant social changes in Lübeck, are set in the novel rather earlier than would be historically accurate.[39] It was possibly a means whereby Mann could distance himself both emotionally and artistically from the characters and events of the novel, where a novelist of an earlier generation of nineteenth-century Realists might have preferred to build a distancing framework into the work—with Tony as storyteller? At the same time the earlier fictional ending seems more chillingly final with no possibility of any continuity into a new century. The historical evidence of this continuity, for example, the simple fact that the original of Tony lived on till 1917, emphasizes how capriciously Mann was prepared to treat authenticated fact when it suited his artistic purpose. His own account of the composition of *Buddenbrooks* in *Bilse und Ich* (written in 1906) emphasizes his own total contempt for the purely factual:

> When I began to write *Buddenbrooks,* my home town did not possess much reality for me . . . I was not absolutely convinced of its existence. It, and its inhabitants, meant very little more to me than a dream.[40]

Buddenbrooks as "dream poetry" is a tempting thought in the context of this chapter, but of course the meaning of the words quoted and the purport of the whole piece *Bilse und Ich* is the right of the poet to create a new reality from the materials he may find in experience, whether his own or other people's. It was hardly a new idea when Mann enunciated it, but he does so more unconditionally and directly here than anywhere else, even going so far, after a reference to the fundamental distinction between the

world of reality and the world of art, as to assert that "the true
lover of language would always rather risk antagonizing a whole
world rather than sacrifice one single nuance".[41] This statement
is made in a newspaper article in reply to an attack by an ignorant
philistine small-town lawyer on an artist, and the artist's irritation
may perhaps have tempted him to formulate his position in rather
extreme language. On the other hand, such full-blooded 1890s
æstheticism from the pen of Mann and not from Stefan George
may persuade us to see *Buddenbrooks* as a work much more "of
its period" than it is usually considered to be when it is viewed,
as it most usually is, as marking the first but very traditional
stage in Mann's career as a novelist.

Before coming to consider what it was that *did* attract Mann
to write the novel if it was not "the purely factual" (amassing such
a huge amount of factual information in the process) and what
some of the "nuances" were which he was prepared to defend so
passionately, it is worthwhile to recapitulate the main outlines of
the story in relation to the structure of the novel and in particular
to the passage of time in it. Part One is devoted entirely to a
family celebration which occupies the late afternoon and evening
of one day in the autumn of 1835. First of all, only members of
the family are present, to be joined a little later by a group of
guests, both family and "outsiders". Everyone participates in a
huge dinner-party. Then all engage in after-dinner conversation
or billiards after which the gathering disperses, its members well-
satisfied with their evening and themselves—and so to bed. The
arrival of an offensively worded letter from a black sheep member
of the family who has married beneath him has coincided with
the day of the festivities, but it is not allowed to disturb either the
party or the sleep of the participants afterwards. The "abrupt"
opening, a snatch of trivial if animated dialogue, has been noted
by W. Rasch[42] as a favourite turn of the century technique which
he sees as a means of suggesting that the story is only an excerpt,
part of a greater totality which may otherwise remain invisible.
While this first part concludes naturally enough with the retiral
of the family to bed, the events of the day have not vanished for
ever, for "hopes, fears, and ambitions all slumbered",[43] no doubt
to reawaken. Part Two is almost the same length as the previous
one, but its action extends over a period of seven years from 1838
to 1845 : it brings the birth of a daughter, the death of two grand
parents and various episodes from the childhood and youth of
Thomas, Tony, and Christian. Part Three, almost twice as long
as the preceding one, relates Tony's romantic adventures—her
courtship by a man whom she loathes, the interlude, where she
meets a man whom she might love, her renunciation and

decision in the interests of the family to marry the "wrong" man—
and the brief termination of Tom's love for a pretty shop-girl.
These events take the reader from June 1845 till February of the
next year. Part Four, of the same length as Part Three, begins
with Tony's life as a married woman, passes rapidly to revolutionary events in Lübeck in 1848, then back to Tony's misfortune
as her husband goes bankrupt and they divorce; in 1855 the head
of the firm dies. Part Five follows on immediately and also lasts
two years which include Thomas's appointment in place of his
father as head of the firm and his subsequent marriage. Part Six,
ninety pages long, relates the disastrous story of Tony's second
marriage and its break-up in November 1859. Part Seven, much
shorter but covering the five years 1861–6, spans the first eighteen
months in the life of Hanno, the new heir to the firm, and the
election of his father to the supreme honour of a senatorship, an
honour which is conferred on him just at a time when he is
beginning to lose all feeling of pleasure in his work. By the end
of Part Seven the Prussian campaign against the Austrians over
the Schleswig-Holstein dispute has been successful and Lübeck has
supported the winning side. Part Eight is the longest of all, culminating in the grandiose celebrations of the centenary of the
family firm, an event marked by public tributes and general
excitement. Hanno's special effort in honour of the occasion
unfortunately leads only to disappointment and tears, and indeed
the whole musical entertainment laid on as the climax of the
celebration party is strident and unharmonious and the bad news
which is brought this time is less easily shrugged off. The celebration is flanked by the marriage of Tony's daughter and by the
subsequent arrest of her husband. In the meantime Hanno is
growing up, a sickly child used to swallowing revolting medicines,
passionately fond of the piano and of a toy theatre he has received
as a Christmas present. By the opening of Part Nine only seven
years of the story are left (1870–7), and more than a quarter of the
novel. This part, however, is short and covers only a few months
from the death of Thomas's mother to the sale of the family home.
Part Ten takes up the story almost without interruption in 1872
to portray in detail the last three years of Thomas's life and the
state of mind in which he spends them—his thoughts about himself
and his own life, his feelings towards his wife and his son are
shown through the tedium of day-to-day life, and then comes the
final desperate longing for spiritual illumination from the works
of Schopenhauer and lastly the visit to the sea undertaken in
the hope that at least his over-worked nerves might be restored.
In January 1875, he dies and is buried with all due pomp. The
concluding Part begins with the aftermath of Thomas's death,

the sale of the house and the firm and continues with the longest single chapter in the novel, which is an account of a typical day in the life of Hanno, a day of torture and horror at school and of blissful escape into music when he is released. After his death from typhus we are shown the female survivors of the family, grouped together all in black, baffled and disconsolate at the experiences of the past years and months with little remaining faith in the future.

The narration, then, is in chronological sequence, even on the occasions when the events narrated take place many miles apart, for example, when Thomas is in Amsterdam, or Tony is in Munich, or Christian in South America, and it uses the traditional techniques of third person narration, epistolary form, the introduction of family papers to give a flashback to the earlier family history, and the use of dialogue to narrate recent or more distant events. However, the events of forty years are not related at an even pace or according to a simple continuous rhythm of ups and downs. The narration of the happenings of a few hours may occupy as much narrated time as the events of years, perhaps because this approximates much more closely to our experience of the passage of time—in this connection one may note that the manner in which Hanno's experience of the sheer endlessness of his school holidays is shown[44] points forward to much more elaborate experiments in *The Magic Mountain*—and perhaps because the "timing" of the events in the novel does not fall into a pattern. The fact that many apparently trivial events are included in the story and many apparently important events (e.g., the Franco-Prussian War) are excluded from it is part of the same purpose. E. Lämmert has argued most convincingly[45] that the time structure within the novel is designed as part of this pattern which is the formal embodiment of the theme of the work, namely decay and disintegration. He shows that Mann is here using the most conventional of means (the chronicle novel structure) in an individual and highly sophisticated way which again points forward to the treatment of time in *The Magic Mountain*. If one sets Part One aside as an introduction, it is the case that a steadily increasing number of Parts is spent on each decade of the action—the first decade is covered by Part Two, the second by Parts Three and Four, the third by Parts Five to Seven, and the fourth by Parts Eight to Eleven. This may seem chance, or coincidence, or of little possible relevance or interest to the critic, but there are at least two good reasons why it would be unwise to dismiss this piece of hidden literary arithmetic as meaningless. First and most important, Mann can explore the process of disintegration with all its symptoms at progressively greater length and in greater depth as the process itself gets an increasingly stronger grip on the family and above all on Thomas. This process is marked, for example, by an increasing tendency to introspection which finally becomes obsessive with Thomas; where earlier in the novel the narrator could be content to record speech, gesture and behaviour as external indications of thought and feeling, he now penetrates into Thomas's mind and motivation and presents them from *within*. Secondly, Mann's half-superstitious fondness for playing with numbers and their possible significance is more familiar to the reader from *The Magic Mountain* and has been noted as an aspect of his personality which spills over from his life into his writings[46]—it is an example of the artist's right to play both with his material and with his readers which Mann missed in the Naturalist novel by G. Hirschfeld and which becomes an element in his own irony.

We are informed by Mann[47] that the germ of *Buddenbrooks* was his interest in the story of "the hypersensitive latecomer Hanno" and possibly also of Hanno's father, and that all the rest (half the finished work) was thought of originally as nothing more than leading up to this. It would be wrong to maintain that Mann's original love for and presumably identification with Hanno are obvious in the finished novel, if by this is meant that the author's sympathies are very evidently on one side. The final work with its sense of gain and loss at both ends and for both sides is much more complex than that. Mann's original choice of subject—the emotional, psychological, and artistic sensitivity of a sickly boy who is also heir to a once rich tradition—could anyone mistake the period in literature to which this belongs? Especially when the detail is added that as a boy he plays in a garden with a fountain ringed by purple irises ! ! Equally complex is the terrible awareness of "life as a masquerade" which has come to Thomas gradually but with rapidly increasing intensity as he has continued to act out the masquerade and which is implanted early in the mind of his son who watches him receptively, ready for such insights. He does not recoil indignantly from this knowledge as his father would like him to or avoid the kind of occasion where he is likely to learn more. Instead he absorbs unquestioningly with wide-open eyes this knowledge about life. This acceptance of what he can see about him is not to be confused with his grandfather's acceptance of the values of his society as right. Hanno is like Hofmannsthal's Claudio a looker-on, a spectator, unable to be part of life or to participate in it, but life has the power to force the sickly boy into participating—at school. This situation, too, is favourite thematic material for the novel (and drama) in the early years of the century. In addition to Hesse's *Unterm Rad* and Musil's *Verwirrungen des Zöglings Törless,* one need only think of Rilke's stylization of childhood throughout his poetry and the bitter personal memories of the five years he had actually spent at a military academy of which he wrote in *Mir Zur Feier* (in 1897 and 1898) that they had robbed him of half his strength.[48] For obvious reasons the military academy lends itself particularly well as a symbol of inhuman tyranny and brutalization. Hanno attends only the "Realklassen" of an ordinary high school. It is Hanno's great misfortune, however, that it has been reformed in the name of "progress" and of the "Prussian spirit" triumphant since 1871— the two being generally considered almost synonymous. As a result of the reform the former humanity of the school's atmosphere and of its instruction have been replaced by the more "forward-looking" concepts of authority, duty, and the categorical imperative. Mann has made very explicit (e.g. "This school was a state within the state") that this establishment reflects *and* symbolizes the values of a modern Prussianized Germany which can only be abhorrent to any sensitive human being, but more than this, that the school is also a microcosm of Life itself. The view that life operates as a kind of Prussian drill by which the sensitive individual is crushed, a view put forward at length in the account of the school day, has also been hinted at in an earlier chapter in the picture of the four and a half year old Hanno who is able to play safely in the garden while the Prussian armies set off for action and return victorious only because he is young enough not to be "cut to a pattern, drilled, lengthened, shortened, corrupted" by life.[49] The subjectivity of Mann's identification with his hero is perceptible in the tone of the description of the day at school : it is as seen through Hanno's eyes that the individual teachers and classmates and the atmosphere of the whole building are presented; the picture is heightened, too, by Hanno's dread on this typical occasion that his lack of preparation will lead to some fearful explosion. The degree of identification is shown more directly in the earlier account of Hanno playing in the garden by the narrator's sudden use of the first person plural as he meditates on the certainty that a child's freedom "to see, hear, laugh, dream, and feel amazement", [49] its unawareness of duty or remorse will be cut brutally short as life gets *us* in its toils. (The only other use of this first person plural in the novel is also startling and significant : in the context of analyzing Thomas's "vanity" immediately after his election to the senate, the narrator begins a new chapter with the words : "The desires we feel and the enterprises in which we engage are conditioned by certain needs of our nervous systems which are very hard to define in words.")

Hanno has no means of putting up a fight against his school tormentors, against his school, or against life. Unless his friend Kai is there to fight for him his only hope is to escape—either once a year blissfully to Travemünde or to his beloved music which he enters as his private kingdom curtained off from the outside world. Hanno's playing and improvizing at the piano are shown as an escape into a welter of Neo-Romantic emotionalism which fulfils and satisfies him (even sexually) and procures for him his rare "moments heureux" when time has no reality. And then, abruptly, it is all over—such happiness and the art which produces it are to be condemned as immoral, pernicious and more than half in love with death. This is the author's brutal conclusion and Hanno's death is the logical outcome: it follows immediately after the extended description of Hanno's improvization at the grand piano in language pretending to be that of an impersonal clinical report but in fact closely paralleling the preceding account of the piano playing both in the actual phrasing and in the different stages in the course of the disease. It is as drastic a judgement as the end of *Death in Venice* on the decadent form of art and artist that was particularly cultivated in life and literature in the 1890s. The affinity of "das Dekadent-Genüßliche" at that time for Neo-Romantic music, especially the works of Debussy, Chopin and Wagner (the two last being Gerda Buddenbrook's favourite composers) has been noted in detail by R. Hamann and J. Hermand.[50] The narrator does not deliver this judgment in the first person, it is true, but he does at the end of both the passages concerned switch to a solemnly moralizing tone, of a kind that is absent elsewhere in the work.[51]

However, Hanno is not the only artist, nor is his the only art, produced by the Buddenbrook family, for the novel may be considered not only as the story of a chain of interlocking generations subject both physically and psychologically to Naturalist laws of heredity but also as a kind of "Künstlerroman". The "artistic" lives of Thomas, Tony and Christian span the course of the action from beginning to the end (or almost in Thomas's case). None of them, of course, is a true or complete artist, but they have the makings of one in some important aspect, which may be the reason for Gerda's ironic remark that "the Buddenbrook hands are just right for playing the piano, only they had never set any store by it".[52] Thomas, Tony, and Christian are very close in age (another instance of the re-ordering of historical fact by the author), if not, outwardly at least, in character. Thomas shows his latent artistic gift last of the three at the stage when his whole life has become the public acting out of a rôle whose content has lost all meaning for him. Despite and because of this he enjoys performing—the emptiness of the part allows him to concentrate on his technique with fastidious care. His satisfaction is in creating an illusion for his public to believe in and in feeling their enjoyment of it; without them he relapses into lethargy and melancholy. Christian, on the other hand, is acknowledged even as a child to be a highly entertaining mimic—an "ape" as his grandfather calls him only half angrily. And lazy and irresponsible as Christian is in matters of business, as a mimic, impersonator and clown, he works hard. His nerves suggest a "decadent" artistic sensitivity, but they do not prevent him from observing the speech and gesture of other people with the closest attention, and from practising his imitations till they are perfect. All of this he does with no thought of offence to others or of impropriety even when his subject is the sounds uttered by his own father as he is dying.[54] But he remains a dilettante whose taste for enjoying himself is too strong to let him ever sacrifice his own pleasure to the perfection of his performance and so his adventurous existence becomes more and more dissolute till in the end he is committed by his wife (whether for honest motives or not) to an asylum. And Tony? Her very first appearance in the novel is as a child-performer sure of her success in the indulgent family circle, delighted to rattle off her catechism as a party piece even though she has little understanding of it or control over the flow of her own words once she has started. Her performances as a story-teller remain a source of family entertainment and pleasure throughout the novel. Thomas especially enjoys her animated accounts of her own experiences and seeks her company in order to be lifted out of his own despondency. It is an unselfconscious artistic gift which the reader may sample both in her manner of speech and her letters with their pictures of her two attempts at setting up house as a married woman, and the inability to stop, or to "shape" her material is a reflection of her lack of self-awareness and self-consciousness—it is also of great benefit to her emotionally, however, in its almost cathartic effect. In a striking passage near the end of Thomas's final visit to Travemünde Mann almost presents her as a parody of Goethe's Tasso—she need never fear suffering, as the need to suffer, the very possibility of suffering, is lifted from her by her spontaneous urge to translate her feelings instantly into a stream of words :

And then she talked about her own life. She talked well, she entertained her brother capitally. This child of fortune, so long as she walked upon this earth, had never once needed to suppress an emotion, to choke down or swallow anything she felt. She had never received in silence either the blows or the caresses of fate. And whatever she had received, of joy or sorrow, she had straightway given forth again, in a flow of childish, self-important trivialities . . . She was not consumed by the inexpressible. No sorrow weighed her down, or strove to speak but could not. And thus it was that her past left no mark on her.[53]

This composite of different facets of the nature of the artist which the novel provides is incomplete without the mention of one small figure from outside the Buddenbrook family, namely Hanno's friend, Kai. Like Hanno, Kai is the last heir, not of a middle-class but of an aristocratic family whose only survivor apart from his father is an aunt who writes romantic fiction for popular consumption. As a child Kai makes up fairy-stories and he later progresses to reading E. A. Poe unobserved during his lessons at school. E. Lämmert has pointed out[56] that Kai's stories may resemble the structure of *Buddenbrooks* in that "they were short and simple at first, but they expanded and grew bolder and more complicated with time".[57] It is an attractive idea that Kai is Hanno's antithetical counterpart as an artist and that the qualities still half-hidden in Kai's childish beginnings as a writer may be an intuition of a principle important to the book's mature author for "the interesting thing about Kai's stories was that they never quite hung in mid-air, but were based upon a reality which he presented in a new and mysterious light".[58] Moreover, Kai, unlike the other characters in the book, can use words with deliberate precision to "master" the threats of his unsympathetic environment, to render it harmless and comic. Examples of this are his nickname for the otherwise terrifying headmaster "The Lord God in the Garden"[59] or his interjection "unfortunately gone mad"[60] later in the school day. As a minor figure Kai fades out (though he is given a mention in the last chapter) so we cannot know his future, but perhaps in him the prophecy of his fairy-tale would have come true as it did for Mann himself—he might have reached a position of very high distinction.[61]

Finally, what of the narrative art with which *Buddenbrooks* itself is told as distinct from the different forms of art and the artist which are shown within it? The elaborate care with which a network of associative parallels ("Bezüge") is constructed within the novel has been analyzed by E. Lämmert.[62] These frequently rely on the simple principle of repeating and varying single words, phrases, details of a situation, even whole situations. Some of the more obvious of these have already been indicated in outlining the action of the novel earlier in this chapter, for example, the family celebration in honour of the new house at the beginning and the later more public one in honour of the firm; Tony's successful party-piece at the beginning and Hanno's disastrous one, followed

by a more successful attempt at public performance when he may
play a tune he has composed and not have to recite a poem; Tony's
visit to Travemünde, Hanno's holidays there—both happy and
carefree—and the last visit paid by Thomas and Christian; the
latter scene with its all-male company, depressing, monotonous
weather and the sense of decay and disintegration on every side
as a parallel to the very last scene of the book, all females this time,
the forebodings of the other scene amply confirmed and rain still
beating at the windows; the opening scene as a counterpart to the
last one; typhus in relation to piano playing: the list is unending,
and includes many of the "insignificant" details noted by Rilke. It
may be that we are to understand these æsthetic parallels and
connections as an expression of Mann's belief that reality too is
composed of them. The element of self-conscious arrangement
which is so evident in the novel may well appear forced and
strained if it is interpreted in this way. But could it not be that
the compositional element is to be taken as a serious artistic game—
one of the qualities Mann so missed in the Naturalist novel he
reviewed. The word "game" is one he uses in passing of the composition of *Buddenbrooks* in a reference to his own Lübeck
experiences and memories as the material "with which he wanted
to play—to play seriously".[63] "His serious game"—it is not a far
remove from this phrase to the notion of artistry ("Artistik") which
H. Schwerte[64] isolates as one of the two concepts unifying much
of the diversity of German literature at the turn of the nineteenth
century. It is also one which leads far into the twentieth. It applies
with perfect aptness even to the precision of the dates in the
novel: the fact that critics have so far been unable to discover
any mistake in them is usually taken as evidence of Mann's conscientious Realism and the desire for authenticity. It could also
be seen as much more lighthearted both for Mann himself who
had to draw up the crossword puzzle and solve it in the first place
and for the reader. It is part of the artistic game Mann plays
that the occasional dates are slipped in irregularly and unobstru-
sively but sufficiently often for the reader in his turn to "work
them out". More important in this respect for the tone of the work
as a whole is the trick played by the narrator in which he first
makes a statement apparently in the rôle of detached observer
and then reveals that, after all, he was merely quoting one point
of view—that of one of the characters involved. The simplest
example of this is the startling but seemingly serious announcement, "And thus began Tony Buddenbrook's third marriage"
which is followed to the reader's discomfiture by a new paragraph
beginning: "Yes, this really was the right way to put it. The
Senator himself, one Thursday afternoon . . . had called it that

and Frau Permaneder quite relished the joke."[64] Much of the verbal irony of the novel should not be taken metaphysically but as part of this half-joking game with the reader. It is, however, in the construction of the whole work—in the combination, overlapping and simultaneous use of traditional, contemporary, and more experimental novelistic techniques that this "modern" playful artistry is most complete.

NOTES

All references to works by Thomas Mann are to the *Gesammelte Werke* (*G.W.*) (Oldenburg, 1960) except in the case of references to and quotations from *Buddenbrooks* where the English translation has been used, with some slight modifications in the Penguin edition (1957).

1. H. Schwerte, "Deutsche Literatur im Wilhelminischen Zeitalter", *Wirkendes Wort* XIV (1964), pp. 254–70.
2. S. George, *Blätter für die Kunst,* quoted from *Auslese 1904–1909* (Berlin, 1909), p. 8.
3. H. Carossa, "Das Jahr der schönen Täuschungen", quoted from C. Baier (ed.), *Selections from Hans Carossa* (Edinburgh, 1960), p. 15.
4. *G.W.,* XI, p. 378.
5. R. M. Rilke, *Sämtliche Werke* (Frankfurt a.M., 1955–66). V, pp. 360–94 and VI, pp. 1349–54.
6. Ibid., V, p. 364.
7. S. George *Blätter für die Kunst,* quoted from *Auslese 1898–1904* (Berlin, 1904), p. 15.
8. "Im Spiegel", *G.W.,* XI, pp. 329–33.
9. T. Mann, *Briefe 1889–1936* (Frankfurt a.M., 1961), p. 5.
10. Ibid., p. 3.
11. P. Scherrer, "Bruchstücke der Buddenbrooks–Urhandschrift", *Neue Rundschau* LXIX (1958), p. 282.
12. *Briefe 1889–1936,* p. 65.
13. P. Scherrer, op. cit., pp. 258–91; and "Vorarbeiten zu den Buddenbrooks", in: P. Scherrer and H. Wysling (eds.), *Thomas–Mann Studien I* (Bern and Munich, 1967), p. 210.
14. *Briefe 1889–1936.* p. 11.
15. H. Wysling, "Geist und Kunst", in: *Thomas–Mann Studien I,* p. 210.
16. *G.W.,* XII, p. 141
17. Cf. accounts by (*a*) M. Amaya, *Art Nouveau* (London, 1966), pp. 123–141; (*b*) S. Tschudi Madsen, *Art Nouveau* (London, 1967), pp. 133–36 and 173–81; (*c*) N. Pevsner, *The Sources of Modern Architecture and Design* (London, reprint 1968), pp. 78–79, 90–91.
18. e.g. R. Hamann and J. Hermand (eds.) *Naturalismus* (Berlin, 1959); *Impressionismus* (Berlin, 1960); H. Schwerte, op. cit.; W. Rasch, *Zur deutschen Literatur seit der Jahrhundertwende* (Stuttgart, 1967); J. Hermand, "Jugendstil–Forschungsbericht", *Deutsche Vierteljahrsschrift* XXXVIII (1964); C. David, "Stefan George und der

Jugendstil", in: H. Steffen (ed.), *Formkräfte der deutschen Dichtung* (Göttingen, 1963), pp. 211–229.

19. F. M. Fels, "Die Moderne", *Moderne Dichtung IV* (1891), p. 81.
20. B. Coghlan in J. M. Ritchie (ed.), *Periods in German Literature, I* (London, 1967), p. 229.
21. W. Rasch, op. cit., pp. 1–49; the reference is to p. 43.
22. *G.W.*, XII, p. 89.
23. *G.W.*, X, pp. 555–58
24. *Ibid., p.* 556.
25. H. Wysling, op. cit., p. 207.
26. *Briefe* 1889–1936, p. 177.
27. Ibid., p. 179.
28. R. Hamann and J. Hermand, op. cit.
29. P. Pütz, *Friedrich Nietzsche* (Stuttgart, 1967).
30. A. Arnold, *Die Literatur des Expressionismus* (Stuttgart, 1966).
31. *G.W.*, XI, p. 109.
32. H. Wysling, op. cit., p. 162.
33. Quoted in P. Scherrer, *Neue Rundschau*, LXIX, 1958, p. 275.
34. R. M. Rilke, "Thomas Mann's *Buddenbrooks*", in: *Sämtliche Werke* V, pp. 579–581. (This is also included in English translation in H. Hatfield (ed.), *Thomas Mann* (New Jersey, 1964).)
35. Ibid., p. 579.
36. W. Rasch, op. cit., p. 28.
37. *Buddenbrooks*, p. 512.
38. J. M. Ritchie, op. cit., p. 193.
39. Cf. P.–P. Sagave, *Réalité sociale er idéologie religieuses dans les romans de Thomas Mann. Buddenbrooks. Montagne Magique* (Strassburg, 1954), p. 11.
40. "Bilse und Ich", *G.W.*, X, p. 15.
41. Ibid., p. 41.
42. W. Rasch, "Das Problem des Anfangs erzählender Dichtung. Eine Beobachtung zur Form der Erzählung um 1900", op. cit., pp. 49–59.
43. *Buddenbrooks*, p. 40.
44. Ibid., pp. 489–97.
45. E. Lämmert, "Thomas Mann: *Buddenbrooks*", in: B.v. Wiese (ed.), *Der deutsche Roman vom Realismus bis zur Gegenwart* (Düsseldorf, 1965), p. 199.
46. Cf. G. Mann, *Thomas Mann 1875–1965* (Bonn, 1965), p. 7.
47. *G.W.*, XI, p. 381
48. R. M. Rilke, "Mir zur Feier", in: *Sämtliche Werke III.* Cf. E. C. Mason's comments in *Rilke sein Leben und sein Werk* (Göttingen, 1964), p. 13.
49. *Buddenbrooks*, p. 342.
50. R. Hamann and J. Hermand, op. cit., p. 156.
51. (a) "Es lag etwas Brutales und Stumpfsinniges und zugleich etwas asketisch Religiöses, etwas wie Glaube und Selbstaufgabe in dem fanatischen Kultus dieses Nichts . . . etwas Lasterhaftes in der Maßlosigkeit und Unersättlichkeit, mit der sie genossen und ausge-

beutet wurde, und etwas zynisch Verweifeltes, etwas wie Wille zu Wonne und Untergang".

(b) "Wallt es dann in ihm auf, wie ein Gefühl der feigen Pflichtversäumnis, der Scham, der erneuten Energie, des Mutes und der Freude, der Liebe und der Zugehörigkeit zu dem spöttischen, bunten und brutalen Getriebe, das er im Rücken gelassen; wie weit er auch auf dem fremden, heißen Pfade fortgeirrt sein mag, er wird umkehren und leben". *G.W.*, I (a) p. 470, (b) p. 474.

52. *Buddenbrooks,* p. 392.
53. Ibid., p. 13. "Ein Aap" is here translated as "a young monkey".
54. Ibid., p. 203.
55. Ibid., p. 521.
56. E. Lämmert, op. cit.
57. *Buddenbrooks,* p. 406.
58. Ibid.
59. Ibid., p. 561.
60. Ibid., p. 574.
61. Cf. ibid., p. 406.
62. E. Lämmert, op. cit.

BIBLIOGRAPHY

(a) For details of Mann's own works readers are referred to: H. Bürgin, et. al, (eds.), *Das Werk Thomas Manns. Eine Bibliographie* (Frankfurt a.M., 1959).
For secondary literature they should consult:
K. W. Jonas (ed.), *Fifty years of Thomas Mann Studies. A bibliography of criticism* (Minneapolis, 1955).
K. W. Jonas and I. B. Jonas (eds.), *Thomas Mann Studies II* (Philadelphia, 1967).
(b) A useful survey of recent literature on *Buddenbrooks* will be found in the notes to E. Lämmert's interpretation in B. v. Wiese (ed.), *Der deutsche Roman vom Realismus bis zur Gegenwart* (Düsseldorf, 1965). Most recent is H. Lehnert, "Thomas-Mann, Forschungsbericht", *DVjs.*, XL, 1966, pp. 257–298; XLI, 1967, pp. 599–654; XLII, 1968, pp. 127–157.

Kaiser's *Bürger von Calais* and the drama of Expressionism

XI

Kaiser's *Bürger von Calais* and the drama of Expressionism

R. W. LAST

B Y the end of the 1830s, the urban English novel had Oliver Twist asking for more ; in the meantime German literature was still preoccupied with rural themes. It was not until nearly half a century later that it belatedly sought to catch up with the rest of European letters and tackle the problems of man in an industrialized environment. Held back by an outdated political and economic structure, Germany did not really become an industrial society until after unification. Then it too, in a more concentrated form, betrayed all the symptoms that had long been evident in France and England : the shift of population to towns and cities, the rise of the proletariat, terrible squalor and exploitation of this new labour force, and the change in social, moral and political ideologies that sought to contain the transformation of society. Literature too stirred itself to examine the new situation and in the Naturalist movement came to some pretty depressing conclusions. As the machine dominated society, so the Naturalists saw blind, impersonal forces controlling and determining the destiny of man. Man was conditioned by heredity and environment, socially and spiritually enchained; man had been devalued, and the Naturalists, in their rôle as observers and recorders of reality, particularly unpleasant reality, faithfully charted the decline and fall of human dignity.

If the Naturalists had their backs to the wall, others had their faces firmly turned towards it, despairing of society, withdrawing into an hermetic exclusivity, backward-looking, preoccupied with æsthetic and other issues remote from the harsh realities of the turn of the century. But, around 1910, another change in outlook occurred :

Then came the artists of the new movement. They no longer dealt in the fine frisson. They no longer presented the naked fact. For them the instant, the split-second of impressionistic creation, was but an empty husk in the mill of time. They were no longer subject to the ideas, exigencies and personal tragedies of middle-class and capitalistic thinking.

For them Feeling spread out into infinity.
They did not see.
They beheld.
They did not photograph.
They had visions.
Instead of the rocket, they created the constant ferment.
Instead of the moment, the extended effect in time. They did not put on a glittering circus parade. They wanted the experience that endures.

Above all, against the atomistic, fragmentary sensibility of the Impressionists they set one great all-embracing Cosmic Feeling.[1]

In spite of this uncompromizing revolutionary fervour which characterizes Expressionism, and marks it off sharply from all that had gone before, the Expressionists share both the Naturalists' awareness of the social and spiritual problems of man, and also an involvement in the irrational, the æsthetic, the otherworldly. But the Expressionists were content neither to accept the world and record it as they found it, nor to turn away and dream. They sought both the re-establishment of man as the centre of all things and the recognition of the universe as a totality.

Of course Expressionism, like any other movement in art, was as varied as the number of its participants; but if it has a focal point, one work that lies at its centre and conveys most fully both the purely technical and also the moral, social, and philosophical aspects of the movement, that work is *Die Bürger von Calais*, by the dramatist Georg Kaiser.

Georg Kaiser (1878–1945) produced such an immense variety of works, and was so prolific a dramatist, that an early critic was prompted to demand :

Is this man, who shines with so many colours, perhaps not an individual at all, but the drama production company of some unknown Young German movement, which uses the registered trade-mark "Georg Kaiser" merely as a legal technicality?[2]

Kaiser had so successfully and deliberately distanced himself from his works that it seemed impossible to refer them all back to a single common point, one source from which they could all have derived their inspiration. Even now that the dust has settled—some of it, regrettably, on Kaiser's work—it is still not easy to reconcile many contradictions. However, in an essay, *Vision und Figur* (1918), Kaiser himself sought to define his mission as an artist—which he saw as overriding all other considerations in life—and to penetrate through the confused exterior to the guiding principles beneath:

> The Vision calls us to singleness of purpose. (Only thus will it reveal its meaning.) . . . The Vision is everything—because it brings all things together. It embraces heaven and earth and the heavenly earthly figure of Man. The figures who embody the Vision take many forms . . . The casual observer stares at the turmoil. He can see nothing but turmoil. He poses the paradox: Where is the unity, which I am supposed to be able to comprehend here in one glance? . . . The writer uses many forms to create one single thing: the primordial Vision . . . What kind of Vision is it? There is only one kind: that of the Regeneration of Man.[3]

This utterance, in which he typically conceals himself behind a rhetorical mask, is more descriptive than explanatory, for the range and nature of his "Vision", like that of the Expressionists at large, seems to shift abruptly from one work to the next: in *Zweimal Oliver* (1926), the New Man born of the Vision becomes a Mad Man; in *Von morgens bis mitternachts* (1912), he gets nowhere at all, and keeps returning to his point of departure; in *Rosamunde Floris* (1936–7), the New Man is a woman, who destroys all about her—and ultimately herself—in a grotesque black comedy which seems to pour scorn on the very idea of "Newness". Perhaps Kaiser's vision can more adequately be interpreted as an attempt to establish contact between transcendent and immanent, between "heaven" and "earth", to render the "figure" transparent so that the Vision behind can be observed, to erect a kind of slippery pole reaching up into infinity, on various parts of which he places his central figures, and observes their struggles. The "turmoil" arises in the mind of the observer, not only at the spectacle of the embattled participants, but also because they are most frequently making only a partial comment on the Vision from a narrow standpoint: some, like Oliver, have their eyes fixed upon the sky, but it is either heavily overcast or dazzling with the blinding light of the sun; others, like Rosamunde and the bank clerk in *Von morgens his mitternachts,* stare at the ground, fearfully clawing away from the morass beneath them. The earth too takes on many forms: contemporary urban society, an abstracted battleground, a small family group, an industrial monolith. And the Vision also is seen variously as a brave new era, or total destruction, or as a primitivist retreat; it may seek to encompass the whole of humanity or offer release in eroticism just to two lovers.

Only rarely is the whole length of the slippery pole explored, in an attempt to translate into dramatic terms the totality of the

Vision in all its implications. The work which makes this attempt in its fullest and most "classical" form is *The Burghers of Calais* (written 1912–3, first performed 1917), thereby giving the most comprehensive picture of its author's Expressionist Vision.

The citizens of Calais are in something of a predicament : the English, convinced that the new harbour poses a military threat to Albion, have laid siege to the town, and the townsfolk have withstood the beleaguerment for many months; but now they can hold out no longer, for the French forces of liberation have been routed. Two courses of action lie open to them : they can either, as Eustache de Saint-Pierre, a venerable and respected business-man, urges, accept the surrender terms, which demand that six of the citizens offer up their lives as a surety for the safety of the rest of the population; or, as the garrison leader, Duguesclins, demands, they should defy the enemy and go down fighting to the last man when the ultimatum expires and the English storm the town, which they threaten to do on the next morning. Eustache's arguments prevail, and he is the first to volunteer for self-immola-tion. However, seven instead of six volunteers come forward; and it is resolved that the seventh, that is, the one who will be released from his bond with death, will be chosen by lot. The volunteers (apart from Eustache) severally take leave of their friends and dependents; but Eustache tampers with the lot-drawing, keeping the others still in doubt, because, he maintains, they are not yet in a fit state of mind for their sacrifice. Instead, each is set out at the sound of the bell early next morning, and the last to arrive on the market place will be spared. This duly occurs, and the last to arrive is Eustache—dead : he has committed suicide that the others in their new-found altruism might go forward together to their deaths. But, as they are about to depart, an envoy appears from the English King to announce that the Queen has given birth to a son; in celebration of this the six are to be spared. Eustache is hailed as the New Man, and his mortal remains are elevated in the growing morning light before the façade of the church.

Kaiser was first drawn to the subject by Auguste Rodin's sculp-ture, *Les bourgeois de Calais* (1884–6), and his second source was Jean Froissart's *Chroniques de France* covering the period of the siege (1346–7). But, if Kaiser treats his sources here in anything like the same way as he does in plays like *The Jewish Widow* (1911) or *Alkibiades Saved* (1920), a study of such extrinsic material can offer little guidance towards an understanding of the intentions of *The Burghers of Calais*. And so it seems to be at first sight.

The statue by Rodin, as one critic has been at some pains to point out,[4] has virtually nothing in common with the play, at least as far as content is concerned. Rodin was commissioned by the burghers of Calais to execute a monument to the heroism of those, who, in the early stages of the Hundred Years' War, offered up their lives for the safety of their fellow citizens, and who must have been among the very few martyrs to have survived the experience of their martyrdom. The statue depicts the six about to set forth for the English camp, despondent and overwhelmingly weary : the whole composition evokes both their reluctance and the supreme effort required to overcome it and submit the self to the greater need of the community. It demands the utmost critical ingenuity to correlate even some of the figures with Kaiser's volunteers, even ignoring the awkward fact that he swelled their ranks to seven, and that, when they set out in the play—already calmly and positively accepting their fate—the bearded old man of the statue (Eustache) is not present among them.

Froissart, too, offers only a welter of contradictions. According to him Jean de Vienne was leader of the garrison—in Kaiser, it is Duguesclins, who by all accounts was nowhere near Calais at the time of the siege, and was anyway far too young then to have been entrusted with a position of such importance. (Not to mention the distinct possibility of Duguesclins' finding himself on the wrong side.) The French chronicler insists that the volunteers numbered six, that they set off immediately, and were saved by the pleadings of the English Queen, "qui moult estoit enchainte".[5] In *The Burghers of Calais*, they are increased to seven, they do not set off, once they have been trimmed down to the right total, until the following morning, and are spared by the actual birth of a son (in fact, it was a daughter) to the Queen. The play ends on a note of resounding triumph, whereas the prospect for the actual citizens of Calais was far from pleasant : mass expulsion to provide accommodation for the English army of occupation. Besides all this, Kaiser also changes the cause of the siege to the construction of the harbour. So, apart from minor considerations like the names of some of the characters, and the motif of the bell which Kaiser takes up and extends, Froissart seems to offer about as much by way of illumination as Rodin's sculpture.

But Kaiser was not primarily concerned with subject-matter when he saw the Rodin group : he was seeking means of rendering his Vision of man into dramatic terms, and he recognized a similarity of method and intention in the statue : Rodin was not interested in the historical sacrifice of six late mediæval burghers, but in the Idea of sacrifice. He sought to penetrate through the specific event in order to arrive at a general and universally valid statement about sacrifice. He tried to portray, not one historical sacrifice, but Sacrifice. And in so doing he did not aim at the representation of reality; the artistic whole he saw as something essentially different from the natural entity.[6] He was quite content, for example, to sculpt a headless striding figure if the subject required such treatment, just as in *Les bourgeois de Calais* the robes of the figures are suggested only : in contrast, heads, arms, and feet are carved in great detail. Through gesture and the use of physical space, Rodin has both concentrated upon essentials, minimizing the impact of the secondary, and expanded these essentials into a universal expression of sacrifice. The composition thereby becomes stylized, and moves away from the representational level to a more abstracted plane.

This was what drew Kaiser to Rodin's sculpture : although Rodin is by no means as ruthless, and works rather from the specific to the Idea,[7] Kaiser noted the affinities between them, and from this grew his intention to impose upon the historical events of the siege of Calais his Expressionist Vision of regeneration, as Rodin had imposed to some degree on the historical moment his more timebound insight.

The domination of Kaiser's will over his material can readily be seen at work in the "characters" of the volunteers.

Of the volunteers, only the Fifth Councillor remains silent throughout the first act. Even when he comes forward to join Eustache, striding resolutely and with the formalized posture of a man deep in concentration, he utters no word. He takes leave of his business associate with the same calm deliberation : only for a brief instant does his inner turmoil rise to the surface, but almost immediately he regains his self-discipline. Such is the extent of his characterization. He is neither explored in depth, nor is he a mere cipher. He is not a businessman; he is The Businessman. He is the essence, the Idea of Business become flesh. Similarly, the Fourth Councillor is the incarnation of The Husband, the Third The Son, Jean d'Aire is Age, and the brothers de Wissant Youth. Severally and collectively they become The Old Man. They are the representatives of the common mass of mankind, lost in the maze of existence, darkly aware of their own humanity, but shackled by a dread of losing their tenuous hold on life. They demand certainty (*Gewißheit*), a selfish security in a world which they do not comprehend and which they regard as essentially hostile. When threatened, they seek desperately for a leader, and find one in Duguesclins. He, too, is The Old Man, but where they are fearful, he is aggressive : he strikes out blindly at the enemy in his frenzy (*Rausch*). Where they cling on to their lives, he rushes into an orgy of self-destruction. His code of conduct is

likewise founded on the superior claims of the individual in
conflict with society; it is a code of honour and shame, attack
against counter-attack, an eye for an eye, and is the mirror image
of the craving for certainty.

This is the vicious circle which Eustache seeks to break, by
recognizing and acting upon the necessity of man's collective responsibility for his destiny, and his ability to control and master his
environment. The two concepts are irrevocably bound together :
the man who is afraid of the world about him either strikes out
blindly at the dark forces he imagines are conspiring to overwhelm
him, or shrinks into himself to create a semblance of security
within his narrow circle of family and acquaintances.

Duguesclins is pictured by Eustache about to dash into battle
thus :

> What else is there for you to do?—You pull the peak of your
> visor down over your eyes and are blind and deaf behind its
> shield. Exactly as you stand here too, blinded and deafened!
> You are enveloped in a darkness that hides your deed from you.
> This way you cannot see it—this way it shrivels up—this way
> it becomes small—no longer frightening to dare to do it!—
> G.K., p. 125).[8]

When he closes the visor, he cuts himself off from the world,
insulates himself from his fellow men, becomes his own prisoner.
In the same way, each of the volunteers, in the leave-taking scenes,
stresses his own importance at the expense of the rest, isolating
himself from social responsibility. To begin with, Eustache sees
this characteristic withdrawal of the Old Man purely in terms of
individual versus society, and seeks to open the eyes of his fellow
citizens by encouraging them to participate in the construction of
a harbour for Calais, an artifice which would demonstrably control
the forces of nature, remove the causes of their timorous or bellicose
attitudes, and thus prove the superior powers of a unified community over the physical world. And this they did :

> (We) drove the dikes out into the sea—forced back wave upon
> wave—broke their anger and tempered their unrest—until the
> new bay rounded out—broad and smooth as on no other coast :
> we opened a gateway into the sea—now ships were to glide out
> on voyages to prosperity! (G.K., p. 112.)

But at the first sign of danger, the citizens—to the utter bewilder-
ment of the now despondent Eustache—reverted to their former
superstition and fear. Duguesclins voices his reaction to the
English army of invasion :

A shark has swum through the sea from England—to fling breakers against the coast of France with the thrust of its angry tail. (G.K., p. 114.)

The ships were to sail forth *on* the subdued sea; the shark thrashes its angry passage *through* the boiling waves. For the citizens, the English have become the minions of the forces of nature wrathful at the insolent bravado of man, who now seek to destroy the harbour and restore their due supremacy. In other words, it could be said that the citizens view the world through Naturalist eyes.

Eustache is forced to recognize that his plans have failed, hence his motionless silence for a considerable part of the first act, during which it must be assumed that he too is forced back into despair at the apparently irresistible power of the forces against which he sought to pit his feeble wits.

It is only when the English Officer announces the surrender terms that Eustache realizes that there is a way out of the situation, and that he had ignored two vital factors in his attempt to weld the weak individuals of Calais into a strong community : firstly, he had endeavoured to create a new communal spirit within the framework of the *status quo*, that is, to appeal to enlightened self-interest—greater prosperity through the harbour—by means of an evolutionary process—the construction of the harbour; and, secondly, he had appealed to men's bodies only, to physical effort and the promise of subsequent physical well-being. What is demanded, he now recognizes, is not a gradual improvement in the standard of living within society as it is, but a sudden change in the whole of society, founded upon a new concept of the rôle and nature of humanity : not evolution, then, but the Expressionist *revolution*.

So Eustache sees, in the possibility of self-sacrifice (negation of the previously held superior demands of the individual) for his Vision (that of a new kind of society, through the regeneration of man), a means of effecting the sudden transformation of all mankind, of paving the way to a new Golden Age for man on earth.

On the level at which Kaiser's dramas are acted out, it is frequently the case that logical progression is subservient to the driving thrust of the individual's urge towards renewal, and the Expressionist writer forces chance into an "inevitable" path towards renewal. Thus it is, in *Oktobertag* (*The Phantom Lover*), that Catherine turns fantasy into reality by an act of will : she determines that the child she is carrying is not that of the butcher's boy Leguerche from whom she conceived it, but of the officer—

Jean-Marc Marrien—whom she once saw fleetingly, and now loves with overwhelming passion. The logic which renders this true is not that of an external law, but stems from the inner impulse of the individual. It is a real victory of mind over matter, in which the Vision imposes its pattern through an individual upon the material world. And such is the case also in *The Burghers of Calais;* for Eustache recognizes that it would be impossible for him to execute his plan with five other volunteers only, five Old Men who would undergo no fundamental change, but simply substitute the certainty of death for that in life for which they yearn.

Eustache must therefore break the vicious circle within them, must first convert them into New Men before he can use them as agents in the regeneration of mankind as a whole. It is for this reason that Kaiser causes Eustache to "will" seven volunteers in all to come forward, outwardly motivated by the fact that, after Jean d'Aire, who is so near to death that he feels he might as well die in a good cause as on his sickbed, comes forward to make the total five, his two prospective sons-in-law dash forward simultaneously in a protective gesture that is at the same time an expression of youthful rashness as a counter to Jean d'Aire's worn-out fatalism. And when the seven are gathered together, there is general consternation, but Eustache reacts *almost joyfully;* for he has now drawn up a group of men ready for the process of renewal; when they realize what has happened, their personalities will become fluid as they founder in a half-world of uncertainty, and he will then be able to mould them into a new and higher state of certainty.

The opening act of *The Burghers of Calais* can be seen as the first step in this direction, the exposing and discrediting of the Old Order, of contemporary society, and the hope that something new might emerge. In this situation Kaiser has fastened on two of the principal social targets of Expressionism : the selfishness and self-destructiveness of capitalism; and war, the inevitable constituent of a culture founded on the sanctity of private property and the stubborn separateness of the individual.

The second act sees Eustache preparing the volunteers for their sacrifice.

The initial leave-taking scene is a kind of anticipatory parody of those that follow : in it, Jean de Vienne, the leader of the council, expresses to Eustache his fears as representative of the people : up to now, they have at least been aware of their predicament, and shouldered the burden of the siege as an unwelcome but inevitable fact; but the present new lack of certainty after a long and desperate battle for civic survival is too much for them to endure :

Uncertainty has shattered their previous unshakeable calm. The long wait for an end to the proceedings in this hall stings them with sharpest anguish. It renders this torment—and it is torment!—intolerable . . . We have drawn the bow too tight— we must remove the arrow from the bowstring before it is sent flying to strike home with—perhaps—deadly effect. (G.K., p. 132.)

Throughout Jean de Vienne's long speech, Eustache remains *silent,* as he had been also at the commencement of the previous act. But now the reasons are different. Instead of the situation having run away from him as before, he now says nothing because he is no longer thinking on the same kind of plane as Jean de Vienne : his eyes are fixed on the Vision; he has left behind him the vicious circle of certainty and frenzy, which still torments the other citizens.

Silences such as this are characteristic of the Kaiser New Man in similar circumstances, and demonstrate the magnitude of the aspirations of the Expressionist Activist. Between the Old and the New the gulf is vast; it can only be bridged by an instantaneous, revolutionary change from fear to confidence, from blind panic to total mastery. Eustache has now already become the New Man— he is not, as has been argued, a superhuman figure from the outset—and has undergone the process he is about to induce in the other volunteers : ridding himself of the dross of *idées reçues* which have shackled him in the past, and determinedly facing the supremely difficult task that lies before him. Hence his mood is one of (very) quiet optimism as he patiently listens to Jean de Vienne's tale of woe.

The Burghers of Calais reveals as much through what it leaves unsaid as it does through word and action; and the paradoxical nature of the situation, although never fully explicit, becomes clearly apparent at this point. Six men are about to join Eustache to be purified and ordained for their mission; outside, the whole population trembles in fear of its life. The latter, when they know who the volunteers are to be, may well—and almost certainly will—revert to their old state of preoccupation with their own selfish security. Perhaps they will spontaneously respond to the inspiring example of the volunteers; but the fact remains that, whereas Eustache tried to convert the whole community in his first mistaken attempt to create a new order, he now has only six men before him. This tension between the tiny group and the vast mass of humanity underlines the immense difficulty of the struggle that Eustache has undertaken, and seems to throw the outcome into stronger doubt. The frequent interruptions of

Jean de Vienne as the seven meet, and the final rush of citizens up to the room, both serve to stress the power of mass hysteria and the terrifying consequences of anarchy. A further consideration : it is indeed true that Eustache is now the effective leader of Calais, having taken over from Duguesclins, but the populace have followed him because he is a strong leader, not because he is a good one. They have not the ability to judge between them, another indication of the gulf between Old and New. Still, the fact that the volunteers intuitively recognize the validity of Eustache's cause offers some consolation, even if they recant in the leave-taking scenes—or insist on going to their deaths for the wrong reasons. But does it? The Fifth Councillor—the first to volunteer—is a hardened businessman, and his motives are in all probability the advancement of commerce by his sacrifice, that is, his death will allow the harbour to remain unharmed; the Third Councillor is, to put it mildly, emotionally unstable, swamped by an over-possessive mother; the Fourth can see no further than the small family group of which he is the head; Jean d'Aire comes forward only because he will die soon anyway; and the de Wissant brothers are now driven primarily by a lust for fame and immortality. In the leave-taking scenes, the first three insist that they will be the ones to be saved; the other three insist on going to their deaths. In each case the motivation is totally misguided and in the second part of this act Eustache finds himself confronted with a task of the greatest difficulty : welding this egocentric heterogenous collection of Old Men into one single New Man.

The setting in which Eustache succeeds in bringing this about is curious in many ways.

Although *The Burghers of Calais* is a drama of long speeches and counter-speeches, the visual is at least equal in importance to the spoken word; and Kaiser, although himself having no pretensions as either painter or sculptor, shares the awareness of many other Expressionists in regard to the uniquely powerful impact of visual experience. Although he professes no interest in the fate of his dramas, once written, they are composed with public performance, not private reading, in mind. There are moments in the action, as, for example, when the de Wissant brothers stand poised on the steps before joining the others round the table in Act Two, which are strongly reminiscent of the sculptural techniques of Rodin : a split-second of tension halfway between motionlessness and movement. In fact, the whole play could be seen in terms of a progression from one such moment to the next on successively higher tidal waves of tension. Gesture too is strictly controlled and highly stylized. And Kaiser exploits to the full the visual potential of the acting area as a whole : he makes constant use of different levels : there are steps of some kind in each of the three acts, and movement up or down is infused with the greatest significance. In the vast assembly hall of the first act, the citizens crowd on a platform looking down on the ranks of councillors, and at ground level stands the tiny figure of Eustache pleading his case. Perspective is also critical : time and again elsewhere in his dramas Kaiser employs a glass door to suggest areas beyond the immediate setting, and the second act of *The Burghers of Calais* offers an important variation on these techniques. The leave-taking scenes take place before a tryptich, which illustrates the harbour before, during, and after construction. Significantly, it is the central panel that depicts the completed harbour, and through this part each of the volunteers goes, up a couple of steps, to the back part of the set. When this tapestry is drawn back, the following emerges to view :

> *The room now revealed has considerable depth. High walls and the broad ceiling are encrusted with decorative minerals and stones from all corners of the earth and with glittering sea shells. A table—near to the step—stands prepared for a meal: seven silver cups, plates. In the middle of the table a bowl covered by a blue cloth. Two unsmiling hunchbacks—servants— have pulled the tapestry right back and go from the sides of the stage to a door left front. (G.K., p. 139.)*

To this should be added the fact that each of the volunteers is decked out in his best and most colourful robes. So it is that, in strong divergence from Kaiser's normal practice, the setting in each part of the second act offers a sharp *contrast* to the words spoken. In the leave-taking scenes, the volunteers renounce their mission, whilst towering above them is the tapestry in silent admonishment. In the second part, the finery of the volunteers and the lushness of the chamber clash harshly with the ascetic message of self-sacrifice and self-obliteration that Eustache offers them. So the abrupt switch from Old to New is underlined by the alienation between setting and characters. The contrast is a grotesque one, highlighted by the representatives of ordinary humanity who act as servants : the cripples.

The grotesque is one of the strongest moral and satirical weapons of the Expressionists; and, in Kaiser's work, physical deformity and disability as a reflection of man's imprisonment within his body in contrast to his boundless aspirations is extensively used.

At the beginning of *The Two Olivers*, both the landlord and Oliver's wife are severely handicapped; in *From morning till midnight,* the pathetic waiter has a weak chest ; and in *Alkibiades Saved,* Sokrates is restricted in his movements by a vicious thorn in the foot.[9] But the grotesque irony of such conditions is specific— in *The Burghers of Calais,* on the other hand, the Idea of deformity is generalised to represent the total incapacity of man to exceed himself. The New Man—he who is to lead the world to regeneration and rebirth—is no ardent youngster, but Eustache, a greybeard of three score years and ten, worn out by the cares of life, who can hardly stagger to his feet to face the immense effort that lies before him.

This second part of the central act has many overtones of Christian tradition and ceremonial, underlining both the eclecticism of the Expressionists, who borrowed themes and motifs from any and every source that would give a greater impact to their Vision; and also the ecstatic, quasi-religious nature of their search for moral regeneration. Here Christianity is used both as a point of reference, and also to demonstrate its inadequacy in the face of the problems confronting the twentieth century.

The speeches of the volunteers apart from Eustache, in which they admit they have been dominated by self-interest, have about them the subdued self-abasement of the confessional; the long table and the sharing of fruit and wine (plus the suggestion of the seventh as "betrayer" of the cause) is a direct borrowing from the Last Supper; and Eustache himself, about to go to his death and resurrection, becomes a Christ-figure. But *The Burghers of Calais* can by no stretch of the imagination be termed an orthodox religious drama, in spite of such overtones, and others like the church in the background of the third act, or the magic numbers of three (acts) and seven (volunteers). Kaiser is simply taking over from the Christian tradition, as he took over from Froissart's chronicles, those things useful to his purpose.

The Burghers of Calais, it is true, is religious in the sense that it seeks a bond between transcendent and immanent, but the Christian legend is not essential to it : it could equally well be described in Platonic terms, a drama depicting man moving out from the flickering light of the cave by an arduous educational process into the brilliant sunlight of the realm of Forms. What differentiates *The Burghers of Calais* from Christianity is its Expressionist anthropocentricity : Eustache is not promising a new life in Heaven; he is promising to bring Heaven here and now down to earth.

He effects the transformation of the volunteers by breaking them out of the protective shell they have fabricated about themselves, by forcing them to become aware of their existence within time and space. Life is not a succession of fragmented days, its actions

dictated by the whim of the moment; and the same holds true for
the individual units that make up the sum total of humanity. The
volunteers must not be divided against each other, nor in revolt
against the task that lies before them, for they are "deeds and
doers already fused into one—as today into tomorrow!" (G.K.,
p. 152.)

So they go off to contemplate these words in the course of the
night. In the last act, Eustache is again silent for the first part—
and not even present; and, in the market place, the volunteers—
now become the New Man—prepare to set out. When it is
discovered that six volunteers have gathered, and that Eustache is
not among them, the tension mounts. Significantly, the citizens
split into two choruses, reflecting the two aspects of the Old Man :
some cry "Send out the six!" (Gewißheit); others "Find Eustache
de Saint-Pierre!" (Rausch). Up to this point at least, the citizens
are no different from what they were at the commencement of
the drama, alternately fearful for their security, and madly
striking out at the forces they believe are seeking to crush them.

Into the shouting and confusion hobbles the ancient, blind (!)
figure of Eustache's father, the two crippled servants bearing
Eustache's body on a litter. In a long speech, Eustache's father
hails his son as the New Man, and the six as his immediate disciples.
They set forth—the moment of departure (Aufbruch) is critical
as a renunciation of the Old and dedication to the New—but are
halted by the English Officer, who announces that they are to
be spared, for that night the English Queen has given birth to a
son. For the sake of this new life their lives are to be restored to
them. The drama ends amid jubilation, a triumph for Eustache
and his Vision. At least, it appears to be a triumph, until one
examines it more closely.

The citizens stand silent. Nearby the blast of trumpets.
THE ENGLISH OFFICER
The King of England!
*Jean de Vienne and the Councillors stand waiting. The light
floods over the church front above the door: its lower part
represents a deposition from the cross; the frail body of the dead
man lies limply in the sheets—six stand bowed over his litter.—
The upper part depicts the elevation of the dead man: he
stands free and untrammeled in the sky—the heads of six are
turned up towards him in wonderment. (G.K., p. 170.)*

Eustache has reached his Vision; but what of the others? The
citizens stand *silent*—the significance of silence has already been
discussed—and therefore uncomprehending. The councillors *wait*
—for the coming of the English forces. The six *stare up*—towards

the remote figure of Eustache. Eustache is *elevated*—again the significance of physical space. Citizens and councillors are looking about them on the same level; they have not changed their attitudes. The six look up, in aspiration—but not attainment. It is all very well for Kaiser to say in theory that "advances made by the few will be caught up with by all",[10] but Eustache is far above the rest, on a totally different plane. He is at the goal, the Vision, whilst beneath the English King is about to enter. The New Man of Calais is dead; the New Son of the English King, a ruling monarch of the Old, is about to enter and claim the town. This is rendered more potent in that the leading representative Old Man in the first act, Duguesclins, has defected to the English side; so he, too, is about to recapture Calais. It seems very much a Pyrrhic victory.

And the Vision Eustache has attained? It is nothing more nor less than self-destruction. He has reached his private union with death, whilst below, life goes on much as before. We see in *The Burghers of Calais*, then, three stages of advancement towards the Vision—the sequence of events in Expressionist drama tends to take this discontinuous form of stages *(Stationen)*, rather than the conventional, unbroken chain of events leading to the traditional climax and denouement—but a sharp reminder that the Vision itself is unattainable on earth. The first stage is chaos, man trapped in a selfish, unthinking battle for individual survival. Next comes the painful process of self-purification and self-negation. Then the long, arduous struggle for the Ideal. The Ideal, the Vision itself, may be beyond our reach, but the struggle is essential, a bitter and unending conflict with forces seeking to drag us back into the mire. From the end of *The Burghers of Calais*, it is clear that Kaiser allies himself with the Vision; having created an artistic world in which to play out its attainment, he turns his back on life and embraces the realm of art.

For, confronted with the gulf between world and Vision, man has to commit himself to one or the other; it is impossible to effect a compromise between the two. The warning signs of this are clear from the commencement of the drama, particularly in the powerful symbolism, which parallels and develops together with events on the stage. The first act debate between Eustache and Duguesclins, for example, is in many ways a clash of symbols. On the one hand, there is Duguesclins' armour, on the other, Eustache's robes. Duguesclins' visor is mocked by Eustache as cutting him off from the environment, instead of offering protection; the loose robes of the citizens, in contrast, far from leaving them open to attack, play quite a different rôle; Eustache explains :

Your deed becomes mere cowardice—as you hanker after it today!—Its courage falls away from it and swiftly shrivels on the ground. It rustles about your feet—our bare soles grind it to dust—and the wind from our passing robes blows it into the sea!—Where will your torch of courage be tomorrow? Thick smoke suffocates it! It smoulders dully from the hot embers— stagnating out of your blood beneath your rigid armour!— Today you and your blood lie dead before your deed—but shall we not live on in our flimsy robes until the brightness of a new dawn? — — (G.K., p. 126.)

The robes allow receptivity to the environment, whereas armour cuts Duguesclins off from his surroundings. And this emphasis on the oneness of all things, the bonds between man and man, and humanity and the universe, runs through all of Eustache's symbols. Duguesclins is seen as a flickering, smoky flame that excludes the world from view; and this is set in contrast to the illuminating, clear flame of the new deed :

It burns a clear, smokeless flame—cool despite its heat—gentle in its blinding light. Thus it towers up high—thus you go on your way—thus it accepts you. (G.K., p. 152.)

The central symbol of the play, the circle, seems at first to corroborate the opening up of man's range of understanding that the other symbols brought forward by Eustache suggest : it represents in the first instance the creation of order and confidence out of fear and chaos. In the harbour, it is an open-ended circle; but gains a note of ambiguity in Duguesclins' description of the beleaguering army round Calais as a shimmering ring. Circle becomes sphere in the balls used for the lot-drawing; and at the same time, too, it is the vicious circle of the Old, and the closed ring of the volunteers. This alternation from circle to sphere, from closed to open ring,[11] underlines the impossible dilemma which confronts Eustache. His aim is perfection, a realm sufficient unto itself, but he realises that, unlike the Platonic sphere of the sun, it is unable to radiate light and enlightenment upon humanity. It is not the fulfilment, but the negation of life. Eustache attains the Ideal, but discovers that the Ideal is death. The "message" of *The Burghers of Calais*—and Expressionist drama has a moral purpose —is, therefore, that, in spite of Eustache's Herculean efforts, regeneration in reality is possible only for the individual : for mankind as a whole it is a lost dream.

That Kaiser is content to leave the paradox unresolved under-lines the acutest problem of Expressionism : the gulf between the temporal and the absolute. Kaiser takes the Activist path, plotting out the stages—chaos, purification, setting off, struggle, Ideal—in a vain attempt to reconcile them. For the Expressionist the moral purpose of art lies in expounding this tension : either in satirical, negative terms, or unwordly flights of ecstatic fancy, or with the positive, missionary fervour of Kaiser.

All the techniques of the drama are enrolled in the artist's singleminded dedication to his Vision : the paradoxical nature of the Vision finds its expression in the tortured abruptness of the language, with its impersonal rhetoric, its concentration of emotions at fever pitch to a single word, and, at the same time, its vast expansiveness. Psychological analysis has no place in this drama, and character, plot, psychological motivation become rudimentary or vanish altogether. The old drama of pity and fear is dead and past; the new is impelled along by the "energy"[12] of the dramatist, his irresistible urge to give expression to his faith in the future of humanity.

The settings become abstracted and stylised. Physical space, sound-effects, movement, lighting : all conspire to evoke the immense state of tension, the vast forces at work.

It is the representation on stage of the path to an Idea, of a vain aspiration towards the rebirth of humanity. But, if the aspiration is vain, hope still remains; if the Expressionist New Man is beyond attainment, it is little use sitting helplessly back and waiting for annihilation; the struggle towards renewal is still worthwhile : in fact, it is man's only remaining hope.

NOTES

1. K. Edschmid, "Expressionismus in der Dichtung", in: P. Raabe (ed.), *Expressionismus. Der Kampf um eine literarische Bewegung*, Munich (1965), p. 95.
2. B. Diebold, *Der Denkspieler Georg Kaiser*, Frankfurt a.M. (1924), p. 9.
3. G. Kaiser, *Stücke Erzählungen Aufsätze Gedichte*, Berlin (1966), p. 665.
4. See E. Ihrig, "Die Bürger von Calais. August Rodins Denkmal—Georg Kaisers Bühnenspiel", *Wirkendes Wort*, XI (1961), 290–303.
5. S. Luce (ed.), *Chroniques de Jean Froissart* (Vol. 4), Paris (1872), p. 62.
6. See R. M. Rilke, *Auguste Rodin*, Leipzig (1928), p. 61.
7. Edschmid, p. 100, calls Rodin "a prisoner of the moment in time".
8. G.K. = 1966 edition. (See note 3 above.)
9. See B. J. Kenworthy, *Georg Kaiser*, Oxford (1957), pp. 1–21.
10. "Dichtung und Energie", G.K., p. 683.
11. See R. W. Last, "Symbol and struggle in Georg Kaiser's *Die Bürger von Calais*", *German Life and Letters*, N.S. XIX (1965–6), 201–9.
12. See "Dichtung und Energie", G.K., p. 682.

264   PERIODS IN GERMAN LITERATURE

BIBLIOGRAPHY

There is as yet no complete edition of Kaiser's works, the vast majority of which are out of print, but the three versions of *The Burghers of Calais* have all been published. The names of some of the characters in the first version (Stuttgart, 1958) together with sections of the text and the punctuation, have been modified in the second (frequently published, most accessibly in the *Am Born der Weltliteratur* series, Bamberg & Wiesbaden (1953 and subsequent editions)), and the third (G.K.). A translation, by J. M. Ritchie & R. W. Last, appears in J. M. Ritchie (ed.), *Georg Kaiser—Five Plays* (London, Calder & Boyars, in press).

H. Denkler, *Die Bürger von Calais. Drama und Dramaturgie,* Munich (1967). A detailed teacher's handbook on the text which says little that is new.

B. Diebold, *Der Denkspieler Georg Kaiser,* Frankfurt a.M. (1924). Somewhat out of date, but still an invaluable document.

B. J. Kenworthy, *Georg Kaiser,* Oxford (1957). A penetrating study of the whole of Kaiser's work.

B. J. Kenworthy (ed.), *Die Koralle, Gas I, Gas II* (London, Harrap, 1969). Long introduction to Expressionism and Kaiser's Expressionist plays.

R. W. Last. "Kaiser, Rodin and the Burghers of Calais", *Seminar V* (1969), pp. 36–44. An analysis of the impact of Kaisers sources.

W. H. Sokel, *The writer in extremis,* Stanford, Calif. (1959). A study of the nature of Expressionism, which explores Kaiser's work in some detail.

A bibliography of Kaiser's work, including information on available English translations, can be found in G.K.

Contributors

DR. J. M. RITCHIE — *Reader in German, University of Hull*

ELIZABETH BOA, M.A. — *German Department, University of Nottingham*

M. A. L. BROWN, M.A. — *German Department, University of Hull*

DR. K. G. KNIGHT — *Head of German Department, University of Kent*

R. W. LAST, M.A. — *German Department, University of Hull*

DR. MARGARET MCHAFFIE — *Senior Lecturer, University of Glasgow*

M. J. NORST, M.A. — *German Department, University of Macquarrie, Sydney*

DAVID TURNER, M.A. — *German Department, University of Hull*

Contents of

PERIODS IN GERMAN LITERATURE

Volume I

ed. J. M. Ritchie